Resilient Kitchens

Essays & Recipes

Resilient Kitchens

American Immigrant Cooking in a Time of Crisis

EDITED BY PHILIP GLEISSNER AND HARRY ELI KASHDAN

Rutgers University Press

New Brunswick, Camden, and Newark, New Jersey

London and Oxford

Library of Congress Cataloging-in-Publication Data

Names: Gleissner, Philip, editor. | Kashdan, Harry Eli, editor.
Title: Resilient kitchens : American immigrant cooking in a time of crisis, essays and recipes / edited by Philip Gleissner and Harry Eli Kashdan.
Description: New Brunswick : Rutgers University Press, [2023] | Includes index.
Identifiers: LCCN 2022020438 | ISBN 9781978832510 (hardback) | ISBN 9781978832527 (epub) | ISBN 9781978832541 (pdf)
Subjects: LCSH: International cooking. | Food habits — United States. | Immigrants — United States — Anecdotes. | COVID-19 Pandemic, 2020– | LCGFT: Cookbooks.
Classification: LCC TX725.A1 R465 2023 | DDC 641.59 — dc23/eng/20220810
LC record available at https://lccn.loc .gov/2022020438

A British Cataloging-in-Publication record for this book is available from the British Library.

rutgersuniversitypress.org
Manufactured in the United States of America

Book design by Regina Starace

Contents

Contents

Preface

The essays in this book come from immigrant restaurateurs, chefs, scholars, food writers, and activists who offer their reflections on the importance of food on their journeys, and especially during the COVID-19 pandemic. The sampling is diverse and unscientific, an eclectic collection of perspectives that, we hope, will inspire readers to seek out new and further stories and think about their own relationships with food and identity during the pandemic.

This book began as an attempt to create a record of the hardships and challenges of the first years of the pandemic, the rough moments as well as the beautiful rituals of resilience that we developed. Personal experiences of isolation, loss, and grief are not always easy to verbalize. For most of us, though, talking about food is easy. That is why this volume consists of personal essays alongside recipes and images. Food is more than a tool for telling stories, as we were reminded during the early phase of the pandemic. Cooking, eating, and drinking became practices of spiritual survival, ways of breaking out of the isolation of lockdown by connecting with our communities, identities, and heritages through our kitchens.

Our collaborators enthusiastically agreed to write about their experiences during this pandemic before any of us had a clear notion of all the trials it would entail. We thank them for navigating alongside us the challenges that come with undertaking such a project in times of great uncertainty and, often, mourning; for the many inspiring conversations we shared; and for the generosity with which they offered their personal stories.

PG and HEK
Columbus, OH, and Philadelphia, PA
March 2022

1

The Lost Year

Spring 2020—Philadelphia

MARCH: THE MONTH OF DENIAL AND GRIEF

I have always wondered why, in the tapestry of memory, some threads are a bright, vivid red, while others have more neutral colors that blend into the background. The night in question was a bright red thread. It was February 29, 2020. Dear friends of ours, a Lebanese and Jordanian couple, had invited us along with several other mutual friends—mostly medical professionals—to their house for *mansaf*. Oh *mansaf*. That quintessential celebratory dish. A Bedouin dish, in fact, enjoyed across Jordan and Palestine. If ever there was a wedding, a birth, even a death, this was the dish prepared, a dish that could feed a crowd. *Mansaf* is always served family style. The serving dish is often so large that eight people could comfortably sit around it, and that is what people traditionally did, using their right hands to scoop up rice and fall-apart tender morsels of lamb with a sauce made of dried yogurt.

That day in February, we opted for individual plates and spoons; we were in Philadelphia, after all, not back in Jordan. But we used the same serving spoons, we gathered in a small place, we snacked on the same cheese board and passed around drinks and plates of dessert. "The Virus" was not a way of life back then, it was a new topic of conversation.

"It's going to blow up, it's going to be big," one of the hosts, a senior medical professional, told us.

"Come on!" everyone said, the flowing wine tempering our outlooks and usual anxieties.

"I don't care if it's Ebola," I joked, "as long as I can head back home to Jerusalem next week!" It had been a long winter, I missed my family, but I also had a photoshoot scheduled in Jerusalem for my upcoming cookbook. Nothing, not even a virus, was going to get in the way of my going back.

The rest of the night is a blur, but I know I went to the gym early the following Monday. I had to burn off all the *mansaf*. Another regular gym-goer—an eighty-year-old doctor—and I were the only ones in the conditioning class at eight o'clock in the morning. The teacher handed us wipes and said we had to be a little extra careful now.

"Is it really that bad?" I asked the doctor, an infectious disease specialist, while trying to hold a plank.

"Who knows," he said, "seems to mostly be affecting the elderly and not much worse than the flu." He let his arms flop, the plank seemingly a bigger challenge than the virus.

I chose to believe him. Why would I believe the alternative scenario, the one that would cancel my trip and change my life?

But what if I had entertained the idea that COVID-19 would blow up in the United States as well? What if I had prepared for the worst even as I prayed for the best? What if I had stocked up on gloves and wipes and even considered buying masks? What if I had planned for the possibility of my girls being out of school and my ability to work from home out the window? Mostly, what if I had bought extra flour and yeast? The journey to find them later took me almost two hours away to Allentown, Pennsylvania.

Hindsight is 20/20. Foresight, on the other hand, could benefit from a pair of glasses.

March started, and I went to New York City for a meeting with my publisher about my upcoming cookbook. I picked up my girls from their school as usual and took them to the dentist. I kept appointments and coffees and lunches. There was a murmur in the air, a suspicion of what was to come, but hope is what we humans live for, and I hung on to its very last thread even as I called my parents several times a day to learn if any travel restrictions had been issued. I clung to my plans like a piece of burlap cloth, afraid of one small change, one string coming loose, and the intricate web I had woven falling apart.

The *Times of Israel* became my first port of call every morning. Flights were being banned left and right, quarantines were being enforced in government facilities, and I needed something to tell me what to do. I debated moving up my flights, but then what would happen if we got stuck in Jerusalem longer than the planned four weeks? Worse, what if we caught the virus and passed it along?

Travel, and the inherent freedom found in the ability to move from one place to the next, was what ironically kept me grounded and feeling safe in life. Yet, in the end, the primal desire for protection trumped my selfish desire for that stability. I worried for my parents' health—my father was in his seventies and a smoker, my mother in her sixties with hypertension—and I canceled our flights indefinitely.

I sat sipping sage tea late at night as I got off the phone with the airline, the same tea I drank throughout my childhood at my grandparents' home. I found a strange sense of calm in its warm sweetness, the one I had tasted thousands of times before. It was the only thing that seemed to make sense in a world that was coming apart at the seams. "Come on, it's late," my husband said. "Go to sleep, you'll figure it all out tomorrow." I should already have been asleep, but I couldn't let go of that sweet scent, the last thin thread connecting me to a childhood I could not go back to.

My daughters' disappointment tugged at my heart, but it was my inability to be there for and with those I loved that really shattered any perception of control I had previously held. In fact, I had been living outside my hometown more years than I had spent growing up in it, but no matter where life took me, I had found comfort in knowing that whatever happened, I was one flight away from my family. The ability to fly, the luxury of free movement, meant that being grounded or being far away was just a perception, not a physical obstacle. But now, for the first time in my life, I would go for more than a year without seeing my aging parents; I had no say in the matter. I felt helpless.

I remembered my father telling us about the many years he had spent abroad in the United States. He would write letters to his parents to schedule a time to call twice a year on the only phone in their village. Perhaps in this day and age, when I could FaceTime every day, my reaction was unwarranted. But in that instant, all I craved was the warmth of my mother's embrace, the scent of our home, of sage tea and *za'atar* and *taboon* bread. I craved the connection to a past that had started to slip away, I craved the things that felt like home, whatever that elusive notion might mean.

APRIL: THE MONTH OF COOKING FOR COMFORT

Recollections of my childhood fluttered in and out of my mind over the following days and weeks, the way they always do when I feel most nostalgic. I don't know if my whole childhood revolved around food, but every bold thread of memory seemed to be colored by it. The smell of falafel frying in overused oil on the cobblestone steps of Jerusalem's Old City where I always had breakfast with my mother. Sounds of *ka'ak* cart vendors crying out the price of their goods at the door of our school and the gate to our house. The taste of my grandmother's *maqlubeh*, my aunt's *khubeizeh*, my other aunt's *burbara*, and my mother's bursting stuffed grape leaves made from our vines. I could no longer distinguish between which of those dishes I truly loved and which I craved for the feelings I hoped they would rekindle, for they were all bright threads in my mind.

Those first few weeks of lockdown were the hardest. Our two-bedroom apartment suddenly became a school and two offices, and we had no respite from each other's antics. Zoom also quickly became a verb, adjective, and noun fluttering around our apartment. My daughters hated doing their schooling over it. My work calls had to be scheduled around my daughters' and husband's calls. Even friends we used to meet regularly became virtual figures in our lives. We were all on Zoom until we were zoomed out.

And so, in the middle of one of those weeks, I decided that we would all play hooky. I called Azar supermarket in Allentown. "*Sabah el kheir*," I greeted the woman on the end of the line at 7:30 in the morning. "Do you have *koosa*? What about eggplants? No, no, not the small Indian ones, the Italian ones for stuffing." I was looking for the specific varieties we ate back in Jerusalem, varieties that had to be hunted down in specific stores because they could not easily be found in mainstream supermarkets

After a bit of back and forth we understood each other. She was Syrian, an immigrant whose story may have been drastically different from mine, but if those differences existed, they were masked by a mutual sense of longing for a shared history, and a nostalgia for the dishes of a childhood we would have all shared back in the Levant regardless of background and circumstances. Princes or paupers, educated or illiterate, Christian or Muslim—we all ate stuffed vegetables. Our mothers and grandmothers prepared them, and the whole family shared in them.

"*Habeebti*," she went on, "we also have fresh green almonds and fava beans, come in you'll find what you're looking for."

And so, my husband and I buckled our four- and six-year-old daughters in the back of the car and drove the two hours to Allentown. I was the only one to step out of the car. Mask and gloves on, I looked more like someone going into surgery than into a grocery store, but once I walked through the doors, a sense of calm washed over me. I felt I was back in the vegetable stores of Beit Hanina and the grocers of our neighborhood. I bought *koosa* and eggplant. I got fresh green almonds. I picked up turnips and beets for pickling. I even carried out a large flat of stuffing cabbage. I hate stuffed cabbage, but my mother made it whenever my father found fresh cabbage at the greengrocer when he bought our fresh fruits and vegetables, and so it would be on my dinner table that week even if I couldn't stand its flavor or smell.

I called my mother later that week complaining that my apartment smelled of cabbage, how nobody liked it, and how my six-year-old had only agreed to eat it dipped in soy sauce.

"Why do you even bother?" she laughed. "You've always hated cabbage."

"I don't know," I replied.

Truly, I did not. I always complained when my mother made stuffed cabbage, preferring instead *koosa* and eggplant. It was a back and forth of protests and negotiations, but in the end, she almost always made something else to eat alongside the cabbage. Maybe it was my favorite fried *sambusek* or *kubbeh*. Perhaps it was *maftool* quickly cooked in tomato sauce. Whatever simple dish it was, it showed me how, even as my mother insisted she would not make separate meals for individual members of our family, she worried about what I would eat and what I liked. It may have been a small, even negligible, act in some ways, but in others, it spoke volumes.

When the Syrian lady had told me that I would find what I was looking for in the store, she had been right. But it was not in the ingredients or the flavors. It was in the memories and feelings I was able to relive. It was in the cabbage I hated, but whose presence on the table reminded me that there was someone across the world who loved me beyond measure—someone who still cared what I ate.

I made stuffed *koosa* and eggplants later that week, and we ate that meal with gusto. As we sat back in our chairs, our plates emptied but for the dried-out streams of tomato sauce, my husband thanked me, "It was delicious."

"It was," I agreed, "but it wasn't the same. It tastes different when someone makes it for me, when my mom makes it."

"You want me to make it for you next time?" he joked.

"No, it's just different when it's at home." My dish of stuffed zucchini felt too much like a Zoom call. You saw the person across a screen, you accomplished what you needed, but you left it feeling empty, cheated of the most basic of human desires: contact. My stuffed *koosa*, prepared by me instead of my mother and eaten in Philadelphia instead of Jerusalem, had likewise fulfilled its purpose, but it had also lost its charm.

MAY: THE MONTH OF THE BRITISH BAKE OFF

I have written a lot about how food provides comfort—whether by reviving memories or building new ones and creating a sense of community. In the back of my mind, and in most of my writings, the focus was on Arab food, the dishes of my childhood and the sense of longing they satisfied or the nostalgia they evoked. But in May 2020, it was an unlikely source of food that brought comfort. As we sat at home, isolated and alone, I felt like I had been shipwrecked in a new world without a map to guide me. How much screen time was too much for the girls? How much was too much for us? How do we pass the time when we can't step outside?

I still had work to do and a few deadlines to meet, but the heightened sense of urgency with which I used to approach everything had calmed. What did a deadline even mean when the world around us was literally in the grips of life or death? A sense of pointlessness permeated much of what I did; having my husband and daughters around me was the only anchor mooring me to earth.

My husband, Aboud, and I started watching *The Great British Baking Show* after the girls went to bed. We were too on edge to watch serious shows, and comedies felt frivolous. We just wanted something light and distracting. We had spent five years in London without having seen a single episode, but all the way across the pond we had suddenly gotten hooked on the elaborate displays of fondant-covered cakes, butchered exotic desserts, and, every now and then, perfect sweets we chose to replicate at home.

The nightly ritual soon became an afternoon one as well, with both girls jumping on the bed between us, picking favorites, making bets on who would win, and crying when a favored contestant was asked to leave. For three weeks in May, *The Great British Baking Show* became our escape and our family ritual. The precision of chocolate tempering, the straight lines of icing, and the exact timing of baking became the antidote to the chaos of the world around us.

The cocoon we had built seemed sustainable until I checked the news one night and learned that the mandatory two-week quarantine in government facilities in Israel had been lifted. Quarantine was only required at home now. I called the airline, reissued my ticket, and started packing. My husband, not an Israeli citizen, could not join us. Only passport holders were allowed into the country.

I packed our bags, including a small stash of N95 masks—an added perk of our earlier Allentown trip. I had actually been surprised to find not only these hard to secure masks in the Arab grocery store, but also bleach, face shields, gloves, sanitizer, yeast, flour, and most of the items that were out of stock in mainstream grocery stores.

My husband and I joked in the car about how Arabs always "know someone" and find a way to get what they need. But, indeed, it was surprising, amid broken networks and supply chains, to find all these provisions in sufficient quantities. Was the demand just not as high in Allentown? Had they been prepared? Or were Arab provisioning networks much like our communities: tightly knit, generous and trusting, finding no need for panic and hoarding? Perhaps when fear of not being cared for wasn't a factor, or when community preservation superseded individual gain, store runs that left grocers depleted just did not become a thing. Whatever the reason, it was how we found ourselves prepared to safely take our flight.

We left May 22nd with the intention of completing the photoshoot for my cookbook at my parents' home during our visit and returning in July before the end of our lease in Philadelphia to help my husband pack up our apartment and move to the house we had purchased in December and were currently renovating.

But life, as always, had other plans....

Summer 2020—Jerusalem

JUNE: THE MONTH OF QUASI-QUARANTINES

Traveling in and out of Israel has always been a source of anxiety for me. I may have been an Israeli citizen on paper, but I was Palestinian by blood and birth, which relegated me to the #6 security category, the strip search line, the additional interrogations. Basically, the royal second-class citizen treatment. The brightest threads of travel in the tapestry of my recollections are frayed. They are frayed by fear, indignance, and anger at injustice. They are woven through my trips in and out of my home country, in which an occupying power would take any measure to make me feel unwelcome. Still, it is my home, it is where my roots run deep. It is where I continue to return, even as the journey wounds my pride.

This time, however, COVID-19, at least momentarily, seemed to present a greater "risk" than the Palestinian mother with two young children arriving at an empty Ben Gurion airport. As we passed through security on our way in, the only questions revolved around our body temperatures and quarantine locations. I gave border patrol the address of my family's home: Abdel-Rahman el Dajani Street, Beit Hanina. She asked for a house number, and it took every ounce of control for me not to crack a joke. We had only received street names a few years back, I myself wasn't sure what our house number was. In the end it was a pointless question because she could not find our street in her system anyway. We settled for a vague address of Jerusalem followed by a phone number.

"Someone will be coming to check on you periodically to make sure you're quarantining," she informed me, "so make sure you do." I nodded my head and walked out into arrivals.

My girls ran toward my father and balked a foot away from him, hands outstretched. "Mama said we can't hug you for two weeks."

"Don't listen to her," he chuckled, then squeezed them both, his smile—in spite of being hidden by a mask—betrayed by the folding accordions around his eyes, compressed more than I had seen them in a very long time.

I had wondered throughout the previous months what must be going through the minds of the elderly. My parents, initially afraid, had been pushing us to come, telling us not to worry about them. If given the choice, would a grandparent want to go a year without seeing their grandkids, or would they risk their health for the pure pleasure that was the cuddle of a child who gave their life meaning? Was it a question of quantity versus quality of life? Was it even a zero-sum game? Had the tables shifted and were children now forced to become the "responsible" parties making decisions on behalf of parents, enforcing separation in the name of preservation? I wish the answers were clear, I wish there was a right or wrong way to do things, but it seemed to me it was like the insurance industry: no guarantees, all about statistics and mitigating risk.

We had taken all precautions for two weeks before leaving Philadelphia and kept on N95 masks throughout the empty flight. Still, I kept my distance from my parents those first few days: no hugs or kisses, sitting at the far end of the dining table, windows always open. Looking back, I'm not sure who was deluding whom. Had any of us been ill with the virus, our methods of "quarantining" would have certainly still provided ample room for transmission. But, right or wrong, family is the most revered unit in Arab society, and the idea of separation for protection struck us as counterintuitive

Less than 24 hours after arriving, the house phone rang.

"Is Reem Kassis available?" the voice on the other end asked. It was police officers calling to ensure I was indeed home, quarantining. My mother brought the phone to me and the gentleman on the line asked a few perfunctory questions. "I need to see you to make sure you are home," he finished.

"Ok, just make a left at the first roundabout and we're the second house up the hill," I explained. He refused. My house was in an Arab neighborhood, and he did not want to drive up to it. Still, he insisted he must see me. But I could not leave the house since I was quarantining.

Catch-22.

"I'll wave at you from the window," I finally suggested. The police officer parked on the main road separating our Arab neighborhood house from an Israeli settlement, waving to me through tree leaves. I opened the window and waved right back.

The story repeated itself a few times during those first two weeks and then again, two weeks later, when my brother arrived. Was it not ironic that when it came to services and rights, Palestinian citizens of Israel were a demographic threat with second-class treatment, but when what happened to us could affect someone else in the country, we suddenly became an equal priority? Perhaps then the solution to the long-standing conflict was intertwining one population's positive outcomes with the other's. I suspect this outlook might be too naive or hopeful, and soon after the threat of COVID-19 dissipates we will reclaim our second-class status and its associated "benefits." After all, decades of resentment stemming from feelings of unfairness and oppression do not dissipate overnight.

Still, in the summer of 2020, as I flew home to work on my cookbook, it seemed like common threads could exist. Yes, those threads would always be pulled precariously taut, and a little tug would give rise to complicated feelings and questions, but that July I focused on the sliver of hope, no matter how unwarranted. My photographer was an Israeli who, during the photo shoot, made his way from his home in Tel-Aviv to ours in Jerusalem on a daily basis, often crashing in the guestroom if the day of shooting had stretched too long. By the time my mandatory two-week quarantine was over, summer was in full swing, and the photo shoot for my cookbook was finally set to start.

JULY: THE MONTH OF DELUDED DISTANCING

I knew that when shooting started for the book I would be somewhat exposed to other people and unable to visit relatives I had gone over a year without seeing. So the weekend between the end of quarantining and the beginning of photo shooting we drove up to the Galilee to visit my aunt and uncles. We did not wear masks, but we said we would not hug anyone. I held on to that plan until I stepped out of the car and my aunt looked at my daughters, tears in her eyes, and embraced them, kissing the tops of their hair instead of their cheeks. My cousin then looked at me. "Is it okay?" she asked, her hands outstretched. I nodded, and she engulfed me in a hug that tugged at the threads of my heart and mind alike, reminding me of our childhood tussles, but also reminding me of just how much I had craved human contact over the last four months.

It was not natural for humans to go so long without physical touch, and while we had all taken precautions with regard to work and going out, family back home seemed to be the exception to the rule. Family was refuge, not risk. True, it was summer. People had become complacent, and the harsh second wave had not yet arrived. But I couldn't place a finger on why this complacency had set in. Was it plain and simple fatigue? Was it a sense of delusion? Or a deep-set idea that family protects, it doesn't harm? Was it denial of the severity of the circumstances? Was it a sense of security in numbers? Whatever it was, I felt a sense of safety being back home—no matter how misguided—like I was in the eye of the storm rather than spinning on its periphery.

If there's one thing Arab societies are good at, it is sidestepping uncomfortable conversations. There is a premium placed on diplomacy and niceties because God forbid you offend someone by asking an uncomfortable question. When the photo shoot started, we didn't discuss masks, we just instinctively kept a few feet away from each other. As I ran up and down stairs between two kitchens, plating and replating, I marked the dishes that had not been touched by the photographer's or his assistants' hands and set them aside for later consumption. Anything that had been touched by a hand was reserved for the person who touched it, if they chose to eat it. Everything else was tossed out.

Throughout those few weeks, people came and went—different assistants, prop stylists, and friends—no kissing, no hugging, no sharing plates. But we were all in the same house, talking, moving past each other. With the benefit of hindsight and what we now know about COVID-19, I ask myself, "How could we have been so blasé about the whole thing, simply assuming that by being a few feet apart and not eating from the same plates we were safe?"

We were basically playing a game of Russian roulette. It was either complete lockdown and no interaction, or complete disregard of medical advice. But even growing up we had always been a society of extremes, had we not? Israeli or Palestinian, right or wrong, left-wing or right-wing, Christian or Muslim. As a Palestinian citizen of Israel with a Christian father and a Muslim mother, I grew up straddling all the gray areas in a society that defined you by the presence or absence of light rather than the shades in between. Now, too, I struggled to walk on one side of the track.

Those last months of writing the cookbook under these circumstances helped it take a different final shape than the one I had originally imagined. My second cookbook was an attempt to show a modern snapshot of an Arab kitchen, traced throughout history. I had realized early on that you could not understand a modern Arab table without understanding the rich, deep history of the region. When COVID-19 hit, the disconnect from people I cared about and a place I called home sent me into the arms of food, allowing it to embrace me, to wrap me warmly in a blanket of happy memories when neither kin nor country could be touched. I may have always known, but at that point I finally understood, just how powerful food was in defining the relationship between people, place, and identity.

Those last few months of entwined thoughts and emotions, of circumstances that could not be disentangled from each other, of choices that were interdependent—much like an Arabesque pattern of infinitely intertwined shapes—and the parallels I saw between them and my cooking gave rise to the title of the book: *The Arabesque Table*.

When we think of COVID-19 and social distancing, most of us probably imagine being forced away from friends or elderly parents, not from our nuclear family. But both choices and circumstances dictated that my daughters and I were separated from my husband for the whole summer. We had purchased a house back in December, which needed a gut renovation. COVID-19 delays forced my husband to stay back in Philadelphia to ensure that it would be ready for us to move in by the end of our lease in July. But that would turn out not to be the case.

Even though he would have loved to join us for just a week or two, he was not an Israeli citizen and would not have been allowed into the country, even as his wife and daughters were there. We settled for FaceTime calls. Each call either started or ended with a question about when we could return. Our lease had ended, and our new home was still under renovation, COVID-19 having delayed it by more than just a few weeks. The wait continued.

Reem Kassis and her daughters in her parents' kitchen in Jerusalem

Maqlubeh and *mahashi* are the traditional foods my mother always has on her table, the ones that remind me of my childhood, the ones she always makes when I go back. But two months into our wait, my daughters were craving the foods that reminded them of their own home and routines. "Sushi, sushi, sushi," Yasmeen, my six-year-old, chanted when asked what she wanted us to cook each day. Shrimp tempura sushi, to be specific, and so my mother, in a bid to bring her some measure of comfort during a summer that had been both one of the best and one of the most difficult of my daughters' lives, found a non-kosher sushi place (shrimp is not kosher) an hour away in Tel-Aviv. We took the trek to pick it up, picking up the corners of my daughter's mouth along with it. Hala, my youngest, craved the gelato ice cream I often got for them on their walk home from school. The *rukab* ice cream purchased from the man with a cooler walking the streets of our Jerusalem neighborhood in the evening did not cut it, so my father drove to the German Colony to a gelateria called Aldo to bring her a piece of the childhood she craved, the one she had been separated from for months.

It all sounds so mundane, but for a child of that age, the comfort and satisfaction that a certain flavor or experience gives rise to is enough to become a prominent thread in their memories, one that keeps them tethered to their past and their families, even as life stretches them in countless directions.

My daughters cried for missing their father in August, just as they cry now for missing their grandparents back in Jerusalem. That is the curse of the immigrant, you always leave pieces of your heart in different places, with no easy way to unite them all. We finally decided to head back, even if the house was not done—camping in the living room sounded much more exciting than it actually was—and we flew back to Philadelphia not knowing when we would see my parents again.

Fall and Winter 2020—Bryn Mawr

SEPTEMBER: UPROOTED

Soon after we moved into our new house and renovation work started to wind down, we did what adults are expected to do: we bought plants. From past experience I knew that in spite of my best intentions, I had a tendency to kill plants off. Even the notoriously difficult to kill snake plant met its demise in my last apartment. My green thumb was more of a brown one it seemed. I promised myself this time would be different.

I read up, I bought potting mix, fertilizer, and planters with proper drainage. I potted the ficus plants and the Chinese evergreens, the philodendrons and spider plants, and everything in between, saving the lemon tree for last.

The tree was stubborn. Try as I might—wet soil or dry—I was not able to pry it out of its plastic planter. When I finally did, the roots were all tangled up, like threads that had been unspooled then gathered back. With every attempt to loosen them for repotting, I felt them break in my hands, my heart along with them. I came to see myself in that tree. I was the one who wanted to leave Jerusalem and my small maternal and paternal villages for a bigger world. I excitedly packed my bags at seventeen with a burning fire inside me and an appetite to take on the world. I made the choice to leave, and yet, fifteen years on, not a day goes by where I don't wonder why I made those choices.

Would I make the same choices if I were to go back? I probably would. But that, again, is the curse of the immigrant: you leave because your options are better outside, but the price you pay for those options is the constant sense of uprootedness and the constant questioning. The world of opportunities may be bigger outside, acceptance more easily afforded, but there is no real sense of belonging. Where are the friends whose parents went to school with my own, whose grandparents taught in the town school and whose aunts were the town midwives and their uncles the store owners, the lawyers, the doctors of the town? This small world I speak of might not exist in most places anymore, but something about connections to the past give us a sense of stability, a feeling of firm ground beneath our feet, the absence of which makes our daily lives nothing but bouts of vertigo.

COVID-19 highlighted this for me, like it did for many others. Where our daily lives, our work, and our friends might have offered temporary distractions from some of life's bigger questions, the extended time at home—especially when dealing with questions of life and death—brought those issues to the forefront. "I don't know where I would be buried if I died," I said to a good friend of mine one day while we were walking outside. She stopped and looked at me. "I was thinking the same thing this week!" she said. She was an Israeli, I was Palestinian, but here in the suburbs of Philadelphia those differences faded. When you're an immigrant, anything that reminds you of home feels pleasantly familiar. "Two of my friends were talking about it last week," she went on, "we still don't have an answer!" We both laughed and offered up comical suggestions, from cremation with every child receiving a portion to plans to stay alive indefinitely.

We did not come up with an answer because, truly, there is none. I never understood that having a town to call my home, a lineage to trace, a community I could count on for life's defining moments, was something valuable. And yet, when issues of life and death become salient, when separation becomes a way of life and travel is not within reach, you start to understand why lineage gives life meaning.

The lemon tree has since blossomed, small buds of lemons slowly appearing. I check on it every day, watering when necessary and smelling its blossoms when I miss the ones from my family's land. I had uprooted this sapling and replanted it, and for a while it was touch and go. There is no telling how many of those lemons will take hold and grow or how big and strong this tree will ultimately be. But for now, sitting in a south-facing window with plenty of sun, the tree has no choice but to continue on.

OCTOBER: THE MONTH OF JOYLESS COOKING

Fawaz Turki, a Palestinian poet exiled after the 1948 war and raised as a refugee in Beirut once said: "For my own generation . . . our last day in Palestine was the first day that we began to define our Palestinian identity. . . . It had never occurred to anyone to define it, or to endow it with any special attributes. Until we were severed from it."

I understood what he meant only after I left Jerusalem to make different countries my home. I learned that lesson, yet again, when I moved into our new home, with its giant kitchen, under the cloud of COVID-19, because we only come to recognize the preciousness of what we take for granted the minute it is pulled out of our grasp.

When planning our new kitchen, I had dinner parties in mind with everyone fitting around the kitchen island as I put finishing touches on dishes. I envisioned weeknight dinners with friends and weekend gatherings with relatives becoming easier and less crowded as every person had a seat with ample space. I heard the sounds of children running around, laughter in the house, food and drink amply flowing. I had dreamed of weaving threads that would embellish my recollections when I grew old. But COVID-19 meant those kinds of gatherings were nowhere on the horizon, that the tapestry of 2020 in hindsight would remain devoid of color.

Our first weeks in the new house were quiet. I made dinner every night for the four of us and we built a new routine in a new place. Both my daughters had birthdays—quiet affairs where we had to slice cakes across continents over zoom—but there was comfort in having each other and having the structure of this ritual. Still, I found myself not enjoying cooking. Granted, I now had a five-year-old and a seven-year-old who found something to criticize in every dish I made. They proclaimed favorites one day only to shun them the next or went on strike and stared at the rest of us as we ate, satisfied with a glass of milk and a banana for dinner. But while these things might have made me question the point of cooking, they were not the reason I lost the joy in it.

You see, for most of the last decade, I have been cooking on a regular basis. In small part, this was for recipe testing, but in large part it was the way I had learned to build a community in the different cities I found myself inhabiting. It was how I got to know people, how I made new friends even when everyone said it was hard to make good friends in adulthood. It was how I built ties and some semblance of roots even as I, and later my family and I, continued to flutter from place to place.

For some people, a splattering of paint against a canvas revives memories of a long gone past. For others, it is the hum of cords on an oud or buzuq that brings the good old days reverberating into the folds of a modern life. For me, it was always food that melted away the walls around me and built up those of my childhood's kitchen. It was food that gently tried to coax my roots into their new planter. It was food that built my community and gave me a sense of purpose in it. And when it ceased to serve that purpose, it ceased to thrill me the way it always had.

NOVEMBER: TRYING TO FIND MY *NAFAS*

A year and half ago, I was at a Georgetown symposium on Middle Eastern cuisine. After a short lecture I gave, a woman in the audience asked what made the food of our mothers and grandmothers so special. She wanted to know why, even after following a recipe to a tee, someone else's food could taste better to us. "*Nafas*," I told her. *Nafas* means breath or spirit in Arabic, but when talking about food it alludes to that intangible element, that thing that made my mother's stuffed *koosa* taste so much more special than mine. A few months later, this kind lady, Zeina Azzam, who I later found out was also Palestinian, reached out to tell me she had written a poem inspired by my answer. I was touched and humbled by her gesture, by seeing how two people can relate and understand each other across time and place and circumstances, by virtue of sharing a common nationality.

For much of the pandemic, life was about damage control: how to work from home with kids around, how to keep the kids abreast of their academics, how to buy groceries without waiting in line, how to ration what you bought so you wouldn't have to make a grocery run, how to maintain contact while physically distancing, how to enjoy a semblance of a normal life safely and so on. In November I finally realized that it had ceased to be a question of dealing with the pandemic and had instead become a way of life. Masks at this point were so common in our life we found them lying around everywhere from our entry table and kitchen cabinets to our car and jacket pockets, just like kids' stray socks and lost coins.

Like those scattered masks, it seemed to me that my joy and love for cooking had also been scattered. I would cook the same recipe I had made countless times before and not find the satisfaction in it, some element of flavor eluding me. I was angry at life and its injustices, I was stressed and anxious about the future, and I was longing for the warmth and closeness of my community. All those feelings seemed to be dripping from my fingertips into my food as I chopped and stirred. My *nafas* had changed, and my food along with it. As I struggled to bring back those elements, I could not stop thinking back to Zeina's poem. I dug through my papers and read it. Then I read it a hundred times over:

Nafas in the Kitchen
By Zeina Azzam
For Reem Kassis

The Palestinian chef
says nafas is like a spirit,
an undefined knowing
that lives in the act of
preparing food

as if ancestors
reside in the knives
that chop and slice,

the parers and the
juicers, the measurers
and the tasters.

Nafas flows from the scents
of spices from childhood,
the deep colors of
beets and saffron,
the memories of how
to stuff a grapeleaf
just so,
pick mallow leaves
from their stalks,
grate nutmeg resolutely
with a coarse metal shield.

You can't teach nafas,
she stresses,
just like you can't implant
a memory, a presence.
It seeps into generations,
forming something bigger
than both the pinch of salt
and the generous stewing pot.

Nafas is the sigh
that emanates from
the core, the inhale
and exhale into air,
to share.
Even zaatar, she says,
breathes between cultures,
travels thousands of miles
to bring nafas
to new homes,
kitchens in exile.

It has been a process since then, and many are the days when my *nafas* is strained. But every time, before I cook a dish from my childhood, a dish that promises to strengthen the threads connecting me to my past, I reread that poem. I read it and remember that food is not just about satisfying a craving or a desire, it is not just about me remembering the "good old days." No. Cooking those dishes is a way to honor those who have come before me, it is a way to allow my ancestors' *nafas* to shine through the food, it is a way to weave their stories as a thread through the tapestry of today's life, and in so doing keep them alive.

Granted, it might not be possible to replicate the same experiences and flavors of a childhood when one is thousands of miles away from home and loved ones. But I had my own children now, and I knew that everything I cooked would one day be stamped not only in their minds but coded into the DNA of their emotional connection to their childhood and culture. The poem reminds me that even as I struggle, my ancestors struggled before me, and the only choice we have is to march on, to weave the threads of our existence—whatever color they may be—into the tapestry that covers our history.

DECEMBER: THE BEGINNING OF THE END

The first dish I ever made after leaving home was *maqlubeh*. I was a freshman at university in the United States, and I had never cooked a meal from start to finish prior to that day. I remember calling my mother so many times she finally told me it would be cheaper for her to fly to the United States and cook it for me than to foot my telephone bill. I eventually crossed the courtyard of my dormitory into a building with a cockroach-infested communal kitchen without the right size or kind of pot. While I don't remember how I fried the eggplants or cooked the chicken or drained the soaked rice, I do remember flipping (*maqlubeh* means flipped over in Arabic) a giant platter of *maqlubeh* that everyone who had stayed behind for spring break freshman year enjoyed a serving of. Tucked away in a locked album on Facebook is a photograph of one of my friends eating straight from the serving platter. The dish is unrecognizable next to my mother's and grandmother's, even next to the more expert creations I put out today. But fifteen years ago, it was a red thread in my mind along which I traveled the six thousand miles from Pennsylvania to Jerusalem.

Today feels starkly different from those days. For the first time in fifteen years, I cannot cook for friends. Simple phrases like "come over for dinner" or "stop by for coffee and a cake"—my language of food, my means of communication—have been taken away from me. Yes, I can still speak, and I can still write, but there are instances where words fail and where food can communicate feelings both more subtly and more powerfully. Today, I find myself suddenly silent.

At every turn in my life, new jobs, new universities, new cities, my table has hosted more diners (and, in most cases, eventually friends) than I can count. Looking back at all the people who have remained meaningful throughout my life, regardless of where this life has taken me, I can almost always point to an early encounter over food. As I mourn the end of this lost year, I also mourn the lost opportunities to deepen friendships and cement new ones. I mourn the people we lost, and the stories and histories forever lost with them. I mourn physical touch, the reassuring hugs and shoulder pats, the relaxed sharing of food and small spaces, and all the gestures that may take years to come back, not because of the virus, but because of the trauma it has left in its wake.

As I write this paragraph, the beginning of the end seems near. My parents and most of my family back in Jerusalem, in a small country technically always at war, have received both doses of the vaccine, while we, in "the greatest country on earth," have no indication of when we might be eligible, let alone how or where we will receive it once we are.

But a new president has been sworn in. Alongside him, the first woman, daughter of immigrants, half Indian, half African American, vice president is making dreams bigger for little girls. Vaccinations promise to embark on a better trajectory now.

2020 is finally over.

Many are the times I said, "I've just written 2020 off." Indeed, I want it to be the year that never existed. It was the year we didn't buy the annual Christmas ornament with our growing family members' names on it. It was the year we didn't celebrate holidays or birthdays with loved ones. It was the year my girls were home from school, and life turned upside down. It is the year we all want to forget. But even as we put it behind us, I have an inkling 2020 will not disappear into the background. No. Years from now, for those of us lucky enough not to have succumbed to its grimmest reaper, 2020 will not be a neutral thread in our memory, nor will it be a lost year. It will be a woven string of bright red. A reminder that health, family, and connection with others are what really matters in life, and a lesson in cherishing those things lest they be snatched away.

Bryn Mawr, Pennsylvania
January 2021

Malfoof (Stuffed Cabbage Rolls)

Serves: 4–6

My mother only makes this dish in the winter because that is cabbage season in Palestine, and the plants at that time are watered only with rain, which gives them the best taste. Abroad, I can't afford to be as picky, so as long as I find a good green cabbage, I buy it, and malfoof is on the menu. "Good" green cabbage means it feels light when you pick it—not dense—and that's exactly what you need to be able to take the leaves apart. If you can't find Middle Eastern or green cabbage, savoy and sweetheart are also good alternatives. Some people add lemon and crushed garlic at the end of cooking, but I prefer to cook it with the whole garlic cloves and serve the lemon juice mixed with chili flakes alongside it for the best of both worlds.

Method

Fill a large stockpot, wide enough to hold the entire cabbage, with water a little more than halfway up the sides. Sprinkle in some salt and bring to a boil.

With the tip of a sharp knife, make a circular incision at an angle around the core of the cabbage until it loosens up and you can pull out the core entirely. Once the water in the stockpot is boiling, carefully drop the entire cabbage into the pot and boil for about 5 minutes. As the leaves start to soften, use metal tongs to pull out one leaf at a time and set aside on a large platter or tray. Once you are left with the cabbage heart, you can take it out entirely and set aside with the leaves to cool.

Meanwhile, prepare the stuffing by combining the rice, olive oil, spices, and salt in a large bowl. Add the meat and mix with your hands, breaking up any lumps of meat, until everything is well incorporated.

For the cabbage

Water

Salt

1 Middle Eastern green cabbage, about 4.5 lb (roughly 2 kg, see note)

8–10 garlic cloves, skin on

2 ¼ cups chicken, lamb, or beef broth (about 500 ml)

For the stuffing

1 ¼ cups short grain rice, rinsed, soaked for 15 minutes and drained (about 250 g)

3 tablespoons olive oil or melted butter

1 teaspoon salt

1 teaspoon nine spice mix

½ teaspoon ground cumin

½ lb minced lamb or beef meat (250 g)

To serve

½ cup lemon juice

1 teaspoon red chili flakes

Plain yogurt

To prepare the leaves for stuffing, set each one on a cutting board and remove the tough stalk in the middle, leaving you with two halves. If each half is very large, you can cut them in half again. You want each piece to be roughly the size of your palm with a somewhat regular shape.

Place about 1 teaspoon of the stuffing at the bottom edge of each leaf and spread lengthwise, leaving roughly 1 inch (at least 2 centimeters) empty on each side. Tightly roll each leaf up without folding over the edges. If the edges are not neat once rolled, use a knife to slightly trim them, making sure to leave some empty space on each side so the rice has room to grow without escaping from the leaves during cooking.

Place the cut stalks in the bottom of a large pot (if you prefer to have a few leaves stick to the bottom for that crispy, browned flavor, do not use the stalks and place the leaves directly in the pot). Arrange the leaves, seam side down, snuggly in the pot and tuck the unpeeled garlic cloves between them as you go along.

Pour the broth over the cabbage leaves, and place a plate on top to prevent them from moving around while cooking. Taste the broth and, if not salty enough, adjust the seasoning. Cover the pot and bring to a boil on high heat, then reduce heat and simmer until the stuffing is fully cooked, the leaves are very tender, and the liquid is almost entirely evaporated, about 60–90 minutes. Check on the leaves periodically to make sure the liquid has not completely evaporated; if it has and the leaves are not fully cooked, gradually add more liquid and continue to cook until done.

When done, remove the pot from the heat and allow it to sit for 10 minutes.

To serve, place a large, inverted serving platter over the pot. Using a hot pot holder or dish towel to protect your hand from the hot pot, place one hand over the platter and another under the pot, then flip the pot over and set the platter down. Slowly lift up the pot allowing the leaves to settle down into the platter.

Serve with lemon juice mixed with chili flakes (to be spooned over the leaves) and a side of yogurt. Leftovers can be stored in the fridge for three days.

Note: It is also possible to microwave the cabbage. Put the cabbage into a large shallow bowl and microwave on high for 5–7 minutes. Take out and peel off as many leaves as possible. Once you reach the center or leaves that have not softened enough, return the rest of the cabbage to the microwave for another 5 minutes. Another alternative is to freeze the entire cabbage overnight, remove the following morning, and allow it to defrost, at which point the leaves will have softened enough to be removed individually. This method is by far the easiest if you have a large freezer. The downside, however, is that some of the leaves will become brown around the edges.

Quarantine Cooking in an Improvised Household

2

STEPHANIE JOLLY: The first identifiable COVID-19 case in New York City was registered on March 1, 2020, arriving on Qatar Airways Flight 701 from Doha.[1] "I was almost on that flight," I blurted out without looking up from the newspaper. I said it more to myself than anyone else. Nearly four weeks into the stay-at-home order, to read the paper over tea and breathe without difficulty already felt like a miracle born from a thousand lucky coincidences.

I had instead flown a day earlier, returning from some inadvertent medical tourism in Nepal. The trip was initially supposed to be for a wedding, but after the sudden discovery of a lump on my neck and faced with a significant wait for an in-network referral, the young doctor who had seen me for all of fifteen minutes pursed his lips before declaring, "I would suggest getting seen while you're abroad, if that's an option." It was outside Pokhara, my husband and I the lone guests of an otherwise deserted resort, which, just weeks prior, had been booked to capacity by Chinese tourists, that I received an email bearing the results of my first biopsy: papillary carcinoma.

Two weeks later, March 3, I sat in the exam room at the New York Thyroid Surgical Center in Columbia University's oncology pavilion. It was such a relief—an exhalation after a breathlessly stressful period—after days of shock and research and phone calls, cutting through one band of red tape after another. Surgery was scheduled for early

If you have a home, you think you can hide from death. This year, more than any other year, that idea has settled. Stay home, stay safe. If you have no home, walk to one.

— Tishani Doshi,
"How to Write an Elegy in the Year of Dying," December 31, 2020

April 2020, with pre-op appointments in a few weeks. I flew home to Kentucky.

I returned to New York City for a work trip on March 14 in the midst of a rapidly evolving situation days before the rest of the world pivoted toward working from home. Though a remote employee for nearly a decade, I was scheduled for a few weeks of in-person studio shoots in Manhattan. Before I left, there was a brief talk about worst case scenarios: the risks between getting locked down *in* the city—away from home where the chance of COVID exposure was higher—or getting locked *out* of the city without any way to enact my cancer treatment plan.

The office shut down two days after I arrived, but my lymph node biopsy was still on the books. As far as I knew, so was my surgery. I never imagined I would have to have a plan in case the city got redzoned. Or if my surgical team got sick. Or if I got sick. Or if the hospitals were overwhelmed.

I called Krishnendu, a longtime friend with whom I had grown increasingly close over the years, who conveniently lived just north of the East Village, close enough to the hospital where I was to be treated. I showed up with the small carry-on suitcase and computer bag I had brought for my business trip, neither of us realizing at the time that we were in essence moving in together for the foreseeable future.

KRISHNENDU RAY: The weekend of March 1, 2020, I had just returned from Toronto after delivering a talk at the Center for Diaspora and Transnational Studies. Overbooked, as usual, I jumped right into a conversation on street vending in Delhi and New York for a Heritage Radio and Gastronomica podcast. My teenage son Rudra was away at college in Pennsylvania. Other than the disturbing news from Stephanie a few weeks earlier about her cancer diagnosis, nothing appeared to be amiss. I called my brother, a critical care physician in Delhi, to wish him a happy birthday. We wondered if there was a degree of overreaction on the part of public health officials.

There was a surreal inertia as I continued preparing for talks and presentations, as if nothing was going to change. Later that week, staff members came to express their anxieties about the rising tide of the virus in the city, deepening their concerns about their commutes. I decided to rotate and stagger staff schedules to reduce exposure and anxiety. On March 11, New York University moved to remote instruction and set up round-the-clock training sessions for teaching via Zoom. The in-person advisory board meeting of the Street Vendor Project was canceled. Plans to fly to the South by Southwest symposium on March 13 were scratched. Rudra's spring break coincided with NYU's, and he was sent home on March 14, giving me precious little time to prepare and plan for a suddenly remote curriculum. Weekly meetings with the program directors and department chairs were established to deal with contingencies and manage the crises. Faculty and staff Happy Zoom Hour was added to address the isolation and anxiety. Rudra's return to campus was canceled.

Stephanie Jolly and Krishnendu Ray documenting a lockdown meal

The news from Italy transfixed me. Images of overwhelmed hospitals, stretched doctors, and nurses sobbing in front of cameras with scared journalists seeped terror into my veins. I did not talk about it, hoping to avoid the curse, but I was morbidly riveted by the numbers. The figure was still low for New York City, only 702 cases, with most infections among the overcrowded immigrant residences in Queens. In those neighborhoods about 15 percent of the workforce is in the restaurant business, compared to 6 percent citywide. Affluence and square footage are inversely related to risk.[2] Cases grew exponentially over the next two weeks, to 21,066 in the United States and 6,266 in New York City. The city had suddenly gone silent—with all nonessential services closed—other than the wailing of ambulances speeding past my window on First Avenue, reminding me of the final stage of the illness.

With Stephanie and Rudra in the household, it was no longer about me. I was worried about two things: bringing the bug home and exposing Stephanie as she waited for her cancer treatment and, to put it directly, dying, leaving my son to fend for himself. I scrupulously sanitized every door handle each time I left the apartment, wearing my mask and carrying a clutch of antiseptic wipes. The fear was unrelenting.

I could not reveal my panic at work because I had to motivate people to work calmly. I could not panic at home to people already worried about their health. I could not panic on the phone with my brother and my parents, as I worried about my father's potential exposure given his stage 3B lung-cancer diagnosis that my brother had been treating over the previous two years.

To work through my terror, I took a walk down First Avenue, past the Korean greengrocer, which was shuttered, moving west to Second Avenue. My heart seized when I realized I was now walking past an improvised trailer truck morgue with a thrumming refrigeration unit outside one of NYU's smaller hospitals. All I could hear was the deep hum of the condenser. There was no one around. Not one car. Not one person in a city of 8 million with 66 million tourists. Momentum carried me past the truck, ears buzzing with blood pressure. I did not breathe until I crossed the street to Stuyvesant Square Park, incongruously resplendent with a flowering dogwood. I turned around at the giant English Elm by the western gate, crossing to the other side of 2nd Avenue this time to avoid the truck, impatient to return home, keeping the information to myself. My fears entombed.

Phase 1: Tension

SJ: "What are you thinking about dinner?" he asks.

Christ, I'm starting to hate this question. It has barely been twelve hours since the last dinner; my cup of tea from this morning is still sitting on the table, cold but not yet emptied. In fact, I am hardly thinking about food at all, other than the logistics surrounding its procurement and provisioning. I am thinking we should use what we have rather than go to the store again to appease someone's craving. I am thinking we have leftovers piling up that we will need to eat or throw out. I am thinking that the frugality I have inherited across generations has trained me to look at what we have and then make a plan. Except we don't really have anything. Nothing that I would consider to be a successful larder at any rate, in good times much less *these* times.

I do not believe I have ever lived anywhere without some form of emergency rations. There were the jars of canned crops in the root cellar of my grandparents' farm. Preserves and dry goods lined the shelves of my suburban childhood garage. There was even a large, plastic garbage bin full of potable water and nonperishables under the back deck at one point, presumably to safeguard against the house itself collapsing during an earthquake or eruption, threats that always seemed to loom large in the shadow of the Cascades. Be prepared. It was the Girl Scout motto instilled in my mother and then in me, but I suspect it was more than that. I lose track of how many great-great-greats I have to count back to find an ancestor who wasn't working the soil for a living and all the insecurity that entails. In my student apartments there was enough pasta and potatoes to ride out most situations. In my house in Lexington, I can imagine the freezer full of last season's apples, blueberries, and pumpkin; a few roasts and some chicken; plenty of butter from when it was last on sale. There is the garden, with herbs and the promise of early spring greens. There are lentils and onions and canned tomatoes. I know the inventory so well that I can direct my husband over the phone to the location of whatever ingredient he cannot find: bottom shelf, far left, in the corner behind the rice—that is where you will find an unopened container of cornstarch. I have always been careful never to run out of the staples "in case of emergency."

Now the hypothetical scenario always lurking in the back of my mind is real, and when I open the cupboards of my adopted kitchen to see what I am equipped to hunker down with I find a tin of anchovies, more than a dozen packets of Thai curry paste, frozen peas, a few cans of various stock, half a pound of rice, and taco shells.

Every day, Krishnendu goes to the store and purchases just enough to make the meals envisioned for that afternoon. Every morning we have to make a new list. The bread is good, but it lacks preservatives and gets hard overnight. The herbs add a brightness to the plates and to the palate, but they quickly wilt and need to be replaced. It is an endless cycle of grocery shopping, day after day, meal after meal. We are supposed to be staying inside.

I have not figured out how to articulate how frustrating it is to have something as temporary as a meal risk exposing us—exposing me.

But it is more than that too—it is also the feeling of being unhomed and reliant on the mercy and generosity of someone else. That feeling compounded when the cooking, the grocery shopping, the meal planning—domestic chores I have often complained about being saddled with—were suddenly wrested from me. There are two adults in this household, but only one of them has the autonomy to make purchasing decisions or the authority to decide what to feed his son. Nor can I protest too vocally about the rhythms of a household I have rather abruptly—gratefully—been allowed to be a part of. So I am called to the table and served my meals at the designated time like a child. In other circumstances one might call this hospitality, but it doesn't feel that way. Of what little control remains, I have further lost the ability to choose what I eat or when.

I can tell my presence is adding an additional burden to the already stressful circumstances, compounded by my perceived unwillingness, if not inability, to take part in the daily ritual of "feeling in the mood" for some dish or another. I forget to eat when I am stressed, until I binge on an entire bag of chips or chocolates, in which case I forget to stop. Snacks ... I have mixed feelings about adding them to the shopping list, partly because I do not want to expose my embarrassing coping habits and partly because I do not want to create a reason for him to spend any longer outside these walls than necessary or spend money on items he wouldn't otherwise purchase were it not for me.

And then there is the graph that I made one night, plotting the number of cases per capita between two neighboring states, Kentucky and Tennessee, one with and one without stay-at-home orders and state protections. I posted it on my personal social media page, thinking it might encourage a few extended family members and acquaintances on the fence to adhere to the guidelines if they could visualize the impact their actions might have. It found its way to a local media personality who reposted to legions of followers and it too "went viral." It was now also spinning out of my control. So, in addition to everything else, I found myself fielding interview requests from CNN and local news networks, all the while trying to ignore trolls on Twitter.[3]

The question about dinner has been lingering in the air, as I stare beyond the wall ahead trying not to say something rash like "I don't know" or "I don't care."

"I'm not hungry yet, so. . . ."

Not the worst response I could have given.

"What type of answer is that?! You don't wait until you're hungry to think about dinner. Dinner isn't about being hungry; it's about having dinner. You have to make a plan."

But to me it is about hunger. This is why I, too, want a plan—so that we can have enough food to not be hungry. Anything can be a meal if it satisfies your appetite; if you are not hungry, don't consume the calories. I grab a notepad and start listing the leftovers in the upper-right-hand corner and days of the week down the side.

For three days I catalog the perishables in the kitchen and track which ones need to be eaten before they go bad. To say Krishnendu is enjoying the cooking would be an overly positive distortion, but he is doing it, and from what I can tell he does not want to relinquish the burden to others. Maybe he doesn't think someone who fails to religiously eat proper meals knows how to cook? Maybe he doesn't trust me to account for his and Rudra's preferences? Burgers. Steak. These are not exceptionally complicated meals to conceive of.

The next time the question comes I am more prepared.

"I am thinking we should do a pasta, but not a meat sauce—something lighter, fresher."

"A dry pasta, a carbonara."

"No, more like with butter and white wine."

"I'm not seeing it."

What is the point of my suggestions if they have to be something that he has already imagined?

"I can do it."

We had fresh tomatoes and herbs from yesterday's grocery store run, of course. While the linguine boiled, I sauteed shallots and garlic in butter, added white wine, and simmered until tossing everything together in the pan before plating, garnished with basil and grated parmesan.

I washed the pans in the sink before bringing three bowls out to the table to await the verdict.

"The pasta is overcooked and needs more salt."
I thought it was good.

KR: Other than my son, I don't like other people in my space, but even he has acquired new young adult smells and attitudes that are difficult to tolerate without some effort. Since his mother left, nearly a decade ago, I have gotten used to making decisions on my own. Knowing I can run to a store almost any time of the day to get supplies that I want has been a comfort.

I come from the lower middle class in India, having grown up in the shadow of scarcity. My father was a salesman, my mother a stay-at-home mom. We got a refrigerator in the late 1970s, and we did not own a car or a telephone until after I had left India to immigrate to the United States. That is partially what drives my desire to fill my home with books and flowers and fresh ingredients. It is a way to signal comfort and affluence, not just of crude capital but of more evanescent cultural capital. I have become quite insistent on my newfound opportunity to signal cultural achievement. Fresh flowers, so fragile and vulnerable to rot, underline the performative aspect of cultural capital. In the Bourdieusian sense, more fleeting, unnecessary things represent the taste of affluence. I have always loved fresh flowers, for as long as I can remember, but the obduracy to obtain them was new. I want them at the dining table, which has now also become my workspace.

No one needs fresh flowers to survive, but I need these walks, these errands, to stay sane and away from the crowded apartment. I resent the new need to generate consent, to be agreeable all the time. I resent the perpetual presence of others in my space. I resent eating canned food. Now, more than ever, I want to cook each meal fresh. There is an obsessiveness in me now about fresh cilantro, mint, basil, rosemary, and dill. I have never been like this before. Angry, picky, insistent about quotidian things, in spite of the risk of contamination. Perhaps because of it.

More than anything else, I resent the presence of another adult in the household unwilling to plan meals. It is making me unreasonably upset. The end of meal planning was a symptom of the disintegration of my family. Throughout the 2000s, my wife's mental health declined into the depths of paranoid schizophrenia, and I read its most acute symptoms as her refusal to cook and eat together as she locked herself in her room, adding lock, after lock, after lock to the door. I created an alternative world of dinners with my school-aged son. Instead of eating at the dining table we ate at the coffee table in the living room. When Mom was in the psych ward, we would cook dinner and bring it to her. If she was tolerant of us, we would sit with her and do homework while she ate. If she wasn't, we would return home, and I would put Rudra into a long, warm bath. Then every night we would either read Sherlock Holmes stories or *The Ranger's Apprentice*, dozing off. I would get up, pour myself a glass of wine, and begin to read, write, and edit. The night's prep for the day's work ahead. We went through the same rituals of caretaking day after day for a decade.

It was more than a decade ago that my wife went to live with her parents, but here I am still struggling to accommodate another adult within the household, a woman refusing to cook and eat together in the right way. In middle-class urban India, no one eats just because they are hungry, and no one refuses to eat just because they are not hungry. I am also older than Stephanie, so my antipathy toward her normlessness in meal planning has the edginess of generational conflict. Meals are commensal, and it is the job of adults to make them so. This disorganization of mealtimes touched the third rail of my migrant domesticity.[4]

Phase 2: Emerging Routine

SJ: The shallot pasta gives me a foothold in the kitchen, and with it the growing confidence to assert my thoughts. The next night, I am invited into the kitchen to make the cucumber salad, up to this point prepared with rough cut cucumbers, avocado, cilantro, and lime. I am tired of it.

"What if I make a different type of cucumber salad?"

"How? With what? Okay, we'll see. Try it."

I could hear the skepticism in his voice, tempered by his conscious effort to be more agreeable.

I sliced the cucumbers into thin coins and sprinkled them with salt before adding rice-wine vinegar and a spoonful of sour cream, topped with fresh basil. Sour cream, of all things, a unifying staple between our individual kitchens that neither of us can fully explain, apart from our similar belief that it makes almost any dish better. There were no leftovers.

From then we began to cycle through our individual go-to dishes—ramen with egg (cooked "exactly 11 minutes and 20 seconds for the right kind of runniness" I learn) and bok choy one night, then orzo with feta, cucumbers, and tomatoes the next. For a time, hearing "I put the sauce on the side because you cannot handle the heat" feels like an accusation, but as my distinct contributions to the household palate are embraced, I slowly accept it as an observation, if not an act of consideration.

We discover that our skills are complementary: I prefer the knife-work of vegetable prep and the creation of salads and sides, while Krishnendu prefers the seasoning and searing of meats. I find he cuts the vegetables too thick, and he thinks I don't use enough salt or heat. Sometime between noon and two o'clock, when we have a break between meetings, we head into the kitchen to warm up the leftovers for lunch, maneuvering around each other in the small kitchen like dancers practicing the choreography. One steps to the right while the other opens the fridge; one squeezes in close to the sink while the other walks behind to get to the microwave; a duck of the head while the cabinet above is opened. Plates, napkins, silverware. Ice in one cup but not the other. The confines of the space necessitate coordination, which requires communication, which has opened the door to collaboration.

There is a busy-ness to it that holds the rest of the world at a distance. Everything is now on pause—the biopsy, the surgery, the treatment. I have subscribed to the daily dispatches from the chief of surgery, who updates the staff and interested public about the hospital's pandemic response and his team's priorities.[5] I read them hoping for answers, but instead I hear the words of a man desperately trying to portray fortitude and hope to a staff under siege. I have deliberately avoided the "cancer as a battle" metaphor since the diagnosis—I will go toe to toe with the insurance company and wrestle the logistics into submission, but it is not as though a favorable outcome means that I have "won" my life back. There are no good wars, just like there are no good cancers.

I am coming to enjoy the anchoring of mealtimes as a way to break up the monotony. As the workdays blend together, meals become the measure of time. "Last Tuesday" could have been yesterday or forever ago, but "the day we had made the potato corn chowder" has a useful resonance.

We read in the paper that there is a shortage of yeast as everyone turns their attention toward making bread. "Who are these people," I wonder, "who now have so much extra time on their hands?" Perhaps they are not obsessively doom-scrolling statistics, or managing departmental transitions to remote, or compulsively reading every open access article on PubMed looking for clues to survival. I hadn't for a second thought about baking bread, though it causes me to remember that biscuits exist. My maternal grandmother spoke about "making biscuit" regularly, but I watched her make them approximately zero times; any biscuits I ate growing up came from the little refrigerated cylinders that pop open when you smack them on the counter.

As COVID cases across the United States reach 350,000, I make biscuits for breakfast—1 stick frozen butter, grated, tossed into 2 cups all-purpose flour, 2 tablespoons baking powder, and a half teaspoon baking soda and salt. Stirred together with 1 cup of milk, soured with vinegar, kneaded 8 times onto the counter. I use the rim of a glass as a biscuit cutter, which inevitably smushes down the sides. It is the best solution we have.

The next day I go out. It is wet and cloudy and empty, which is to say a beautiful day for me to finally do some grocery shopping. It is only the second time I have left the apartment since I arrived. The soundscape is largely sirens, a few birds, and the occasional helicopter. The shops on 1st Avenue are all boarded up; the family-owned grocery across the street will close this week. Those who are out give wide, suspicious berths and avoid eye contact—as if we have all become walking gorgons behind our masks. It is starting to feel normal, which is itself discomforting.

I buy ice cream and flowers. Cucumbers, spinach, beets, goat cheese, manchego, feta, and rice. Asparagus, potatoes, and lemons. All the alliums: shallots, scallions, and red onions. Mint. Bacon. Apples. Provisions to sustain the illusion. If you are eating well, how bad could it really be?

The following Saturday, I repeat the biscuits and this time add a hollandaise. I Google how to poach an egg. "By the time this pandemic is over," I think, "the only reason I'll need to eat at a restaurant is because I don't want to cook."

Krishnendu is insistent that Rudra seize this opportunity of having someone around whom he can learn to bake with, like he used to do with his mom. In the evening he can sometimes be cajoled to assist me with a dessert, but my unreliable protégé more often leaves me standing about in the kitchen waiting for him to come out of his room so that we can begin, or he immediately disappears the moment the last step is complete, saddling me with his mess in addition to the regular dishes. He has been the only member of the household to take up the sudden craze for sourdough, and we make room in the fridge and countertop for the off-smelling jars of starter. It feels a bit like we have acquired a new pet. Am I responsible for feeding this thing on the days he forgets? I decide that I'm not; unlike a sentient animal, I feel no moral obligation for its survival beyond occasionally pointing out that it looks sad and hungry.

For Rudra's nineteenth birthday, I bake a chocolate mousse layer cake covered with ganache. I deceive myself into thinking that I am doing this for him, but as I force everyone to gather around the table at midnight (squarely in the birthday boy's waking hours) to sing, it is evident that this household has zero traditions around birthdays and that blowing out the candles on a cake is a novelty performance they are putting on entirely for me.

At the end of April, the biopsy confirms the presence of cancerous cells in my lymph nodes. Later that week, I get a call that surgery has been scheduled for the following Tuesday. "[We are now] performing emergency surgery and surgery that is considered urgent on a case by case basis," reads the email from Columbia. The hospital is still overwhelmed with COVID-19 patients.

After over a month of stasis it now feels like it is happening too fast. I am relieved it has been scheduled; I am distressed that it has been classified as urgent. I am scared to die and I am afraid of what life will be like without an organ that regulates my metabolism. Even if there is enough time for anyone else to travel into the city to be with me beforehand, there are no flights, and there are no visitors allowed.

Without a restaurant open to have what could be my last hurrah we take to creating the restaurant experience at home with what we have—to minimize exposure at all costs, the grocery trips are put on hold. We pull out a cabbage from the produce bin and replicate the vegetable side from one of our favorite New York City restaurants Simon & the Whale: thick slices of cabbage, partially steamed, then roasted with homemade preserved lemons and prosciutto, to replace the speck (cured pork). Never has cabbage felt so fancy.

KR: In *The Migrant's Table*, I wrote how cooking and eating are conserving impulses among immigrants, showing how middle-class migrants, especially men, insist on a Bengali dinner every night.[6] Dinner in a Chicago suburb can be even more Bengali than one in Kolkata. Breakfast and lunch are where there is rampant hybridization. With dinner, the door is shut on the public American world of commerce and professions, creating a private enclave of culture underlined by the unambiguously Bengali dinner of steamed rice, fish in mustard sauce, and sauteed greens seasoned with *panch phoron*.

I think this is why I have resisted too much variation in my cooking—I cook to replicate; almost all innovation has been accidental. I have adapted—adding new dishes like steak; mashed potatoes with milk, butter, and black pepper; steamed broccoli; Polish-American style kielbasa; and pierogies to an interracial household—but the point always was to get it as close to my mother's Indian cooking of rice, *daal*, and mustard fish or my ex-wife's Irish or Lithuanian grandmother's home cooking.

Now I find that not only are we cooking better and more adventurous stuff—new kinds of salads with fennel and kohlrabi, using specialty vinegars and herbs such as tarragon, dill, sorrel, and sage (newer for me); sweeteners such as honey with attention to provenance, molasses, and *guarapo*; larger cuts of meat, such as pork shoulder and leg of lamb, than I had dared on my own given the South Asian grammar of my cooking—we are also getting better at sharing the space of the living room for our meetings, reading, and writing. I sense that Stephanie and I have come to enjoy the intensity of work in each other's presence; I have come to enjoy working in hers. We now know at least one-half of what work is for the other. There is a lot of editorializing and commenting on our own readings. She reads out sections of Ibn Battuta's *Rihla* (Travels) where he complains, "I stayed for eleven months at the court of this Sultan [in the Malabar] without ever eating bread, for their sole food is rice,"[7] and compares them to her recent reading of Marco Polo's memories of Malabar where he notes that "the staple foods are rice, meat, and milk."[8] We have quite a laugh at how quickly these elite male travelers appear to judge the local women sexually, marry them, abandon them, and move on. She is beginning to edit my writing more intensively. Explaining to me the grammatical rules I am breaking. Apparently, my prepositions are all out of place—at, of, in, to, by, with—presumably a problem that non-native speakers exhibit. I am beginning to understand the specificity of my errors in writing in English.

And then there is the *New York Times*. Everyone reads the paper version of the NYT delivered every day to our door. Rudra usually picks one news item and poses questions about it or proffers some opinion that is usually more centrist than mine. If Stephanie is already leafing through the newspaper with her breakfast when I get up, she makes it a point to hand me over the main section, moving on to pick at one of the other sections instead. I feel a little guilty; sometimes I make a vague noise to suggest that she can keep it, but I do not insist. I presume the patriarchal privilege of getting the front page when I sit down with my tea and toast, topped with cold smoked salmon, avocado, crème fraîche, and sometimes with cilantro, depending on whether I have had the opportunity to refurbish our supplies. Privileges are tough to concede.

On Wednesdays, she reaches for the NYT food section and offers up what she sees as a suggestion for dinner. I have almost never cooked from this before. There is the bean and sausage soup with parsley by Melissa Clark. Then the baked salmon with Dijon mustard, mayonnaise, lemon, and cilantro by Genevieve Ko. "We should make this." She turns the paper around for me, putting her finger on the green goddess dressing under the title "A Dip for All Your Wilting Herbs."[9]

We are beginning to make lots of interesting stuff on toast, where we chop a little, mix a little, and have something warm and filling so that we can return to work refreshed and reoriented. Chicken salad with green onions but without celery (Stephanie cannot stand its taste, nor can she stand the sound of anyone else eating it; she has all but banned it from the apartment) becomes the perfect lunch break on an intense day. Other days it is the quiet toasting of bread, the spreading of a generous amount of butter and liver pate, and slicing of shallots for a quick pickle. A can of Coke split in two glasses, one with ice, the other without (ironically, it is the born and bred American who eschews the ice). There is an eagerness in the way she brings the plates to the dining table that tells me she enjoys this lunch routine as much as I do.

Phase 3: Cookbooks

SJ: "You look like a Danish murder victim," he says.

We'd taken to watching a lot of subtitled Scandinavian crime dramas, and the four-inch slash across my throat was clearly evident through the transparent collodion surgical dressing protecting my incision. His observation provides the precise form of levity I didn't know I wanted.

For the first few days, I move unmistakably like a woman who just went through major surgery. I expected the healing process to be a function of time: each day a little better. But it is instead the summation of multiple vectors, each on their own timescale, sometimes exacerbating and other times operating independently of the rest. Pain, swelling, drainage, hormones, electrolytes, energy, fatigue, stiffness, soreness, inflammation, and bruising. One gets better, another gets worse. Every day it is a new combination.

Food appears on the table without my help: hot dogs one night, McDonald's takeout another, thin crust pizzas from Posto the following. "I'm in a head fog," I say. I don't know what I want for dinner. I cannot see straight, cannot read, cannot focus on my phone or my hand or anything in front of my face. I eventually remember to remove the scopolamine patch I was given to prevent nausea from the surgical anesthesia. My mind starts to clear, but my body is still swollen and bloated. I regret having told everyone how good I felt the day after surgery. I am desperate for a hug, for any sort of physical affection, but my husband is stranded 900 miles away and Krishnendu will barely look at me. "You're like a colonizing presence," he says, "I need some space."

At seven days post-op I get a call with the pathology results. I can't even yell out, "What are the odds?!" in frustration because I know the odds: 0.8%—Zero. Point. Eight. A rare aggressive variant that signals the journey is long from over. In eight weeks, I will undergo radiation, and in six weeks I will have to cut out all iodine-containing products from my diet. I walk into the kitchen to begin a crème anglaise, the base for an elaborate fresh strawberry tart. Carpe diem. Dinner is a flatbread of butternut squash and brie.

The dining table has by now been completely submerged by the flowers of well-wishers, anchored by a towering bouquet of orchids, hydrangea, snapdragons, and roses from my husband that creates a visual barrier between the forward dining space and the workspace at the aft. The weather has fully turned toward summer, and city restrictions begin to lift. We celebrate my birthday with an elaborate spread of sushi, ordered in from Kanoyama, and Milk Bar cake. The next few weeks are filled with open air markets and rental car picnics outside the city. There is seared salmon over farro and cod in coconut milk curry over rice. We bake whole trout. Rudra receives one-hundred oysters as a gift from his mom and painstakingly shucks a dozen or so every night until they are gone.

I am reading a travelogue on the couch, while Krishnendu is sitting at his computer at the table. "Have you heard of this Alison Roman?"

The "scandal" has been all over social media, but her cookbook is on the shelf untouched. We are curious.

We start with the Buttered Salmon with Red Onion and Dill. As a Pacific Northwest native, I have baked a lot of salmon in my life. Twelve minutes at 325°F? I doubted it, but okay. Never have I baked salmon to such a perfectly creamy texture. The following night, we make Salmon with Soy and Citrusy Charred Scallions and Smashed Cucumbers, Sizzled Turmeric and Garlic Salad. And then Citrus Chicken Rested in Herbs.

We have never eaten so well. And we have never had so much *fun*, learning new techniques, new combinations as we follow along with the vision of someone else. It is as if all the responsibility and decisions involved in dinner have been handed over to others, some third-party cookbook writer who can just tell us what to do and we will execute it.

"What's next?"

By virtue of my prep-station near the sink with a clearer line of sight to the cookbook than from his at the stove, I am the de facto instruction reader alouder.

"It says, 'Place half the peas in a medium bowl. Using your hands, crush the peas. You are looking for crushed, not a puree.'"

"Should we do that?"

I shrug. "Yes . . . ? I mean yeah, right? We should try it."

And then the first of July is upon us and this doorway to a new world of ingredients slams shut in anticipation of the radiation treatment.

No iodized salt allowed in the diet. No seafood. No dairy. No soy. No egg yolks. No seaweed thickeners. No canned beans. No commercial goods. It is a long list of no's that makes even the vegan alternatives to conventional kitchen staples off-limits, a challenge that—in a way—I feel somewhat ready to tackle after over one hundred days of COVID-19 cooking.

I bake a honey wheat bread using noniodized salt and concoct a "not butter" spread with coconut fat and turmeric. Breakfast is covered: tea (with my daily allotted teaspoon of cream) and toast.

Our first dinner is a chateaubriand with roasted cauliflower, blistered scallions, and pureed potatoes, and then the next day a picnic lunch of cucumber tomato salad, guacamole and salt-free tortilla chips, watermelon, and thinly sliced leftover filet. But it gets trickier as the days continue. I suggest dinners that require little to no modification—like Thai-style lettuce wraps with cucumber, mango, and fresh herbs, or seared hanger steak with a homemade peanut sauce, pineapple, and avocado. We sear lamb chops with cipollini onions. But when Rudra wants takeout, I end up making myself a salt-free peanut butter and jelly sandwich. When they want a pre-dinner snack of sushi and charcuterie, I watch them snack while I eat some fruit.

After months of feeling like I had a second home, I find myself back on the outside—an interloper who just wants to eat the same thing at the table as everyone and does not want to have to pretend that a meat patty with salt-free ketchup on homemade honey wheat bread is the same thing as a cheeseburger. Food had become so essential to the rhythms of the household that to be excluded feels extraordinarily inconsiderate and unnecessarily harsh.

When it is time for my RAI (radioactive iodine) treatment, I find a nice little studio in Greenwich Village to wait out the half-lives of the isotope for a week in isolation following radiation safety protocol. I can hear the sounds of the street rise up and waft through the second-story window. It is almost as if I am there, sitting alone at a table in a bustling café, working away, except I am not. In some ways it is the best of both worlds: the noise and the energy of the café in the privacy of my own space, without the need for shoes, or a bra, or a corkage fee for the bottle of good rosé I had in the fridge (thankfully, wine is approved on a low-iodine diet).

We celebrate my return with melt-in-your-mouth salmon on a bed of thinly sliced cucumbers, apples, and radishes, with purple basil microgreens and a new pile of cookbooks inspired by the Indian Ocean world, flagging dishes we would like to make and the ingredients we would need to make them. Ravinder Bhogal's *Jikoni*. Hawa Hassan's *Bibi's Kitchen*. Pomegranate molasses, mint, leg of lamb, *za'atar*, mastic, ghee. New collaborative lists emerge, and the world opens up to us, even if travel restrictions keep it shut away.

Epilogue

SJ: Thinking back to this time recalls such a heavy silence, because there was nothing we could say. The reality, the fear would be too hard to put to words, at least in speech, but to talk of anything else felt like a superficial distraction.

So, we sat, and we wrote, and we worked. He clattering away on his computer and me on mine, periodically emailing each other drafts of our various projects from across the room. Reading each other's words. And then we cooked. Asking which way we should cut an onion or how long to sear the fish. But what we were really saying is "I hear you. I feel it too. The terror. The stress."

KR: After Rudra and Stephanie left, in the fall of 2020, I realized I did not cook that well for myself. Rudra texts me what he is cooking, like the dumpling and chicken stew that he learned during the pandemic, or beans and potatoes in a spoonful of bouillon, topped with a scoop of sour cream and a handful of fresh dill. He tells me he can no longer afford the expensive proteins on his student budget that he took for granted at home. Cold smoked salmon with avocado and crème fraîche—his ritual breakfast at home since he was a few years old—is out of bounds. He tells me he is missing that, but also that he likes the constrained choices he has to make now that he has to manage his own purse strings. Stephanie sent him a huge package of fresh caught frozen salmon that he hoards in the freezer. Searing a piece with crispy skin for himself and each one of his roommates as a special occasion, this is where he comes closest to Bengali cooking, serving it over a steaming bowl of rice. He is building a world of his own in the gaps left by his father.

Retrospectively, the top note of my cooking had been about responsibility and caregiving. So, when for the first time in my life, after almost twenty years of cooking, I was left to cook for myself, I could not do it alone. Social mediation became necessary to what and how I was cooking and eating. My pleasure was in crafting and feeding, but not in a selfless way. It was the pleasure of feeding oneself in the company of others, taking care of myself in taking care of them, crafting something delectable. It was the pleasure of cooking as a responsibility, as material transformation, but also as a performance. Not as mere misrepresentation but as a space of reflection and curation, such as living rooms typically are, with the china cabinet or the netsuke collection. Things for show, things in the right aesthetic order to express a sense of oneself in some relationship to various others, close and far.

Shortly after Stephanie moved into a new home in Raleigh, she sent me a text: "What does your day look like? Maybe we should coordinate a dinner plan. Do you want to try to cook together over Zoom?"

What had started out as a difficult exercise in negotiating space, taste, and work, had become so pleasurably practiced that I missed it once it was gone. Home is where you take care of others, that idea has settled in me, and in doing so it has unsettled my idea of home.

Notes

Epigraph: Tishani Doshi, "How to Write an Elegy in the Year of Dying," December 31, 2020, Scroll.in, https://scroll.in/article/982710/how-to-write-an-elegy-in-the-year-of-dying-poet-novelist-tishani-doshi-on-the-death-of-her-dog.

1. J. David Goodman, "How Delays and Unheeded Warnings Hindered New York's Virus Fight," April 8, 2020, *New York Times*, https://www.nytimes.com/2020/04/08/nyregion/new-york-coronavirus-response-delays.html.
2. For a very useful sequence of events related to restaurants in New York City see Gary He's two-year summary of events from the point of view of four restaurants. https://ny.eater.com/22259333/new-york-coronavirus-pandemic-gotham-di-an-di-veselka-jing-fong-photo-essay.
3. "This is what effective governance looks like," Jolly wrote in a March 19 Facebook post. "Two states of similar demographic and rural/urban centers; two vastly different responses to the pandemic. One immediately declared a state of emergency, strongly encouraged social distancing, signed executive orders, closed schools and later closed all bars/restaurants. The other—did not." https://www.cnn.com/2020/03/28/politics/andy-beshear-kentucky-coronavirus/index.html.
4. "Third rail" is an idiom that alludes to the electrified subway rail in New York City. It refers to a topic that one does not discuss.
5. Craig Smith, "COVID-19 Update from Dr. Smith" newsletter series, Columbia Surgery, https://columbiasurgery.org/news/13691?page=6.
6. Krishnendu Ray, *The Migrant's Table: Meals and Memories in Bengali-American Households* (Philadelphia: Temple University Press, 2004).
7. H.A.R. Gibb, *The Travels of Ibn Battuta A. D. 1325–1354*, trans. With revisions and notes from the Arabic text ed. C. Defremery and B. R. Sanguinetti. The translations completed with annotations by C. F. Beckingham, vol. 4 (London: Hakluyt Society, 1994), 805.

8. *The Travels of Marco Polo*, trans. and with an introduction by Ronald Latham (London: Penguin, 1958), 293.

9. Melissa Clark, "A Dip for All Your Wilting Herbs," April 8, 2020, *New York Times*, https://www.nytimes.com/2020/04/08/dining/green-goddess-dip-coronavirus.html.

Pasta with Shallots and White Wine

Method

Boil the pasta in salted water according to the directions on the box, give or take a minute depending on how you like your pasta cooked.

In a separate pan, while the pasta cooks, melt the butter on medium heat. Sauté the shallot until translucent.

Pour in the white wine and let it simmer for approximately 5 minutes. Toss in half the chopped tomatoes and continue to simmer until the tomatoes start to soften.

Stir in the cream.

Grate enough cheese into the pan that a thin layer covers most of the surface. Stir. If the consistency is still very thin, add more cheese or continue to simmer. If the consistency is too thick add more wine or butter or cream, or all three.

Salt, if you insist.

Add the drained pasta, fresh herbs, and remaining tomatoes into the pan, tossing to combine. Garnish with more herbs and cheese as desired.

1 package linguine, or any other noodly pasta

4 tablespoon butter, give or take

1 shallot, thinly sliced

¼–½ cup white wine, rosé, or sparkling (whatever you have lingering in the fridge)

1 medium tomato or a handful of cherry tomatoes, chopped

2–4 tablespoons (1–2 ounces) heavy cream or half-and-half

Parmesan or another hard, salty cheese

Fresh basil, parsley, or tarragon

Note: all measurements are approximations.

3

Duck Tales

One of the last things I ate before leaving Saigon in early March 2020 was a fistful of one of my favorite street food snacks: lovely, chewy *bánh cam*, sesame balls made of glutinous rice flour, filled with mung beans, and deep fried until golden and crisped. It came courtesy of a masked street vendor who happened to walk by with her basket of treats—and a bottle of hand sanitizer—at just the right time. She was not the only one with hand sanitizer at the ready. The country was already taking precautions against the coronavirus: schools were closed, and reminders about sanitizing and masking were everywhere, from public squares to the back of taxis.

Meanwhile, the United States was just barely waking up to the reality of the coronavirus. On March 15, a few days after I returned to Los Angeles, the mayor ordered all restaurants to halt on-site dining. Takeout and pickup were permitted but only for the restaurants that enforced social distancing protocols. One day later, on March 16, the then president Donald Trump, who had already referred to the coronavirus in an Oval Office address as the "foreign virus" days earlier, doubled down, framing the pandemic as the result of a "Chinese virus." And in June, a Los Angeles council member, citing unconfirmed reports that the virus originated at a wet market, proposed shutting down the city's live animal markets. It did not seem to matter that live animal markets are already regulated by multiple local, state, and federal agencies, and that he himself had never set foot in one.

Unsurprisingly, threats of and actual violence against Chinese- and other Asian-owned businesses erupted that year. And when that spring turned into a very long summer, the tenor of the racist rhetoric hit another note. The murder of George Floyd sparked uprisings across the country, including in Los Angeles. During one especially heated night, the Mozzaplex—the local name given to the block where chef and owner Nancy Silverton runs a trio of celebrated restaurants—was damaged. Soon after, Silverton cowrote an op-ed in the *Los Angeles Times* about that night, recalling that looters "scattered like roaches" when police cars arrived and pondering how the various protests across the country have "really kicked the media into high gear and, remarkably, relegated COVID-19 to the inside pages. (You remember the pandemic, right? That Wuhan, China, bat thing? We quarantined and wore face masks?)"[1]

Tien Nguyen in Saigon

While the op-ed was criticized at the time (as was the *Los Angeles Times*, for running the piece), the Los Angeles outpost of the popular food site *Eater* later saw Silverton's piece as one thing on a list of many things that made 2020 a "rough year" for her. But "on the upside," the site reported, the chef did manage to release a cookbook and open a new restaurant in the midst of the pandemic. That her editorial was dismissed so casually, as if it were a trifle of an incident where she was the only party harmed, and that her harm could be offset by capital infusions to her empire, only served to reinforce the racism in her piece in an environment already caustic with xenophobia.

These semantic attacks, and the institutions that platformed and legitimized those attacks, landed with such devastation at this particular moment because they are not singular. Chinese and Chinese American cooking have been ostracized as sites of contagion pretty much since the moment Chinese workers arrived in the United States and were hired at meager wages to build the foundation of the country's economic engine. So tenacious is the association that there have been various blatant attempts to capitalize on it. In 2017, the trailer for a smartphone game quite literally called "Dirty Chinese Restaurant" was posted online, created by developers who apparently strived to gamify racism (they claimed the game was satire; the game never launched).[2] In the spring of 2019, a white-owned restaurant called Lucky Lee's opened in New York, advertising "clean" Chinese food (the owner claimed she intended "clean" to mean organic ingredients and other markers of the so-called clean eating lifestyle; the restaurant eventually closed). And well into the pandemic, a contestant on *MasterChef: The Professionals* branded her style of Asian street food cooking as "Dirty Food Refined" (she claimed she intended "dirty" to mean indulgent; she eventually deleted the tagline).

But the most instructive recent precedent might be an epic battle waged in the early 1980s in California, with health inspectors on one side and Chinatown restaurants and butchers on the other. Thermometers and knives were drawn, and when the dust settled, the skirmish over Chinese-style roast duck, and how to prepare it safely and legally, would be a pivotal moment for immigrant food culture in the state. It was also a lesson on the opportunities local governments have to support, rather than continue to stigmatize, immigrant foodways—and how those opportunities are too often thwarted by prejudices embedded in policy. These lessons have only become more relevant as this pandemic wears on and the suspicion cast over Chinese food has extended to other sites of immigrant cooking—specifically, to the sidewalks of Los Angeles, where the vast majority of street vendors were forced to shut down at the onset of the pandemic. It was necessary, the city insisted, to protect public health, even as there were no known links between street food and community spread of the coronavirus, and even as the city actively worked to help brick-and-mortar restaurants transition to a model prioritizing takeout and outdoor dining.

These are the two episodes I seek to explore in this piece. In the first section, I will dive into the fight over Chinese-style roast duck and the ways in which officials sought to weaponize science against an immigrant community, only for that community to wield it back with equal aplomb. Though the community emerged victorious, the pandemic has shown that there continues to be an association between the cooking of certain communities of color and disease. I will turn to the tenacity of that association in the second section, where I will examine how Los Angeles's treatment of its street food vendors during the pandemic is reminiscent of the xenophobia exhibited during the Chinese roast duck battles.

Chinese-style roast duck has been popular inside and outside Chinatown since 1959, when Cecilia Chiang put Peking duck on her menu at The Mandarin in San Francisco. That popularity was boosted in 1972, when President Richard Nixon made his historic visit to China; portions of the visit were televised, giving American viewers a chance to watch the president awkwardly wield chopsticks and feast on roast duck and other banquet dishes.

But there was one entity that was not such a fan of the ducks: the Los Angeles County health department. In the early 1980s, the county's health inspectors zeroed in on Chinatown ducks hanging by their necks in kitchens and display windows; they jabbed thermometers into the birds, didn't like what they read, and so ordered them into the trash, often dousing them in bleach or another denaturing agent first to render them completely inedible. Chefs and owners protested that the ducks needed to be hung to dry before and after roasting. They pointed to the long, long history of this method of preparation in Chinese cooking. The inspectors shrugged and pointed to the California Health and Safety Code.

The California Health and Safety Code sets forth the laws governing food safety and handling procedures for consumer food and retail food settings, including restaurants. The purpose of these laws, the Code says, is to "safeguard public health and provide to consumers food that is safe, unadulterated, and honestly presented through adoption of science-based standards."[3] The invocation of science here suggests some measure of neutrality and objectivity, but, as we shall see, the deployment of the Code against immigrant communities shows how these standards are often leveraged against those who don't conform to certain Western ideals. The provision the Chinatown inspectors cited was one that relates to holding temperatures, or the temperatures at which perishable food must be stored in order to prevent the growth of harmful bacteria. At the time of the roast duck purge, the law required such foods be kept either very cold (at 45°F) or very hot (at least 140°F). Having a duck hang out at room temperature for hours and hours? Not even close to being up to code.

For many Chinese restaurants, the temperature requirements were a conundrum. As connoisseurs know, the most prized aspect of this style of roast duck is the skin: It should be bronzed mahogany, with a crackle that shatters. With Peking duck in particular, the true pleasure comes from folding shards of the skin into paper-thin, taco-sized wraps or doughy *baos* smeared with a swish of hoisin sauce and garnished with scallion threads and a sliver or two of cucumber. A good roast duck is a feat; it takes immense care, skill, time, and finesse to achieve a crispy skin while keeping the meat itself tender and moist. To prepare the bird, cooks coat the ducks in a vinegar solution along with a layer of marinade. They then seal the birds' cavities and hang them from hooks to dry at room temperature for several hours before transferring them to a high-temperature oven to roast. After cooking, the duck is hung again for several hours, again at room temperature, to drain. In her *Mastering the Art of Chinese Cooking*, the noted cookbook writer Eileen Yin-Fei Lo directs cooks to dry the bird for ten to twelve hours "in a cool place with good air circulation," and suggests using a fan to speed up the drying time. In his BBC television series, cookbook author and chef Ken Hom has suggested drying the duck for five hours, "or preferably overnight."

These long drying times are crucial. Jacinta Cheng, a restaurateur who pled unsuccessfully with the inspectors at the time of the 1982 duck hunt, described the unsavory effects of missing those drying times. "If we put it in the refrigerator, the skin won't be crispy. If we put it in the heat too long, the meat will be tough and dry. If we cooked it according to the health department," she concluded, "no one would come to buy our duck." The explanation did not move the inspectors, who were remarkably unsympathetic. According to Cheng, an inspector threw out three dozen of her ducks and, in response to her pleas, told her, "I don't care about Chinese tradition. You are in America right now, and this is what you have to do." In total, the inspections cost Chinatown food operators an estimated $100,000 in fines, plus the

Duck Tales

57

loss of product and the humiliation of watching their painstakingly prepared dishes bleached and trashed. Repeat "offenders" were fined $10,000 to $15,000 for each instance. Many were unable to withstand the financial hit.[4]

In its defense, the health department invoked its mission to protect public health. When it came to the ducks, the department chose to act preemptively; as director Norm Michiels told the *Los Angeles Times*, "We've had, historically, cases of food poisoning where this product is implicated, but it's never been proven to be the causative food."[5]

In response to the aggressive health inspectors, Chinatown restaurants rallied. They enlisted the support of Irvin R. Lai, a fellow restaurateur who was the president of the Chinese Chamber of Commerce as well as a prominent community activist. (Those who are familiar with Asian American history and activism will recognize Lai's name: he was part of a group of activists who led the movement for justice after the murder of Vincent Chin in the summer of 1982.) Lai, now, reached out to state assemblyman Art Torres. Torres was a willing ear, but he needed some assurance. A legislative aide, Michael Woo, ferried five three-day-old roast ducks over to a food science expert over at the University of California at Davis.

The laboratory results were decisive: the ducks were safe for consumption. In fact, it was the very method of preparation, including the incredibly dry skin and the high roasting temperature, which created an environment inhospitable to the sort of bacterial growth that would raise food safety concerns. The study concluded even after a few *days* at room temperature, the ducks "would not pose any hazard from a health standpoint." (The scientists in the lab were so confident in their findings that after they completed their analysis, they feasted on the leftovers.)[6]

With his ducks in a row, Torres introduced a bill to exempt Chinese-style roast ducks from the temperature requirements of the Health and Safety Code and instead allow the ducks to be held at room temperature for several hours. The Los Angeles County Board of Supervisors supported Chinese restaurants and the Torres bill.[7]

The same could not be said about the county health department, which vehemently opposed the bill. Shirley L. Fannin, the county's chief of acute communicable disease control, warned that the exemption would swallow the rule: there would be litigation, she said, over more exemptions "since barbecue pork, Chinese style, is not basically different than barbecue pork Mexican, German, French, or fast-food chain style." She saw the bill, moreover, as an attack on food safety regulations as a whole. "The public confidence in clean, fresh food has been built up over many years," she wrote in a letter to the *Los Angeles Times*, "but it can be lost in only a few."[8]

Willful ignorance about the myriad ways to prepare barbecue pork aside, the choice of language here is striking. Even as she offered no rebuttal to the Davis test results, Fannin held steadfast to her idea of what "clean, fresh food" looked like—and it didn't look like a Chinatown roast duck. If this sounds familiar, that is because it is. If you recall, the controversy over Lucky Lee's and the *MasterChef* contestant invoked a similar sleight of language to suggest Chinese cuisine was not "clean." Moreover, Fannin's letter is especially interesting given that Chinatown roast ducks were actually quite fresh; many chefs at the time, particularly those credited with pioneering the local, seasonal ethos of what became known as California cuisine, sourced their ducks from Chinatown butchers precisely because those birds were freshly slaughtered. Michiels, meanwhile, was asked directly about the UC Davis laboratory results, and he responded only, and vaguely, "That information is inconclusive, too." He did not specify how the information was inconclusive, and he offered no contrary evidence.[9]

Despite this opposition, Torres's bill passed easily. As Torres recalled later in an oral history, "The most persuasive argument to all of them [senators] was that in five thousand years there has never been a reported food poisoning by Peking Duck [chuckle] in the history of China or America. So what's the problem? It was a lot of *burrocrats* who just basically wanted to have something to do and the Chinese restauranteurs were having a hard time."[10]

As much as the origin story of the dish helped the bill succeed, it was in some ways a double-edged sword: its history legitimized the safety of the preparation, but it also reaffirmed its perceived otherness. When Governor Jerry Brown signed the duck bill into law in front of news cameras at a restaurant in Los Angeles's Chinatown (Brown was up for election that year and could not resist the chance for a savvy photo op), a spokesperson from the United Chinese Restaurant Association inadvertently affirmed the difficulty in reconciling this tension: "Peking duck is not a Communist plot to get America eating their food," he said. "This duck has been Americanized."[11]

The bill passed, but the controversy remained. "Since the preparation of Peking duck is now exempt from the health and safety code," a microbiologist wrote in a letter to the *Los Angeles Times*, "does this mean the state of California will be liable for any medical costs incurred in any future food infections?"

The jury is still out on that one. Since the bill was codified into law in 1982, there have been no recorded significant outbreaks of food poisoning linked to Chinese-style roast duck, according to Will Kymlicka's study *Criminal Law and Cultural Diversity*. It is also worth noting that the duck legislation anticipated, by decades, a now widely accepted doctrine called Time as a Public Health Control, which allows foods to be held at room temperature for up to four hours before serving or cooking. In 2005, the state incorporated this doctrine in an amendment to its Health and Safety Code § 114000.

The duck bill has left a legacy in other ways. Within the Chinese community, it was a key moment of political activation. The ducks, as Torres said, were "a symbol of a community that was under siege by Department of Health officials. [Chinese restaurants] were being fined five to ten thousand [dollars] a day because they were not cooking duck according to Western cooking standards."[12]

It also set a precedent beyond Chinatown. In 2001, Korean bakeries in Los Angeles successfully pushed for an exemption for *tteok*, a two-bite Korean rice cake stuffed with dried beans, fruit, and nuts popular during holidays, incorporated into California Health and Safety Code § 111223. Under the new law, the rice cakes are permitted to stay at room temperature for up to twenty-four hours so long as certain other cooking and labeling requirements are met. As with the Chinese-style roast ducks, legislatures sent samples of the rice cakes to a laboratory for analysis and, as with the ducks, the results returned negative for harmful bacteria.[13]

Over the last two decades, the state has made similar exemptions for other prepared foods, including fresh rice noodles, which lose their supple texture and become hard and brittle when refrigerated. Mooncakes and *bánh chưng*, the hefty Vietnamese glutinous rice cakes stuffed with luscious pork, buttery mung beans, and sweet shallots, are also exempted. During the public debate over the exemptions for mooncakes and *bánh chưng*, the bill's sponsor, Assemblyman Van Tran, joked it was actually the health department's rules that posed a danger to public safety: "If you put the moon cakes into the fridge, anything that's lower than 40 degrees, it would not taste the same, because it would be basically a hockey puck. The texture of the cake would be a solid object, and it would be a health hazard if you bite it."[14]

The real proof, of course, is in the pudding—or in the mooncakes. When Assemblyman Tran brought in mooncakes and glutinous rice cakes, served at room temperature, to a public hearing, "the crowd gobbled them up."[15] And lab tests validated the safety of both.

But all these years after the roast duck battle, it has proven difficult to sheathe that double-edged sword. The debates over these recent exemptions saw culinary tradition harnessed as either a refuge or a test of assimilation; the Orange County health specialist mentioned earlier, for instance, noted that "as regulators, we may not always fully grasp the significance of tradition. In turn, the community may not fully comprehend the importance of and need for the laws and regulations we enforce."[16] In 2000, as owners of Asian bakeries and restaurants voiced their frustrations, a Los Angeles health department official speculated why Asian foods have become the flashpoint for these specific battles: "Maybe it is the tenacity on the part of that community," he said, "or maybe their products are not as adaptable to the code."[17]

Lawmakers and the media, too, have amplified this otherness by depicting the issue as one rooted in opposition. In the media, headlines ranged from "Moon Cakes Prompt American Culture Clash" to "Balancing Food Safety, Tradition." Discussing the basis for his *bánh chưng* bill, Assemblyman Van Tran said, "You have to find a balance between public health and history and culture," before adding, "It's a classic American story."[18] (He did not elaborate further.)

It is an easy sound bite, this framing of culinary tradition and public health as two sides of a coin. But it is misleading: the two are not necessarily at odds. Chinese-style roast duck, *tteok*, mooncakes, and *bánh chứng* did not receive exemptions because the desire to honor and preserve foodways won over the need to protect and maintain public health. To the contrary, these exemptions were made precisely *because* they fell within established food safety guidelines. Had any of those dishes fallen outside those parameters, it is far from certain that history alone would have carried an exemption all the way to the governor's desk. Supporters of a 2004 bill to allow freshly prepared sushi to remain at room temperature for 24 hours, for instance, failed to introduce any scientific data to support their position. The bill subsequently died in committee.

It is worth pausing here to note that a food producer does not actually *need* a legislated exemption to prepare a dish in ways contrary to the code. Rather, producers can apply for a variance, which essentially amounts to official permission to prepare a certain dish or food their way, so long as their alternate method is deemed safe for consumption. That is one reason why a coalition of health officials opposed the Korean rice cake bill; a legislated exemption, they argued, was unnecessary since the bakeries could just seek a variance instead.[19] But taking advantage of this option is expensive, formidably so; it requires the producer to take on the cost of lab tests and analysis, among other fees. It seems misguided to criticize smaller, independent food producers—who operate on slim margins even on the best of days—for not pursuing an option they cannot afford.

Echoing Fannin's letter to the *Los Angeles Times* all those years ago, officials also continue to be concerned that these exemptions undermine both the department's authority and the public's faith in the health and safety laws. One environmental health specialist in Orange County, which neighbors Los Angeles County and is home to several Asian communities, including the largest Little Saigon in the United States, wrote in 2006, "Health laws are usually science-based, thereby allowing their application to be free from political bias. In reality, however, we often see that the needs and desires of our clients invariably come into conflict with those laws. If left unresolved for too long and depending upon the political currents of the day, these conflicts may ultimately lead to legislated exemptions. While these exemptions have been politically crafted to answer specific problems, they often end up undermining an Environmental Health program's broader ability to protect and best serve its community."[20] The specialist specifically cited both the Chinese roast duck and *tteok* rice cake exemptions, the latter of which he considered "a more recent embarrassment." This interpretation of these events is telling in that it reveals the depth of the gulf that still exists. What the department considers embarrassments, after all, the respective communities see as rare successes. For Chinatown business owners, the passage of the roast duck bill meant that the dish—and thus, perhaps, the community that created it—passed a citizenship test. It was, as the United Chinese Restaurant Association spokesperson stated, "Americanized." Moreover, previous studies on how restaurants fare under the gaze of health inspectors have suggested that bias plays a role in how they are evaluated, and at least one study has suggested that an institutional unfamiliarity with certain cuisines and non-Western food preparation methods disproportionately disadvantages immigrant restaurants and restaurateurs of color.[21] Those restaurants are further burdened as they bear the consequences—a lowered letter grade, perfectly safe ducks thrown into the trash—of that cultural gap. And those gaps effectively fix in place the otherness of those foods, the people who labor to make them, and the stereotypes that are the foreigner's constant companions.

Thus, as Yong Chen observes in *Chop Suey USA*, though the mooncake exemption was "seen in the Chinese world as a rare victory of Chinese Americans in upholding their culinary tradition," the entire ordeal "nonetheless discloses again that Chinese food still has a long way to go before it becomes truly acceptable and respected."

Chop Suey USA was published in 2014. Seven years and one pandemic later, Chinese food has yet to achieve a level of acceptance and respect that would protect it from being scapegoated and attacked. But it is not just Chinese foodways that have struggled during this time. Indeed, the roast duck controversy is a useful lens through which to examine and understand the attack on other immigrant food spaces throughout this pandemic. This attack has been particularly visible on the streets of Los Angeles. Early on, the city's street food vendors were singled out as potential sites of infection—despite little evidence to suggest that they played any role in spreading COVID-19. In doing so, Los Angeles chose to continue, rather than repudiate, historical prejudices about immigrant cooking and disease.

On March 17, two days after Los Angeles ordered its residents to shelter in place and restaurants to close on-site dining, the city council set its sights on street vendors. "It is necessary to impose a temporary moratorium on street vending in the public right of way," the motion read, "to protect Angelenos from the novel Coronavirus pandemic." The motion also called on the Los Angeles Police Department to work with the county's health department "to establish protocols to effectively enforce the health code."[22]

The city has a historically fraught relationship with its street vendors, but the city's action here surprised me nonetheless. Many restaurants are built around their dine-in experiences, so adjusting to a new model centered around takeout would require time to implement new systems and, possibly, entirely new menus better suited for takeout. Street vending, on the other hand, is outdoors by default and designed to go. One of my fondest memories of street food dining in Los Angeles is scarfing down a Baja-style fish taco just before midnight, the salsa from the makeshift bar splashing on my shoes, when a bus driver pulled up, hollered her order, and received her tacos, fully dressed on two stacked paper plates, inside of the sixty seconds idling at the red light. This could never happen at a restaurant. It seemed likely that street vendors were much better positioned to handle the transition to takeout than many restaurants.

It was surprising too because Los Angeles had just decriminalized street vending. Up until 2017, street vending in Los Angeles was illegal; the mostly immigrant operators who set up sidewalk shops anyway risked being charged with a misdemeanor and, for undocumented vendors, deportation. At the time, Los Angeles was one of the only major cities in the world to outright outlaw sidewalk entrepreneurship. As Mark Vallianatos notes, "The association of vending with immigrant workers and immigrant communities helps explain [a] reason why sidewalk vending is illegal in Los Angeles. From restrictions on Chinese laundries to racially restrictive property covenants, governmental and private land use controls in the city were long tinged by racist assumptions. Although attitudes are changing, sidewalk vending has been viewed as a foreign, chaotic activity—a third world occupation—rather than as an opportunity to encourage business formation, make pedestrian-friendly streets and provide food in low-income areas."[23] Sarah Portnoy further notes in her study of Latino food culture in Los Angeles that vendors are often seen as "'a manifestation of disorder,'" and presumed to be "unsanitary and creating sidewalk congestion in already densely populated areas."[24]

These prejudices were particularly vicious throughout the 1980s, when many refugees from Central America settled in and around the city and turned to selling street food. That, in turn, led to debates about whether the informal economy should be formally regulated, debates often laced with anxiety about how the city sees itself. At one point, the president of a local chamber of commerce wrote to the *Los Angeles Times*, "I don't know any chamber member who would embrace street vending. I do know that they are definitely opposed to street vending in residential areas. We all want to have the access and opportunity to make a living, but there are some standards we have as a society that we have to try to promote and maintain."[25]

Against that backdrop came an earnest attempt to legalize street vending. In 1989, then Los Angeles city councilmember Michael Woo—the same Michael Woo, as it happens, who had chauffeured those Peking ducks to the UC Davis lab earlier that decade—moved to create a system to finally regulate vendors while encouraging entrepreneurship. But developing the system was a long process; with multiple stakeholders and powerful business interest groups concerned about competition lobbying against it, the council took several years to establish the basic framework. In the meantime, other anti-vending measures were drafted, including one to allow law enforcement to seize vendor equipment. That measure was supported by a Los Angeles Police Department supervisor who minced no words linking street vendors with disease: "We are approaching a crisis situation here, and like cancer, it spreads. If you don't eradicate it, it's going to consume you."[26]

When it finally launched, the program barely fulfilled the initial promise of a regulated system. Advocates had pushed to re-zone multiple areas of the city as street vending zones, but only one small pocket in a neighborhood just west of downtown was ultimately created. To set up there, vendors were required to pay a $750 permitting fee, rent designated carts at $250 a month, select from a narrow list of permitted foods to sell, and operate only during certain hours of the day.[27] It is no wonder that so few vendors ended up participating.

In the 2000s, a coalition of vendors and community organizations renewed efforts to create a permitting system that would better serve the needs of the city's street vendors. In February 2017, the city council, galvanized by Donald Trump's racist rhetoric and executive orders targeting immigrants for deportation, voted almost unanimously to decriminalize street vending. The lone "no" vote belonged to councilmember Mitch Englander, who saw the vendors as threats: "We took action to decriminalize [street vending] without coming up with a true plan to say how we'll protect brick-and-mortar businesses and residents," he told *LA Weekly*.[28]

As plans to create a proper permitting system moved forward, other councilmembers representing predominantly white, wealthier parts of the city lobbied, unsuccessfully, to empower brick-and-mortar businesses with the right to prohibit street vendors from setting up on nearby sidewalks. At least one motion attempted to designate entire business improvement districts, including the wealthier parts of Melrose Avenue, Westwood, and Encino, as no-vending zones.[29]

In late 2018, the governor decriminalized street vending statewide and ordered local jurisdictions to implement vending regulations. It still took nearly two more years, but in January 2020—mere months before the onset of the pandemic in the United States—the City of Los Angeles Sidewalk and Park Vendor Permit Program formally launched.

When the program began, there were already an estimated 50,000 street vendors in LA, of which an estimated 15,000 to 20,000 sold food (others sold a vast variety of goods, including clothing, electronics, and flowers). A few months into the pandemic, I spotted a number of vendors, even food vendors, also selling hand sanitizer and cloth masks. My favorite huarache vendor actually pointed me to her lineup of masks as she pinched off a golf ball–sized piece of masa and tugged it into an oval shape (because this is a championship town after all, her offerings included masks outfitted in Dodger blue and Lakers purple and gold). A significant number of vendors are immigrants, refugees, and migrants who grill up bacon-wrapped hot dogs, stuff tacos and *pupusas* with carne asada and other fillings, shake Tajín on cubed pineapples and watermelons, and dunk freshly cut noodles into bowls of warm broth. In total, street vending contributes a little over $500 million to the local economy,[30] and street food vendors in particular have done much to cement Los Angeles's national reputation as a culinary destination.

To kick off the program, vendors were granted a six-month grace period during which time they could operate, unpermitted, without being cited. During those first six months, the agencies tasked with enforcing the law—the city's StreetsLA department (formerly known as the Bureau of Street Services) and the Los Angeles Police Department—would educate the vendors about the new program, and the permit fee would be halved from $541 to $291 to encourage applications.[31]

Nearly one year after the program's launch, there are fewer than one hundred permitted vendors.[32] While the current system improves on the previous one, the barriers to entry are still significant. Both the city and the county regulate street vending, so vendors must navigate not one but two opaque, sometimes conflicting, bureaucracies. The county in particular has extremely specific cart requirements for vendors who wish to sell certain hot foods, such as hot dogs—so specific, in fact, that there is no pushcart on the market that meets those specifications. Even those vendors with compliant equipment face daunting expenses, including high permit fees and commissary leasing costs; all told, the start-up cost to launch a sidewalk operation can add up to as much as $20,000. As the Los Angeles Street Vendor Campaign noted in a letter to the City of Los Angeles Board of Public Works on June 1, 2020, this cost is prohibitive for the vast majority of vendors who make an estimated $10,000 a year in revenue, have little to no access to lines of credit, and cannot afford the time required to navigate the miles of red tape.

Many of these issues were known before the program began. In fact, officials and cart manufacturers had already been in touch about developing affordable, compliant carts. When the coronavirus hit home in March, the city and county had an opportunity to cushion the economic blow to vendors. Instead, they chose to make it worse.

Early on in the pandemic, the city council made two crucial decisions: it decided restaurants were essential to the community, and it decided street vendors were not. The same day the city shut down street vending in March, it also passed a motion in support of restaurants using language that could have applied equally to street food vendors: "Though [restaurant] closures are critical in mitigating the spread of the coronavirus and ensuring the public health of Angelenos, many restaurants in the industry are small, family-owned enterprises that do not have the financial capacity to withstand long term closures. . . . The City should explore opportunities to provide financial relief that complement any State and Federal programs that are made available."[33] What really amplified the cognitive dissonance here was the fact that the council did not actually intend to shut down all street vending. As councilmembers clarified a day later, the motion was intended to enforce the street vending law immediately, cutting short the program's six-month grace period. Given how few permits were issued before March, the motion may as well have been a moratorium. And in broadly ordering that street vending cease in order to "protect Angelenos from the novel Coronavirus pandemic," even as it cited no specific links between street vending and COVID-19, the city leaned into, intentionally or not, the long-standing associations between immigrant cooking and disease. That the city did so with such careless indifference—not even bothering to specify whom the motion was intended to impact—further suggests how it saw the mere existence of street vendors, permitted or not, as a threat to public health.

In May, restaurants were permitted to reopen for on-site dining. In a move to support restaurants, the city launched a no-fee program called L.A. Al Fresco, which allows restaurant owners to bypass the expensive, time-consuming process otherwise required to obtain a permit to set up an outdoor dining area. To facilitate the process, the city quickly set up a website where restaurants could submit their applications. Restaurants were required only to describe their outdoor dining plans and tick off a few boxes attesting to their insurance coverage and commitment to abide by the program's rules (rules that include a distinctly Los Angeles requirement that outdoor seating be no closer than eighteen inches to any star on the Hollywood Walk of Fame). Approval of applications was immediate.

Because L.A. Al Fresco was limited to restaurants at first, permitted street food vendors—who numbered fewer than one hundred and who would have liked to have a seating area for their customers—could not set one up (and, unlike restaurants Al Fresco, they and other street vendors were required to locate 500 feet or more from the Walk of Fame (lest they get in the way of a pandemic tourist snapping a photo of Mickey Mouse's five points). Permitted vendors, very much an afterthought, were included a long month after the program's launch.

Unpermitted vendors have been in an even more precarious position. As many mountains as the city moved to develop L.A. Al Fresco, seemingly overnight, it could not be bothered to move a pebble for vendors. Despite plans to create a remote permitting system accessible at business development centers across the city, would-be street vendors must *still* submit their paperwork in person at the StreetsLA office downtown. And because city buildings were closed at the time for COVID-19 precautions, vendors could not just walk in—they first had to make an appointment.

Though the city's actions (or inactions) have resulted in marginalizing street food vendors, there is one area where the vendors do have the city's full and undivided attention: punishment. In stark contrast to restaurants, which initially were on an "honor system" to comply with the COVID-19 orders issued by health officers, street food vendors are not just assumed to be carriers of contagion, they are also presupposed to be noncompliant. Indeed, it is not a coincidence that the same motion to shut down vending also carried orders for enforcement. In a way, the motion reflects an assumption that has been seeded in the program from the very beginning: the very first topic on the city's FAQ about the sidewalk vending program does not pertain, as one would expect, to the process of getting the permit. Rather, the very first question poses a threat veiled as a question: "What if I don't get a permit?"

(Answer: "Vendors will be fined $250 to $1,000 for not having a proper license of permit.")[34]

In the nine months following the council's March 2020 motion, the city issued over six hundred citations to street vendors. On the county side, published materials to assist vendors with opening (or reopening) during the pandemic highlight—in bright yellow—the fines for opening without a permit. These fines, of course, are levied even as the county itself created many of the barriers that prevent vendors from obtaining the proper permits in the first place. The reopening guidelines for restaurants have no correlating threat about noncompliance.

Toward the end of November 2020, California began to experience a surge that appeared to be more rampant, and more deadly, than what the state had experienced in the spring. The number of new coronavirus cases in L.A. County exploded from 5,150 on November 30 to just over 20,000 on the first day of 2021. The first few weeks of the new year saw an average of 15,000 new coronavirus cases in L.A. County alone. As I finish this piece at the end of January 2021, California has tallied over 15,000 deaths statewide, with some 6,000 deaths in L.A. County. Outdoor dining was ordered closed in late November; a statewide stay-at-home order followed soon thereafter, leaving restaurants, many of which had invested thousands of dollars in outdoor settings and equipment, in a lurch. Bafflingly, despite these grim numbers, concerns over new variants of the coronavirus, and few available hospital beds, the state lifted its stay-at-home directives on January 25. Less than a week later, L.A. County allowed outdoor dining to resume.

In response to the November shutdown orders, a number of Southern California restaurants, including more than a few near where I live, were defiant and refused to close. Many were fined, and health officials threatened to pull their health permits and force them to shut down until the permits were reinstated. It was unclear how the local police would be involved, though, as the county sheriff had stated his intention not to enforce the shutdown order. As he explained to a local news station, these restaurants "bent over backwards to modify their operations to conform to these orders and then they have the rug yanked out from under them, that's a disservice, I don't want to make them more miserable."[35]

Street vendors, who have had rug after rug after rug pulled out from under them, have not been as fortunate. Subject to the policing arms of both the county and the city, they are fined, their food is tossed, their equipment is confiscated. As councilmembers mull over the possibility of keeping the L.A. Al Fresco program permanent after the pandemic is over, street vendors are in limbo: current laws punish them for not having the proper permits. Current policies offer no pathway to compliance. And plans for the future threaten to privatize public space. All in all, the opportunity to support and empower vendors during this time of crisis has been ignored in favor of a path that leans into the continued stigmatization of immigrant cooking and all but tries to guarantee their disempowerment. And it all started with one motion describing street food vending as a threat to public health.

I began working on this chapter early in the fall of 2020, when Los Angeles, and California as a whole, appeared to be recovering from a peak of infections over the summer. It is now January 2021, and Los Angeles is the epicenter of the pandemic. Every day for the past few weeks, ambulances have wailed past my place. Every day for the past few months has felt like one long night. There is an anxious silence muffling the city. The streets are not as empty as they probably should be, but traffic is noticeably lighter. Pedestrians move at a pace somewhere between a fast walk and a headfirst run, as if chased by an invisible, uncertain, force. This is especially true in Los Angeles's Chinatown, just north of downtown. Before the pandemic, the forces of gentrification were already at work there, threatening to sap the soul of the neighborhood as longtime residents and restaurants were displaced one by one (the most popular restaurant in Chinatown was, and continues to be, a Nashville-style hot chicken spot that opened in 2016 in a two-level mini-mall called Far East Plaza). The pandemic has made the future of this Chinatown, like so many Chinatowns across the country, uncertain.

But while xenophobia and the lack of meaningful government action have affected these communities, they have not affected the communities' capacity to organize. Individuals and organizations have stepped in where the government has refused to set foot. Earlier this year, a group of street vendors formed Vendedores en Acción to continue the fight for equity in the street vending program. Inclusive Action for the City, a community development group on the forefront of advocacy efforts for street vendors, launched the Street Vendor Emergency Fund early in the pandemic; to date, it has disbursed over $500,000 in direct cash assistance to nearly 1,200 vendors.[36] Meanwhile, crowd-sourced Google Sheets of Chinatown and San Gabriel Valley restaurants open for takeout continue to circulate, and users in massively popular Facebook groups like SGV Eats and Let's Eat! Southern California are sharing their meals and connecting diners to restaurants.

As the new year begins in 2021 and vaccinations roll out, it is hope that holds space now. Hope in the resilience of community, hope in two shots and a sore shoulder. After returning from Vietnam in March, one of the first things I had (after isolating for two weeks) were *birria de res* tacos, the corn tortillas slicked neon red by a shallow dip into a pool of consommé before hitting a searing hot *plancha*. The vendor was tucked just far enough from the main road, and I happened to be driving by; after a five-minute wait in a respectfully socially distanced line, I devoured my plate in the car. I felt at home.

More recently, I picked up a Peking duck from Ji Rong Peking Duck in San Gabriel Valley. It was packed to go in a pizza box, with the meat, skin burnished bronze, and pliable wrappers all neatly separated into makeshift compartments. The duck was excellent, but I really could not get over the pizza box. It took me back to California Pizza Kitchen's Peking duck pizza, one of many confused yet successful pizzas that allowed the chain to benefit from, and capitalize on, "fusion" flavors in the 1980s and 1990s. You may remember it too; the base slathered with a gingery hoisin sauce and laden with cheese and disappointing shreds of no-skin-just-duck-breast. You may well remember it forming your first impression of California cuisine.

This duck made me smile because if you wanted to appropriate the appropriator, you probably could not do much better than pack an expertly roasted Peking duck so thoughtfully into a pizza box. Now *that* is California cuisine. It felt like restorative justice, if only on a cosmic level.

The pandemic has reminded us of the so many ways policies rooted in ferocious, racist stereotypes are weaponized against immigrant communities. But the duck-in-a-box and driver's-side taco are also reminders. Those each represent the gains and the spaces immigrant communities have claimed. I am wary of romanticizing this—California Pizza Kitchen, after all, just emerged, refreshed, from a bankruptcy, while Ji Rong, and small restaurants like it, are fighting to hold on—but these meals have been reassurances that however hopeless it might feel now, shadows of hope loom large too. Can you hang your hat on a shadow? I'll let you know at dawn.

Notes

1. Michael Krikorian and Nancy Silverton, "Our Restaurants Were Looted: Worry about George Floyd, Not Us," *Los Angeles Times*, June 4, 2020.
2. Greg Morabito, "Racist Stereotypes Run Amok in 'Dirty Chinese Restaurant' Game," *Eater*, September 29, 2017, www.eater.com/2017/9/29/16384674/racist-stereotypes-run-amok-in-dirty-chinese-restaurant-game.
3. California Health and Safety Code § 113703.
4. "Battle over Peking Duck Heating Up," *Los Angeles Times*, March 3, 1982.
5. "Battle over Peking Duck."
6. "Battle over Peking Duck."
7. "Duck Issue Would Be Cooled," *Los Angeles Times*, March 10, 1982, C6.
8. Shirley L. Fannin, "Food-Handling Rules for 'Peking' Duck," letter, *Los Angeles Times*, March 20, 1982, B2.
9. "Duck Issue Would Be Cooled."
10. Art Torres, Interview by Steve Edgington, August 12–14, 2003, transcript, CSUF Center for Oral and Public History for the California State Archives State Government Oral History Program, archive.org/details/oh2004-06-torres/mode/2up.
11. M. Seiler, "Controversy over Peking Duck Finally Laid to Rest," *Los Angeles Times*, July 7, 1982, SD3.
12. Art Torres, Interview by Steve Edgington.
13. Assembly and Senate Floor Analysis, Cal. Assem. Bill 187 Food Labeling and Safety, 2001–2002 Sess., Ch. 204, 2001 Cal. Stat., https://leginfo.legislature.ca.gov/faces/billAnalysisClient.xhtml?bill_id=200120020AB187.
14. Lonny Shavelson, "Moon Cakes Prompt American Culture Clash," NPR, February 18, 2007, www.npr.org/templates/story/story.php?storyId=7480086.

15. David Pierson and Mai Tran, "Can Not Too Hot, Not Too Cold Be Just Right?" *Los Angeles Times*, September 1, 2006, www.latimes.com/archives /la-xpm-2006-sep-01-me-mooncakes1-story.html.

16. John Ralls, "And Now for Something Completely Different . . ." *CEHA Bulletin*, Summer 2006.

17. Daniel Yi, "Delicacies of Asian Cuisine Not to Inspectors' Taste," *Los Angeles Times*, September 5, 2000, www.latimes.com/archives/la-xpm-2000-sep -05-mn-15732-story.html.

18. Pierson and Tran, "Can Not Too Hot?"

19. Bill Analysis, Assem. Bill 187 AB 187 (Liu): Hearing Before the Assembly Committee on Appropriations, 2001–2002 Session (May 2, 2001), https://leginfo.legislature.ca.gov/faces/billAnalysisClient.xhtml?bill_id =200120020AB187.

20. Ralls, "And Now for Something Completely Different . . ."

21. See, for example, Kimberly J. Harris et al., "Food Safety Inspections Results: A Comparison of Ethnic-Operated Restaurants to Non-Ethnic-Operated Restaurants," *International Journal of Hospitality Management*, 46 (April 2015): 190–199. Almost unbelievably, a training manual used by Toronto's public health department between 2004 and 2014 referenced "Chinese-style foods" as a possible source of food poisoning. Laura Armstrong, "Toronto Public Health Removes 'Racist' Document Suggesting Chinese Food Causes Food Poisoning," *Toronto Star*, August 6, 2014, https://www.thestar.com /news/gta/2014/08/06/toronto_public_health_removes_racist_document _suggesting_chinese_food_causes_food_poisoning.html. It would be interesting to explore further the role of food media in legitimizing or correcting these stereotypes. When the New York health agency doled out a "C" to the fine dining restaurant Per Se, for example, local food media rose to the restaurant's defense. As Soleil Ho pointed out at the time, it is hard to be certain the media would have done the same if the restaurant at issue were a Chinese one. Joseph Erbentraut, "This Is Why It's Racist to Call 'Ethnic' Restaurants 'Gross.'" HuffPost, April 11, 2016, https://www.huffpost.com/entry /ethnic-restaurants-food-safety-racism_n_5706984be4b0a506064e771d.

22. Motion, Los Angeles City Council File No. 20-0147, arch 17, 2020, https:// clkrep.lacity.org/onlinedocs/2020/20-0147-s27_Mot.pdf.

23. Mark Vallianatos, "Compl(Eat)Ing the Streets: Legalizing Sidewalk Food Vending in Los Angeles," in *Incomplete Streets: Processes, Practices, and Possibilities*, ed. Julian Agyeman and Stephen Zavestoski (Abingdon, UK, Routledge, 2015), 205–224.

24. Sarah Portnoy, *Food, Health, and Culture in Latino Los Angeles* (Lanham, MD: Rowman & Littlefield, 2016), 89.

25. David E. Brady, "Informed Opinions on Today's Topics: New Proposal Fuels Street Vendor Debate," *Los Angeles Times*, October 8, 1993, https://www .latimes.com/archives/la-xpm-1993-10-08-me-43622-story.html.

26. Amy Pyle, "Street Vendors Eke Out a Living in Fear of Crackdown," *Los Angeles Times*, March 9, 2019, www.latimes.com/archives/la-xpm-1990-07-21-me-1-story.html.

27. Lee Romney, "Group of Street Vendors Licensed in Test of Reform," *Los Angeles Times*, May 7, 1999, www.latimes.com/archives/la-xpm-1999-may-07-fi-34742-story.html; see also Rocio Rosales, *Fruteros: Street Vending, Illegality, and Ethnic Community in Los Angeles* (Berkeley: University of California Press, 2020).

28. Dennis Romero, "Fearing Trump's Deportations, L.A. Begins to Legalize Street Vendors," *LA Weekly*, January 31, 2017, www.laweekly.com/fearing-trumps-deportations-l-a-begins-to-legalize-street-vendors.

29. Willy Blackmore, "Street Food Is Legal, but Vendors Could Still Be Squeezed as New Rules Are Worked Out," *Los Angeles Times*, June 14, 2018, www.latimes.com/food/dailydish/la-fo-re-street-food-vendors-los-angeles-201800615-story.html; Motion 40B, Los Angele City Council File No. 13-1493-S5, October 31, 2018, http://clkrep.lacity.org/onlinedocs/2013/13-1493-S5_mot_b_10-31-18.pdf.

30. Yvonne Yen Liu et al., "Sidewalk Stimulus: Economic and Geographic Impact of Los Angeles Street Vendors," Economic Roundtable, 2015, https://economicrt.org/publication/sidewalk-stimulus/.

31. Los Angeles City Council File No. 13-1493, 13-1493-S5, November 6, 2019, clkrep.lacity.org/onlinedocs/2013/131493_CAF_11-18-2019.pdf.

32. Janette Villafana and Jack Ross, "L.A. Street Vendors Are Caught between COVID and the Law," *Capital & Main*, November 30, 2020, capitalandmain.com/los-angeles-street-vendors-are-caught-between-covid-and-the-law-1130.

33. Motion, Los Angeles City Council File No. 20-0147-S48, March 17, 2020, clkrep.lacity.org/onlinedocs/2020/20-0147-S48_misc_03-17-2020.pdf.

34. "Vending Commonly Asked Questions," StreetsLA/Bureau of Street Services, https://streetsla.lacity.org/vending-questions.

35. Louis Casiano, "LA County Sheriff: Deputies Won't Enforce Newsom's Stay-at-Home Order," Fox News, December 4, 2020, www.foxnews.com/us/la-county-sheriff-newsoms-stay-at-home.

36. "Annual Report 2020," Inclusive Action, 2020, www.inclusiveaction.org/s/2020-Annual-Report_FINAL-FULL-compressed-7bat.pdf.

Cà Phê Sữa Đá (Iced Coffee with Condensed Milk)

Makes 1 cup

When the misery of the pandemic was compounded by multiple heat waves crashing into Los Angeles during the summer and early fall, I found some comfort in taking out my *phin* and making Vietnamese-style iced coffee. This is my basic recipe, but I begin with a few notes:

- The classic way to make *cà phê sữa đá*, of course, is to use a *phin*, a brewer that resembles a top hat and sits atop your cup. For the uninitiated, the *phin* has three parts: the body of the *phin* itself, a filter either dropped or screwed into the chamber, and a lid. You can find *phins* at Asian markets; alternatively, Brooklyn-based Nguyen Coffee Supply has beautiful ceramic ones available online. And if you are ever in Saigon, La Viet Coffee has a custom-made version that is fun to tinker with.

- If your kitchen sink, like mine, clogs at the sight of coffee grounds, you can make cleanup easier by trimming a paper filter to size and placing it at the bottom of the *phin* before adding the coffee. Aeropress filters fit almost perfectly.

- The slow drip-drip-drip nature of the *phin* means it will take a few minutes longer than other brew methods to make a cup. If it is taking too long, it is likely because the coffee is ground too fine, or the grinds have compacted too much. Shaking the *phin* gently to loosen the grinds may help move the water along.

- All that said, if you don't have a *phin*, you can use the coffee brewer you do have.

¾ cup water (175 grams, about 6 ounces)

1 tablespoon condensed milk, plus more to taste

2 heaping tablespoons (15 grams) medium-grind coffee

Ice

- I suggest using medium- to dark-roast coffee that will complement the sweetness of the condensed milk. Beans with hints of chocolate and caramel are especially good with the milk.

Method

In a kettle set over high heat, bring the water to a boil.

While the water comes to a boil, spoon 1 tablespoon of condensed milk into a mug.

Add the ground coffee to the *phin*. Gently tap or shake the *phin* to level out the grinds. Drop the filter in the chamber of the *phin* and apply a bit of pressure to tamp and slightly compact the coffee (if your filter has a screw, screw in the filter just short of tight). Place the *phin* on top of the mug with the condensed milk.

When the water comes to a boil, remove it from the heat, wait 30 seconds, then pour just enough water into the *phin* to saturate the coffee—the water level will be just above the filter. Let the coffee bloom for 30 seconds, then pour in enough water to fill the chamber. As the coffee filters, add the remaining water, then place the lid on the *phin*. The total brewing time will be between 4 and 5 minutes. When the coffee has finished brewing, remove the *phin* (you can flip the lid upside down and place the *phin* on the lid).

Stir to combine the milk and coffee. Taste. If you like your coffee sweeter, swirl in a bit more condensed milk.

Drop some ice into a separate glass. Pour the coffee over the ice and give it a good stir. Enjoy.

4

Cooking with the Lights Off

I do not go into the kitchen very much these days. We have a chef de cuisine who was promoted to that role during the pandemic, mostly because "restaurant" operations have become rather complex. Not to mention childcare and all of that. I do not have the bandwidth to actually cook right now. At all. But I would be lying if I said it was only because of time management issues. It is really hard to feel passionate and excited to cook during this time. The reason that many of us cook is that instant gratification from pleasing others. In the hospitality industry, that is what we live for. When you have a silent, empty building, and your food gets packed into to-go boxes and gets tossed into a bike carrier's bag and ends up cold and upside down in someone's apartment thirty minutes later, it is hard to keep picking up that knife.

What we love most about Kachka is sharing this culture and connecting with our guests. Sometimes it is just a transaction, sometimes people do not want to be bothered; they order what is on the menu, they eat their food, they pay their check, and they go. But when diners engage with us—want to know more—we want to tell them more. That human connection is the most satisfying part of having a restaurant. When that is taken away, it all feels pointless. So that is where we are at right now. It used to be something we put

Bonnie Frumkin Morales spoke with Philip Gleissner and Harry Eli Kashdan over Zoom in February 2021. This transcription has been edited for length and clarity.

our blood, sweat, and tears into because we loved it unconditionally. Now we are indentured to it.

If you search for "Russian" restaurants in most major metropolitan areas, you will usually find a banquet hall that is owned and operated by immigrants from the former Soviet Union (FSU). These banquet halls serve the immigrant community, and so they are very much legitimate. There is a lot of dancing, there are speeches and toasts, and the atmosphere is very vibrant and celebratory. The food has to be plentiful—that is *really* important. But, in order for it to feel "opulent" or "prestigious," in the eyes of most FSU immigrants it should be something French or Japanese or really anything but their own cuisine. The food they are actually preparing at most of these venues is so vaguely authentic that it is almost comical. There is a lot of sushi, for example. For folks who immigrated from anywhere in the former Soviet Union, there is a long-standing, self-conscious, and negative feeling toward their own food. Obviously, the Soviet food shortages and quality issues left their mark on most people's psyches in that way.

So that is how my husband, Israel, and I opened Kachka in 2014. At the time, there was nothing in the United States—and in some ways, globally—that spoke in a way that we thought was relevant and respectful to the cuisine that I grew up eating. So we set forth on opening a restaurant, which is not something that any sane, rational person should do. Israel and I come from restaurant backgrounds, so we know firsthand that owning one is for fools. It is a lot of work for very little return. Back when we were dating, we would always talk about how we would never, ever, ever own a restaurant.

But we became almost *possessed* to open Kachka. It felt like if we didn't do it, this cuisine might never be brought into the light. It became our passion and goal in life: to share this food, this way of eating, and all the culture around it with as many people as are willing to listen—or eat, really.

We are constantly motivated to find ways for Americans to put this cuisine in their mental rolodexes as a normal meal to eat. When you are thinking about whether you are having ramen, or Thai, or pizza tonight, Russian or post-Soviet isn't something that really pops up, and my goal—our mission—is to change that. This drives every business decision we make.

I already knew how to cook; I had been cooking professionally for years. But we had absolutely no idea what we were really doing—we had never owned a restaurant before. We had to find finances—an investor—no bank would lend to us, write a business plan, et cetera. Every little detail like, well, "I actually don't know what you have to do when you hire a person—I've never had to do the actual paperwork. What does that entail?" I know this might be obvious to some, but what we did not know going into owning a business is that there is no manual, and there are no guardrails. From the outside, it would seem that you should not be allowed to just open a restaurant to the public without there being a singular, consolidated body of things that you are supposed to know about doing it. There is your local government and the federal government, the health department, OSHA (Occupational Safety and Health Administration), and on and on. It is a patchwork, sometimes with conflicting regulations, and, so, as a result, you actually have no idea. There have been many times over the years where we have realized, "Oh, we've been doing this wrong the whole time."

Thankfully, this crazy, harebrained idea of ours to open Kachka seemed to resonate with people, because we were busy from day one. From our opening in 2014 until the pandemic, it has been busier year after year. A lot of our success can certainly be attributed to hard work and know-how, but there is an undeniable percentage of a restaurant's success that is intangible—some might call it luck. We are beyond grateful that the intangible part clicked for us, because it could easily have gone the other way.

There are a wide range of reasons people dine at Kachka, as is true for any other restaurant, but there is one type of diner in particular that motivates me: maybe their grandmother is from Riga, or they are an international student studying in America and separated from their family back in Minsk, or they lived in Moscow twenty years ago. It is just amazing how powerful food and smell are in recalling faded memories. We have had several instances of people crying into their bowls of *golubtsi* because it triggers a memory of a lost loved one, of family

Bonnie and Israel Morales in their
restaurant during lockdown

separated by an ocean, of a past chapter in their life. Their mother
hates the food she grew up with—refused to cook it—but at *babushka*'s
house this was what she would always make. *Babushka* died some years
ago, the thread was broken, and they lost that connection until that
moment when the steam from the bowl of cabbage rolls hit their nos-
trils. I never anticipated that such a level of connection could happen
at a restaurant. Though unanticipated, these moments are my most
powerful driver.

The same driving force led to writing the *Kachka* cookbook. I had
an agent approach me who was really excited about what we were
doing. It was just months into our having opened the restaurant and I
certainly did not have the time to write a book, but there had not been
one written on the subject in almost, at that time, thirty years, since
Please to the Table. I felt it was critical to share what we were doing, and
I was not sure if this opportunity would come up again, so you find the
time you don't have in the first place. Again, there was an unexpected

connection made. Readers email me from all over the country thanking me for writing this book, telling me that their experiences mirror my own and that they finally feel seen.

My parents were refuseniks. They were in the Soviet Union and basically said, "We don't want any part of this anymore. We're Jews, we want to go to our homeland of Israel." You had to denounce Communism first, and then you could apply to leave. Then came a really stressful waiting game—it was meant to be a deterrent, most people did not want this risk—because if your application ended up being denied, after you had already said, "I don't want to be part of this," you were basically unemployable. You would live in the margins. My entire extended family, both of my sets of grandparents and all of their siblings, were all going to go at the same time, and they all ended up backing out on my father's side. On my mother's side, her sister and my grandparents ended up leaving a little bit later because of the timing of the applications. So my parents ended up being the only ones. They left on their own in 1979, without knowing for sure if they were ever going to see any of their family again.

In the Soviet Union it was nearly impossible to observe any religion during that time. It is interesting because my mother's grandfather was the kosher butcher in their village, and just one or two generations later there was absolutely no observance. That is how effective Sovietization campaigns were. On the other hand, my father has stories of how they had to make matzo for Passover underground. You would buy a sack of flour and bring it in a suitcase to a neighbor who would bake the matzo. The next day you would pick up your matzo and take it home in a suitcase, all by cover of night. It was highly illegal. The discrimination, anti-Semitism, general inability to thrive, it was all too much, and my parents decided they would not raise children in this place. It was worth it for them to risk everything and leave.

My brother was six or seven at the time. They left by train from Minsk, through Warsaw and into Vienna. My father describes the train car having no heat. It was wintertime, and the toilet was broken, and there was frozen urine on the floor of the train car—inhumane circumstances. In Vienna, they announced that they didn't actually want to go to Israel, they wanted to go to the United States. This was a premeditated, known path, from my understanding. A lot of people applied to go to the United States. Canada and Australia were also very popular at the time. My parents chose the United States because my mother had a great uncle who had left through Cuba before the Russian Revolution. He had already been established in Chicago, and so they asked for that family to be their sponsor. From Vienna, after you said you were going to the United States, that took you to Rome—Ostia, really—to wait for approval to enter the United States. My parents were there, waiting, for a few months.

The whole process was really stressful, obviously. You leave the Soviet Union with basically nothing. The Soviets did not allow you to take anything valuable when you left. My mom painted some of her jewelry so that it looked less valuable, and my dad took his wedding ring and had it melted down into a different shape, so that it looked cheap and hollow instead of solid. They hid valuables in my brother's toys. People also packed what they thought they could sell while they were waiting in Italy. The wait was indefinite, and this was one of the only ways to make sure you could put food on the table. My dad told me about a man in their emigration group who went with an entire suitcase of condoms because he had heard, either mistakenly or as some sort of cruel joke, that in Italy what they really desired were Soviet condoms. So this man shows up to Rome with a suitcase full of Soviet condoms, and they are completely worthless.

When they came to the United States, the Hebrew Immigrant Aid Society being their backers meant that my brother was given a full scholarship to Solomon Schechter, a Jewish private school. My brother came home one day from Solomon Schechter demanding that there be no more pork in the house. When I was a little girl, I remember going to Hebrew school and the whole bit, and bringing back all that, so I feel like all of the Jewish components to our family came from the children. We would bring these ideas home, and then my parents would think, "Well, yes, we left the Soviet Union, we came to the United States for religious freedom, and to not be persecuted as Jews." They could not get good jobs when they were in the Soviet Union, and so they felt like they had to uphold all of this, even though they were not religious.

Now to backtrack a little—I was, for very practical reasons, born the year after they made it to Chicago. My father had a little bit of English, and he also had some training as a computer programmer in Russia. That was, obviously, very important in 1980, so he was very employable, even with limited English. My mother had been a book-keeper, but without any English that is not a very helpful trade. She basically told my father, "Look, I'm not going to be able to find any meaningful work. This seems like a good time to have a second child." That is how I came about. The next logical step for my mother was, "Well, if I'm home already with a child, I can start watching some of our other immigrant friends' children." It turned into a business. She became a home daycare provider for Russian Jewish immigrants. She became an icon in that suburban Chicago community, raising hundreds of children over the years.

At the daycare, Jewishness was purely cultural. In the Soviet Union, because of the anti-Semitism, Jews felt very ostracized. You had to navigate and network. Every once in a while, somebody who was Jew-ish maybe had a leg up somewhere and could help out. Otherwise, it was nearly impossible to thrive—get into a respectable university, find a decent job. The Soviets marked "Jewish" as the nationality on Soviet Jews' passports and in many ways the distinction and anti-Semitism did create or at least enhance the sense of "us versus them" for many, including my parents. So it was a distinctly separate culture. And that extended to their resettled homeland. In the Chicago Soviet immigrant community, which at that time was predominantly Jewish, everyone relied on each other. There was a shared experience.

As an adult looking back on all of this, what reverberates the most for me is just how impossible it is for my parents, and therefore myself, to really identify with a specific nationality. The entire time that my parents lived in the place currently known as Belarus, it was part of the Soviet Union. On top of that, the nationality listed on their passports was "Jewish." But in the United States, Jewish is not considered to be a nationality, and the place that they were born, the Soviet Union, no longer exists. It would be downright unnatural to identify themselves as Belarusian since that country came to exist long after they left. Americans get confused when they say they are Jewish, and if they were to call themselves Soviet, they might be thought to be communists or Stalin sympathizers. So then, I want to know how I should label the food I cook at Kachka. If I don't know what to call the place my family came from, how do I talk about the food of that place? Most of the time, my parents just say they are Russian to make things simpler, and I do too.

I went to school for industrial design, and when I graduated, I landed my "dream job." I was in New York, and it was everything I wanted—and I was miserable. I hated everything about it. I would spend all my time at the Union Square farmers market instead of at my office job. I started showing up later and later to work, leaving earlier and earlier, and one day I quit and went to culinary school. It wasn't quite so instantaneous—I was getting more and more interested in cooking and I hated my job, so I made the jump. It was reckless and impulsive, but I could not shake it. My parents thought I was nuts—they were very, very concerned. But I had caught the bug and I was just obsessed with cooking.

Growing up, my mother hated having me in the kitchen because I had really long hair. I would always go running through the kitchen with my hair down, and she would yell at me and shoo me out of the kitchen because she was worried that one of my hairs would fly off my head and magically end up in the soup or whatever else she was making. It is not a fairy-tale story of, "Oh, my mother taught me all the ways of the Russian kitchen when I was a little girl." No. A lot of what I do now, and the way I have come around to the food, is as an adult becoming curious and going back to my mother and asking lots of questions.

Culinary school means classical French training—mother sauces, all that stuff. I ended up working in restaurants after that, and every place you go is more of the same basic paradigm. I worked in a really modern place at one point, the kind that uses liquid nitrogen and sodium alginate and such; you eat your menu. So I definitely did a wide range of things. I remember in culinary school we actually had this exercise in one of my classes where you were supposed to go through the mechanics of opening a restaurant. The restaurant that I had come up with was this Russian concept. I still have the menu I wrote for it. I laugh at it because it is so pretentious and it is also so insulting. I had taken all of these classic Russian dishes and just "Frenchified" them. It was such a disrespectful thing to do, instead of keeping dishes true to themselves. It is the kind of irreverent thing you do when you don't understand.

There is a dish called *kholodets*, which is basically like meat jello. It is made using bones and collagen, typically from veal or pork, and boiled for a long time. Because of the natural gelatin, that liquid will be firm when it is cold. You pick out all the meat, chop it up with garlic, and you fold it into this aspic, and you set it. That might sound really bizarre to many Americans, but the haute cuisine version of this gets a lot of acclaim and is something gourmands spend a lot of money on at fancy restaurants. I remember that I was home for the holidays, and we were having a big family party. I told my mom, "Don't worry about it. I'm going to take care of the *kholodets*!" I spent four days making this stock, making consommé from it, confiting various cuts of meat, and doing these perfect *mirepoix* vegetables. I was so excited about it, and then I remember serving it and looking around the room at all of my family and them just kind of being, like, "But where's the *kholodets*?" The dish that I described the first time around may not paint a really sumptuous picture to you, because maybe you are not familiar with it, but it is so much more satisfying, and so much more *real*. Not to say that there is anything *wrong* with this refined, technique-driven, fine-dining version. It serves a different purpose. But there was also nothing wrong with the original *kholodets*, so why was I trying to fix it?

For me, the story behind a dish, why it exists, is actually more important than how it tastes because that understanding informs everything. Sometimes it is not a childhood story, sometimes it is some-thing contemporary, something I just learned about recently or that I am exploring on my own. It doesn't always have to have some sort of family tie, but there is always a reason behind it.

The beginning of the pandemic was surreal and emotionally harrow-ing. We were also just caught completely unprepared. "What do you mean, I have to lay off all my staff?" I could not quite understand how I was expected to just tell everyone they didn't have a job anymore.

This may sound really naive, but at the time I felt, "Well, but this thing isn't our fault. It's a virus and it's not our fault, so what do you mean that I, as a business, have to figure it out myself?" After that sort of initial shock, though, we realized that, yes, in fact, we had to scale down and figure out how we were going to proceed. We sat down and laid off forty-five people and retained twelve. We said goodbye to our employees, but they were also our friends. And the twelve of us that were left turned around and started getting ready for takeout service that day, because with a restaurant you cannot just stop. When you expected to do 300 covers in a night, and then suddenly it's nothing, you are left with many thousands of dollars of highly perishable food sitting around. We had no choice but to do our best to sell it. We said our goodbyes—lots of hugging—wiped our tears, and turned around and went back to work. We did not close at all. It was traumatic.

Before COVID-19, we were the kind of restaurant that hated accommodating takeout. It was always on a case-by-case basis. The manager would have to go back to the kitchen and ask if it was okay right now, and the customer had to be there in person and wait while we prepared the order. We didn't really have the right kind of packaging. We didn't have the infrastructure for it. It was a totally foreign concept to us. So we built an online store on our website in a matter of days. We were building the plane as we were flying it, figuring out how takeout even works, and who the credit card processor is, all of that.

We had just opened Kachka Lavka, which is this little deli adjacent to the restaurant, in November, so we had this new little baby deli, and it actually turned out to be the perfect thing for this strange moment because we were positioned to sell groceries. We had three or four cases of toilet paper sitting around, and nobody had toilet paper, so we started selling the individually wrapped rolls that you use in restaurants. Yeast was hard to come by, so we were selling yeast. All the stuff that was not available in stores, it was not because there were actual shortages, it was because the supply chains were broken. We had all these supplies that grocery stores couldn't access, so we were able to leverage that.

Israel and I started doing deliveries all over Portland. We didn't want our staff to do that because nobody really knew how this virus worked, and so everyone was really scared, and no one wanted to go inside people's buildings. We didn't want the guilt that we might put our staff in a dangerous situation, but we needed every sale we could get. It was strange and bizarre, and we were in this place for a few months.

Passover approached during these early pandemic days. We normally do a huge Passover dinner at an event space every year, and this would have been our fourth year doing it. I thought, "Oh, that's really sad that we're not going to be able to do the Passover dinner. Let's do some sort of a special take home box." We prepared a meal box, and it sold out very quickly. We realized that it was something that people wanted.

It felt good for us too. It had been so bizarre to be preparing food in a silent, dark restaurant. We are so used to it now, a year later, but at first the silence and darkness in the dining room felt so dystopian for us. We did not realize how much we missed the driving beat of the music, the clinking of glasses, the low murmur and pops of laughter, the sound of silverware hitting plates. Doing these meal boxes gave us a glimmer of that human connection. That sense of purpose really helped for a few weeks. There were a few different cases where multiple generations picked up the same box. We had a daughter, a mother, and a grandmother all come by at various times in the day, mentioning that they were all having a Zoom Seder together. Even though the three generations would only see each other virtually that day, Kachka became the thread that joined them and there was something haunting about knowing that they all stood in the same spot that day just a few hours apart.

As the scope of the pandemic stretched from weeks to months, it became increasingly difficult to navigate. No one knew anything, and no one was telling us anything. What happens when an employee has an itch in their throat? Would we need to close if someone got sick? In Portland, we were approved for Phase I in our local terms in June. This meant we could have on-site dining. We knew this was an eventuality, so we had been preparing for it some months in advance. We also knew that our employees would not feel comfortable with people inside our space. We have this huge parking lot adjacent to our building, so we turned it into this whole separate, outdoor pop-up restaurant called Kachka Alfresca. Being able to do this really changed things for us. First of all, we had been missing having people around. We could start working out those muscles of being a restaurant. We also knew that there was no way we could really do Kachka the way we wanted to do it in an outdoor parking lot on picnic tables and paper plates, so we wanted to do this thing that just felt really light-hearted and fun—a mental vacation for our guests. It was from another time, kind of, like, TGI Fridays–inspired Russian food. We had a lot of fun with it, and it was summertime, so it was warm, and the weather was beautiful.

As light-hearted as the food we were serving was, our hearts were heavy. There was this overlay of the Black Lives Matter movement and the protests happening. There was a dissonance where, at the same time that we were basically throwing this big, socially distanced party every night and everything was really fun, we were also running around donating food for protesters at all hours of the day—seeing people just frustrated and devastated. Marches and demonstrations were often just blocks away. It rips your heart apart to want to both tear everything down and fight for what's right but also do your best to focus and keep your business from sinking.

And then in July this thing called the "86 List" popped up. There were similar versions in other cities but essentially it was an anonymous social media account that was lambasting restaurants for poor practices and unhealthy work environments. We ended up on that list a few times, and it was gut-wrenching. My husband and I work relentlessly for our employees. To get some of this backlash was shocking to us, more than anything. All we ever do is try to do right by our staff. I quit social media, personally, because I could not handle it. It would make me nauseous. I recognize that everyone was really angry and frustrated, and it was a really, really challenging time. I am happy that people who felt like they could not speak up found a safe way to share, but it was not a constructive platform, and did more harm than good across the city.

Just as those tensions began to ease and the city began to find its rhythm again, there were a series of intense wildfires. The wildfires were the first time since the pandemic started that we had to close the restaurant. For three days, the smoke and air quality in Portland was so hazardous that even inside our restaurant our air filters couldn't keep up. I am not a religious person, but it began to feel like a higher power was testing my resilience.

And, of course, we all knew that winter was looming. The rains and chilly air were waiting for us. It would be too unpleasant to eat outside after October, and there was no way in hell that it would make sense to do dining indoors at that point. We realized that we would have to coast on fumes through the winter and hope we could make it to summer again.

This time around, rather than like it was in the spring, we knew what was coming, we could prepare for it and plan. It felt a little bit more like organized chaos instead of just pandemonium. That's what we have been doing ever since. Right now, my husband and I are actively trying to figure out what we are doing next. That sums up the entire last year: it has been like opening a new restaurant every three months. If I hear the word "pivot" again, I might throw something. You cannot think that far ahead, and you are constantly trying to figure out how to make it work, but you also don't want to invest too much time, effort, or capital because you don't know when it's going to need to change again.

So many times throughout this whole year we thought, prematurely, "Oh, yeah, you know by such and such month everything will be normal." I feel like I have said that so many times that at this point we are too nervous to even think it. It just seems like we are never going to get there. I know part of it is the time of year, the weather, the endless nights of abysmal take-out sales. It's a real head game at this point in the pandemic—trying to keep the mental drive and focus when your mind is starting to give in. In the first few months it was simple determination: "Oh, we can do this for a few months, no big deal. It's kind of fun!"

We have been trying to distract ourselves with work on diversifying the business so it's a bit less fragile in the future. Selling our dumplings frozen to local grocery stores, relaunching our vodka—that is not brand new, but we had put it on the back burner, and we re-released it in December. That's us trying to diversify, trying to say, "Okay, well, maybe we just don't put all of our eggs in one basket and we start thinking about other ways to connect and to continue our mission, without it being in a physical space."

The big question is: When can we start feeling safe to plan further out? We cannot keep thinking month-to-month. We had a PPP (Paycheck Protection Program) loan that we ran through in the first round, and then we just got our second round. That makes all the difference because, both times—right before the first one dropped, and now right before the second one—there was this moment where we knew, "If we don't get this money, we will have to close." Right now, it feels great because we're at the beginning of the second round of PPP funds, and I understand the math. I know that we are going to be able to pay our staff, which will allow us to be able to operate and therefore get some sort of revenue. That is great, *for right now*. But at the end of that, what happens? The funds and the time in which we can use them are still finite, and the point at which we will be able to operate without needing the funds as a crutch is unknown. We don't know when that need will end. As these twenty-four weeks of PPP count down, our stress will continue to go up. At what point does the length of time start to feel like it's not just a little bump but is in fact the way life is now? The source of stress and tension is okay right now. We are making it work within the parameters, and we have this little safety net and that's helping. But what happens next? I don't know. Everybody is in that boat, it's not just restaurants.

I don't have a really strong tie to feeling that I have to cook these dishes at home for my children so that they have them or hold on to them, and I think that might be because I do it for a living, and I sometimes forget about that. Yes, sometimes the food we eat at home is reflective of our culture. We eat probably double, triple the buckwheat that our neighbors do. Probably more than quadruple. But we also make ramen and roast artichokes. We eat everything, and so I don't really think about food at home with the kids as a way to pass on the culture. I wonder, if I didn't cook the food of my childhood for a living, would it be different? I would probably be more conscious of it.

I miss eating at restaurants; I love seeing what my peers are doing. We all use each other, just like in any artistic expression. For the creative aspect and also the technical aspect of what we do, you look to others, you riff on what they're doing. Musicians do the same thing. When you don't have that interplay, your inspiration, the places that you look for something to bounce off of—when those things start to be harder to access it can mute everything. Travel too. I get so much inspiration for what I do by traveling. It isn't always food, sometimes it is just some visual inspiration, or something else. All of those things have fallen away, and so it gets really hard to get excited. Your only outlet ends up being what you saw on Instagram. And *that's* depressing. As a cook, I am languishing.

At the end of the day, this is temporary. It is not going to last forever. I am an adult about it; I understand that this will pass and we are all going to be fine. It is just that right now it's hard to stay positive. I hold on to the knowledge that at some point we are going to be able to feed people in our restaurant and share this with them again. I also know that when we are able to do what we do, people are going to be extra excited. There is going to be so much energy around shared experiences and going out to eat. Right now I am seeing the world in black and white, and when things reopen it is going to be like seeing in color for the first time, you know? And that's exciting.

My Mom's Chicken *Kotleti*

Yields about 8 patties

Method

Place potato and onion in the bowl of a food processor and blend until uniform. Transfer mixture to a large mixing bowl and add all remaining ingredients except for the oil. Mix by hand until uniform.

Heat a large skillet over medium heat. Add about a ¼ inch of cooking oil to the pan. When the pan is hot, use a disher or two large spoons to shape and place four patties in the oil. Cook for about 5 minutes on each side or until the internal temperature reaches 165°F. Transfer to a warming oven and cook *kotleti* in batches until there is no more chicken farce left. Serve immediately.

1 Yukon gold or similar or smallish baking potato (125 g), peeled and chunked

1 medium onion (115 g), peeled and chunked

1 lb ground chicken, dark meat only

1 egg

1 ¼ teaspoon salt (7 g)

1 teaspoon garlic powder

Oil for cooking

5

The Meaning of Martin Yan

In January 2020, the Bay Area–based public media outlet KQED made an announcement on its Facebook page: for "the first time ever," the station would release old episodes of the show *Yan Can Cook!* on its YouTube channel every Monday of the year.[1] The program, hosted by the Chinese-born chef Martin Yan, had been airing consistently on American public television since 1982, making it one of the longest-running cooking shows in the country. But these old episodes had been lost to time. They would include a 1985 episode where Yan fills the cavities of a cucumber with braised pork shoulder, a 1988 episode where he cooks a "Beijing pizza" with hoisin sauce topped with chopped *lap cheong* sausage and mushrooms, and a 1989 episode where he bakes *dan tat*, egg custard tarts the color of dandelions.[2]

Yan needs no introduction for many Americans. He has charmed the nation for four decades now, blurring the lines between education and entertainment. A cheery host who makes cooking seem fun, he works along the same lines as his predecessors Julia Child and Graham Kerr, who had popular cooking shows in the 1960s. Like Yan, both hosts seemed to cook in pursuit of joy. Yan is not just a chef, he is a brand. He has written over two dozen cookbooks. He has sold cookware under his name and owned restaurants.[3] But he has also gained prestige approval: he has won multiple James Beard Awards for his show, along with an Emmy. His popularity likely rivals that of Lidia Bastianich or

Jacques Pepin, faces you are bound to see on public television on a Saturday afternoon. But Yan has been on American television since long before talents like Marcus Samuelsson or Ming Tsai entered the fray. Back in the 1980s, Yan's race distinguished him from most others on food television. From the onset of his career, everything about Yan clearly marked him as foreign—his accent, his skin color, his food. That Yan managed to become a household name in a field that was so overwhelmingly white is remarkable.

I was born a decade after Yan's show first hit American airwaves. Like many Americans, I grew up knowing who Yan was, thanks to his abiding presence on television. In my adolescence, I rarely stopped to appreciate the skill Yan displayed in these shows. To me, he was just a funny guy standing in front of a stove. Perhaps I let myself become convinced that Yan was not worth taking seriously, though pinpointing who, or what, exactly installed this belief in my head feels impossible now. His talent—for comedy, for cooking—rarely seemed like a matter of discussion, and it was thus invisible to me. I simply perceived him as the butt of a joke, ridiculed for his shameless attempts to make viewers smile. Yan appealed to the lowest common denominator, and I naively thought that that alone was reason enough to disregard him.

It would take me years to grasp just how notable Yan's very visibility on television was, and the expertise that allowed him to scale such heights. As an adult, I would step into the culinary world myself, dealing firsthand with its exclusionary, often racist tendencies. Existing in that world became soul-draining; I just wanted to do my job. In search of some guidance, I looked to Martin Yan.

I was not alone in my desire to revisit Yan's work. "Martin Yan Was a YouTube Celebrity Chef Before There Was YouTube," declared the headline of a February 2020 profile of Yan for KQED's online publication.[4] The writer Ruth Gebreyesus posited Yan as the progenitor of modern cooking entertainment, the kind that now lives online. "*Bon Appétit*, along with YouTube celebrities, has placed humor and narrative at the center of their videos," Gebreyesus observed, referring to the Condé Nast–owned food magazine's once-bustling YouTube channel. Months later, this statement would feel fraught. In the summer of that same year, *Bon Appétit* saw an exodus of on-screen talent after assistant food editor Sohla El-Waylly, whose family hails from Bangladesh, leveled allegations of pay imbalances between white talent and talent of color under Editor-in-Chief Adam Rapoport. Rapoport resigned hours after these accusations—along with a photo of him garishly dressed up as a Puerto Rican man on Halloween—surfaced. The injustices at *Bon Appétit* seemed to prompt a wider cultural realization of how deeply embedded racism is within the American food media, though this was not exactly news to those of us who have inhabited the industry for years.

Gebreyesus wrote that article in a time that now feels distant. In those early months of 2020, many in the United States failed to take the threat of a pandemic seriously. Instead, an alarming number of Americans were content to see the virus as little more than a hypothetical nuisance from China, a convenient excuse to discriminate against Chinese and Chinese Americans. This was a mere prelude to the torrent of anti-Asian violence that would stretch into the following year. By March, Chinatowns in major American metropolitan areas had become targets of xenophobia and racism, with restaurants bearing the brunt of such intolerance.[5] Within weeks, the pandemic pushed the United States into lockdown. Staggering shifts would follow. Over the course of 2020, the pandemic would claim hundreds of thousands of lives, exposing an unfathomable level of government mismanagement. Scores of restaurants would close their doors, sometimes for good.

In those months of forced isolation during the spring of 2020 I found myself watching Yan's work on YouTube. He made taro dumplings in one episode, pork spareribs with black bean sauce in another. His gaiety, combined with the clarity of his instruction, even made a shy cook like me want to get into the kitchen. Certain recipes of his called to me immediately, like a hot, sweet, walnut soup he made in one episode devoted exclusively to desserts.[6] He outlined the recipe's arithmetic clearly in the show's corresponding cookbook, *The Yan Can Cook Book* (1981). Just as Yan instructed, I toasted the nuts in the oven until their perfume filled my kitchen, then blended them into a chalky powder. I dropped the dust into a saucepan filled with water, rice flour, and brown sugar until it began to bubble on the stove, stirring it gently over fifteen minutes until the stew became muddy. I splashed it with some evaporated milk, turning the soup tan, and eased it back to a boil. The soup bursts with quiet character, lush and full-bodied; sip it and you are suddenly aware of all the possibilities that a walnut contains.

But I was not necessarily watching Yan because I wanted to cook his recipes. Rather, I was more interested in watching *him*. Though these episodes were older than I was, I found Yan's persona disarming in a fresh, unexpected way. He reached out to the viewer's fundamental desire for pleasure, without apology. Take one 1985 episode, in which he begins by telling his audience they are about to go fishing in the South China Sea. Standing on the studio stage, he grabs a fake fishing rod and pulls a crab out from behind the counter; the crustacean is the size of a small boulder. "Oh, my!" he exclaims. "My worm got away!" The order of the day, he tells the viewer, is crab and bean curd soup.[7] Even when engaging in these hijinks, Yan never lost sight of the fact that he was there to teach viewers how to cook.

As I spent more time watching those episodes, I began to appreciate Yan's gifts anew. But I wondered if there was any struggle lurking behind that confident screen persona. Yan, I figured, could not have had an easy time in the food industry as a Chinese immigrant man in America. America has long made a sport of emasculating East Asian men; I surmised that this may have fueled dismissals of Yan. Perhaps my lifelong misconceptions about Yan had a lot to do with the prejudices of a food establishment that was, and in some ways still is, quite hostile to anyone it deems to be an outsider.

I understood this marginalization acutely. September 2020 would mark four years since I began writing about food professionally, a trajectory I never imagined for myself. Back in 2016, I was a

Mayukh Sen

twenty-four-year-old aspiring cultural critic eager to prove my bona fides as a "serious writer," so I took a gig as a staff writer at a digital food publication because it was the only salaried writing job I could find. The industry often felt inhospitable to me by virtue of things I could not control, particularly the fact that I was brown and queer. But I needed to make a living, so I stuck with the job in spite of the indignities it would expose me to. I would face bold racism from readers and strangers on the internet. With time and rising recognition, I would field slightly more veiled insults from my elders who seemed to resent any crumbs of attention thrown my way. I think of the white editor of a legacy food magazine who publicly chided me for pointing out, in her own words, "how politically incorrect and biased" others in my industry were. I cannot imagine being spoken to in this way had my name been one white folks could pronounce, or if I had looked more like them. No matter how much acclaim came my way from the food establishment, people in power seemed to subject me to constant humiliation. Why stay in an industry that barely seemed to want me?

The seclusion of lockdown urged me to step back and become introspective about what I had sacrificed in those early years when I was trying to make enough money to get by. I realized how often I self-tokenized to succeed, marketing myself as a "queer person of color," a voice who might be able to disrupt the homogeneity of the food publications I wrote for. I am mildly ashamed to admit it, but advertising myself as such was my cynical bid to satiate the white, liberal guilt of those who held power in my industry. I have been reminded of my pragmatic motivations for entering this industry during the pandemic, a time when I—like many other Americans—have lost income that I once took for granted. Publications I once wrote for no longer exist; those that are still kicking have thinned their editorial budgets. I have had to become strategic again. The pandemic, along with its attendant financial stresses, has laid bare the creaky foundations of American capitalism, which disadvantages so many who simply need to survive. As I reflected on my career, I wanted to know what hurdles Yan faced in his ascent, and if he made similar bargains in his career to establish himself. I wanted to see Yan's story in more forgiving terms than the prevailing culture ever allowed me to. I wanted to hear Martin Yan tell me his story in his own words.

Before I even had a conversation with Yan, I knew quite a bit about his early years, a period he has retraced often in prior interviews. He was born as Yan Man-tat at the end of 1948 in Guangzhou, China.[8] Food was all around him as a child. His father, Yan Tak-ning, owned a restaurant in the city that served comforting clay-pot meals, while his mother, Lam Sai-mui, operated a grocery store two blocks away, selling staples like dried squid and salted fish.[9]

Yan was not the first in his family to come to America. Around the 1920s, decades before settling back in China, Yan's father traveled to Portland, Oregon, and tried to find his footing there, opening a café where he served chow mein and Americanized Chinese dishes like chop suey.[10] But he did so during a period of great animus toward Chinese people in the United States. The Chinese Exclusion Act of 1882, which attempted to strangle Chinese immigration into the country, was still influencing broader cultural attitudes. The discrimination his father faced in Portland, Yan would later say, became too much to bear.[11]

Yan's father was in his sixties by the time he returned to China, and he would die when Yan was just five years old. The years after his death were not easy. Circumstances forced Yan to take care of his younger brother while his mother tended to the family business. Hers was a precarious line of work. "Because we had a business—a grocery store— we were labeled capitalist and they shaved her head," Yan told the magazine *Lucky Peach* in 2012.[12] On some nights, he said, he and his family had so little to eat that they would stir-fry marbles with fermented black beans, slurping the black beans off the marbles.

Around the time Yan was thirteen, he finished primary school, and his mother sent him off to Hong Kong, where he lived with a man named Mr. Wong, a family friend whom he referred to as a "distant uncle," though they were not related by blood.[13] Yan would claim in some interviews that when he made the trek to Hong Kong, all he carried was a tiny rattan suitcase, with three pairs of underwear, and small change.[14] There, he got to work at Wong's restaurant and catering business, a multistory venue serving wonton noodle soups and Chinese barbecue. Yan served as a prep cook, but he was too frail to even lift a wok on his own. Instead, he busied himself with tasks like boning chicken and fileting fish, becoming remarkably deft with a knife.[15]

That restaurant in Kowloon City became Yan's life.[16] He ate there, slept there. Each night, he stacked the chairs and made his bed on a wide board sandwiched between two booth seats. Because the restaurant did not have a proper shower, he bathed himself by filling a bucket with water and pouring it over his head.[17] Though apprenticing at his uncle's restaurant was unglamorous work, Yan grew quite fond of cooking in those years; he even thought of studying it at a formal level at Hong Kong's Overseas Institute of Cookery. He did not have enough money to afford the school, so Yan struck a deal with the owner of the Institute: in exchange for free tuition, Yan would shop for groceries and lug them back to the school, which was located on the seventh floor of a walk-up.[18] Yan had an eye toward going abroad, though, just as his father had. He worked to improve his English in his teens.[19] Before leaving Hong Kong, he changed his name on the advice of a missionary: He would no longer be known as Yan man-tat. Now, in the new era of his life, the world would call him Martin Yan.

"I came to America with about twenty dollars in my pocket," Yan tells me over the phone one day in May 2020. Such a claim would probably sound preposterous in anyone else's voice. But Yan, an engrossing storyteller, has a way of infusing this claim with sincerity. He knows how to sell himself. I had asked Yan to recount the tale of how he began his career cooking on television. His journey began in 1965, when, thanks to a sponsorship from a Baptist church, he migrated to Edmonton, Canada, where he would study at the University of Alberta.[20] His time in Canada was short-lived: a chance visit to a friend in California made him realize he might feel more at home in America, so he sought admission to the University of California, Davis. Though he gained acceptance, the tuition was steep. Because he was a foreign student, Yan had to pay about three times as much as his domestic classmates. He needed money.

Near the end of his freshman year, Yan found work in local restaurants in various roles: dishwasher, waiter, cook; jobs that paid measly sums, around sixty cents an hour. He knew those jobs could not possibly cover tuition. His eyes lit up when a friend told him about a woman named "Madame" Sylvia Wu, a Chinese-born restaurateur who owned a popular Chinese restaurant in Santa Monica. Wu, a native of China, was a capitalist success story herself. A savvy businesswoman, she had been operating Madame Wu's Garden since 1959, and was boastful of her ability to attract non-Chinese customers.[21] "I never tire of watching Robert Redford and his two children when they visit my restaurant," she proudly wrote in her cookbook *Madame Wu's Art of Chinese Cooking* (1976).[22] She also happened to teach cooking classes at UCLA. Hearing about her kindled an idea in Yan's head: why not become a cooking instructor?

So Yan took a Greyhound bus down to Los Angeles in the hopes of meeting Wu. She was, luckily, quite gracious with her time. "And I said, can you tell me a little bit about how I can also teach at UC or start teaching cooking classes?" Yan remembers asking her at the meeting. Wu suggested that Yan try to teach cooking at his school's extension program. The gig paid a handsome $18 an hour, a rarity in the era—certainly enough to cover his tuition. But Wu had a well-established restaurant to her name; Yan had nothing to show for his talents. Yan was dogged in his determination, and his drive would compensate for his thin résumé. Once he got back to campus, he marched over to the office of UC Davis's Continuing and Professional Education and told the school's director he would like to teach a cooking class.

"And the director asked me, 'Are you a master chef? How long have you been working in an established restaurant as executive chef?'" Yan recalls. Yan was honest about the fact that he lacked traditional qualifications for the role, like a teaching certificate. The man sent Yan away. But Yan did not give in easily. "So the next day, I went back to bug him again," Yan says. The man would not budge, but Yan kept trying anyway. He returned each day for a straight week. "I figure out I have nothing to lose," he says. "And also, my skin is thick."

Soon enough, the director of the extension program got wind of Yan's tenacity, so he instructed his secretary to tell Yan that he was not at the office. Yan was no fool. He started to suspect that the director was secretly sneaking out the back door of his office just to dodge Yan. Yan, growing increasingly desperate, hid out near the back door before he caught the man. "And he was so furious," Yan recalls. "I was harassing him! And I said, look, I'm serious. If you don't give me a chance, I never, never can stay in this great university. So do me a favor. Help me out." The director begrudgingly invited Yan into his office. "So we sit down and talk and he said, 'Look, Martin, you are driving me bananas,'" Yan says.

As the conversation went on, though, the man's stance started to soften. He gave Yan an ultimatum, telling Yan that he would put an ad in the local newspaper for a class on Chinese cooking. If Yan had a minimum of fifteen people sign up for the class, the extension school would let him teach. "So I said, okay, that's a deal," Yan says. "If I cannot get fifteen people, if nobody signs up, I'll never come back to bother you." Yan went back to the restaurant where he was working at the time and pleaded with each of his customers to join his class. Some were doctors or lawyers; others were spouses of faculty members at the school. His persistence paid off: by the following week, a whopping forty-three people had signed up. But Yan was not yet aware that this new role would require him to reinvent himself.

In spite of his public gregariousness, Yan has long claimed to be shy by nature. "Even now, at home, in my office, I don't talk much," he tells me. "But in front of the camera, when I teach—I go crazy."

While his friends were tending to their social lives, Yan busied himself balancing the demands of work and school.[23] He taught two classes a week. Because most of his students were working professionals, they came to his classes pretty exhausted. He realized he needed to keep their attention; otherwise, they might just fall asleep. There were challenges. "In the beginning, my English is not very good," he says. "I can speak, but very, very intermittently." So he decided to approach the job as if it were an acting assignment. He deliberately constructed a character for the public eye: a jollier, goofier avatar of himself.

Yan drew inspiration from two people in particular: Julia Child and Graham Kerr. He did not know them personally; he just saw them on television, and he adored them. Yan made a daily ritual of watching Child and Kerr, studying their energy. Child was still captivating America with her PBS show *The French Chef*, which had begun airing in 1963. Kerr, meanwhile, was a dapper Scotsman who dazzled live audiences with *The Galloping Gourmet* (1969–1971), the CBS show where he channeled his charisma into making dishes like shoulder of lamb Wellington or prawn soufflé.[24]

Child's shows were models of restraint compared to what Kerr brought to the mix. At the beginning of each show, Kerr would leap over two chairs while cupping a glass of wine in his hands. Kerr's propensity for theatrics may have resonated with the masses, but that recklessness also made him an object of derision for the food establishment. "He's a very great showman who has very little respect for food," James Beard told *LIFE* Magazine in a December 1969 article.[25] As the writer David Kamp would later put it in his 2006 book *The United States of Arugula*: *How We Became a Gourmet Nation*, Kerr's show "committed the cardinal sin of *wanting* to entertain its viewers."[26] But Yan was no snob. He was mesmerized by Kerr. "I said, wow, they are pretty good—not only educational, they are very funny," Yan tells me of his fascination with Kerr and Child. They did not take themselves too seriously. Yan found their levity aspirational. "I told my roommates—I said, one day, I should be on television like them!"

Yan kept teaching at UC Davis through the 1970s as he worked toward a bachelor's degree in food science and nutrition, but circumstances would bring him back to Canada later in the decade. A friend from Hong Kong was operating a restaurant in Calgary, and he needed Yan's help. The restaurant found loyal patrons quite quickly. They included the employees of CFAC-TV, a local television station with offices close by. The station aired a talk show featuring a guest chef each Friday.

Yan's life would change on a frigid Thursday in October 1978, when the station's producer and television station manager frantically asked Yan if he could give a cooking demonstration in place of a chef who had just called in sick. Yan wasn't sure about the proposition at first. He had never been on television. But he figured that the gig could, at the very least, bring more publicity to his friend's restaurant. "So I said, okay. I'll do it just for you even though I have never done any television," he remembers.

So Yan packed his ingredients—his soy sauce, his seasoning, his oil, his meats—into the trunk of his car. By the time he got to the station at 10:15 on the morning of the taping, he could barely even pry open his trunk. Temperatures were so glacial that the food had frozen into immobile blocks on the ride over. "So I told the producer as well as the hostess—I said, well, look, you asked me to come here and cook, but I can't cook because everything is frozen," he chuckles. He only had half an hour for the segment. But it was too late for him to back out. "And then I told the producer and director before I do the show, I said—I've never faced the camera before," he says. "I don't know how to do television, okay?" They assured Yan he just had to look at the camera with a flashing red light. The instructions seemed simple enough. Too bad there were three different cameras.

Yan somehow maintained his composure through filming, bantering with the hostess while he tried his best to make do with the bricklike slab of meat before him. "And then she asked me questions and I started cutting, and I couldn't cut it," he says. He tried to keep his eyes on the red light as it ping-ponged between cameras, unsure of where to focus. "I get totally confused!" he laughed. "And then I guess they probably think this guy is a nutcase."

The recording was, by Yan's estimation, a disaster. "And then after I finish, I figure this is the beginning and end of my television appearance," he says. Just after the recording, though, the director asked Yan to come back the following week; the station's general manager was apparently quite impressed. This time, Yan would have forty-five minutes, not thirty. In spite of his reservations, Yan wanted to help his friend, so he agreed to return. This time, he resolved to put his ingredients in the backseat of his car, not the trunk. Yan planned to make four dishes. "While I'm cooking, the hostess came up and ask me questions—*this this this*—and I barely finished doing two dishes in forty-five minutes," he says. "And then I said, look, I could have done four dishes but you are ask so many questions and interrupt me and I got so confused again!"

Once Yan packed up, the director asked him to meet the general manager of the station. To Yan's astonishment, the man proposed that Yan have his own television program. The station asked Yan to record 130 shows over twenty-three days, a punishing schedule. But the offer was too alluring to ignore: He would be paid CAD100 per show. It would be called *Yan Can Cook*. So he fulfilled his duties. He brought over a chef from the restaurant kitchen to help him out; he hired a dishwasher. He knew how to cook "a couple hundred dishes," in his estimation. Drawing on that repertoire, he recorded five shows per day over twenty-three days. Yan treated the task as what it was: a job. "I never cared about success," he says of recording those initial episodes. "I just want to get out of it."

I feel a pang of familiarity in Yan's confession. Any triumphs that followed his very practical decision were entirely unplanned. I sometimes still ask myself how long I will be in this line of work that I did not consciously seek out in the first place, whether writing about food is my calling in life, if I will be stuck here forever. This internal crisis started to feel especially acute since the start of the pandemic. It is a time in which I have begun to reevaluate the unhealthy ways in which I once bound my profession to my identity. To work through this confusion, I have made peace with one reality: creative work is still work. Accepting this truth has been freeing; it has made the painful aspects of my work a bit easier to swallow. I now know how to preserve parts of myself that I could so easily have surrendered to my job.

Yan seemed to understand this fact quite early on. What Yan really wanted to do, for example, was teach, and he never strayed from this goal. After he finished filming the initial batch of episodes of *Yan Can Cook*, he decided to try his hand at opening a cooking school in Toronto. He went to great lengths to establish himself in the city, going to local malls and handing out brochures until security kicked him out. These efforts did not pay off; after three months of trying to create excitement for his school, no one signed up. He was nearly broke. Coming to terms with the setback, Yan returned to the United States. He went back to

UC Davis to finish his master's degree in food science, earning it in 1977.[27] Television, however, beckoned. The next year, his show began airing in Canada, and it was a hit. The station asked him to come back and film some more segments. Without any other enticing options for making money, he agreed.

He would record more than five hundred episodes of the series over the next four years. Yan was equal parts comic and cook on that show. "What did people call Egg Foo when he was a kid?" he asked in one episode. "Egg Foo Young."[28] Shticks like this brought him a steady stream of fan mail—in 1981, the Canadian newspaper the *Globe and Mail* claimed he received 10,000 letters a year—and some audience members treated him as an object of intrigue because he was foreign. They loved his accent, for example. "I think you are the cutest thing to come along in a long time," one viewer reportedly wrote to him. "When you say 'appwoximately,' we all go cwazy."[29]

Today, these attempts at praise smack of xenophobia and racism, condescending to Yan. Yet I suppose so many of us on the margins have dealt with a version of this infantilization. I recall, for example, the industry veteran who casually referred to me as the "diversity writer" of the first publication I wrote for, diminishing the scope and breadth of my work while implying that I filled an unspoken quota. And I still cringe when I recall the older members of the food industry who have championed me as a voice that is "urgent," "fresh," even "necessary." In my experience, the people who have attached these descriptors to me rarely care to engage with the substance of my writing. They see me purely through the prism of my identity—queer, brown—and believe that these differences automatically lend my output moral gravity. But there is something uniquely patronizing about people not even caring to read your work. The denial of this basic courtesy is a sign that they do not take you seriously, even if they claim to love what you are doing.

Everyone seemed to love Yan for his humor, even the press, though there were signs that he wanted the world to see him as more than "the Galloping Gourmet of the wok," as the *Globe and Mail* once called him. "But I'm not as nutty as people think I am," he insisted to the paper. "Put me in front of a camera and I know I can be a motor mouth. I love to talk and I get very excited about my favorite subject—Chinese cooking. But it's a subject I'm very serious about."

While Yan's show found a devoted audience across Canada, it also aired on stations just south of the border in states like Montana, putting Yan in front of a wide swath of American viewers. Producers from the United States came calling in the early 1980s. In 1982, an especially attractive offer arrived from KQED, a PBS affiliate, in California's Bay Area. The station told him that the American version of *Yan Can Cook* would have a slower shooting schedule than its Canadian counterpart, with no more than twenty-six episodes per year. Yan said yes.

America was not used to seeing East Asian stars like Yan cooking on television. The restaurateur and chef Joyce Chen's nationally syndicated *Joyce Chen Cooks*, a WGBH production, aired between 1966 and 1967. With it, she became the first person of color to host a nationally syndicated cooking show in the United States.[30] The show had visual and aural elements that played up Chen's Chinese heritage, like the presence of gongs and the sound of wind chimes that began each episode.[31] Though she was a warm presence on screen, Chen could sometimes come across as diffident in these episodes too. There was another trait that Chen could not silence: her accent. This may have prevented more widespread affection from the white American public. Producers tried their best to circumvent this through roping in a speech instructor, but that didn't solve the perceived problem at hand. Despite Chen's effort, her delivery lacked the fluidity of a native English speaker. The show lasted one season, unable to attract a sponsor to finance the transition from black and white to color.

Yan rose to prominence over a decade after *Joyce Chen Cooks* halted production. The show stressed Yan's perceived otherness to white Americans in ways similar to *Joyce Chen Cooks*: an animated introduction showed Yan cleaving produce as it somersaulted in the air, accompanied by flute music ripped straight from an Orientalist fantasy. But Yan worked in a different set of circumstances than Chen had. "It's about the time that China and US developing a good relationship," Yan says of the era. Geopolitical shifts in the 1970s opened up a new rush of American interest in Chinese culture, for one, particularly following

Richard Nixon's 1972 visit to China, a diplomatic gesture that widened American appreciation for Chinese cooking.[32] Likewise, as the author Kathleen Collins posited in her 2009 book *Watching What We Eat: The Evolution of Television Cooking Shows*, a health-conscious social wave in the 1980s made East Asian cuisines—especially ones reliant on seafood and vegetables in light sauces—more palatable to American audiences too. And Yan, unlike Chen, was a man. He was exactly what the American market wanted.

Yan enjoyed a steady rise over the next few years. He speaks with great pride about the heights his show has scaled, telling me he has recorded more than 3,500 episodes over four decades as of May 2020. He has recorded segments all over the world—Vietnam, Singapore, Malaysia, China. In segments of his show today, he comes across as more relaxed. Still, the older episodes have their virtues. They are often quite funny, for one. But what is evident, too, is his exceptional talent as a cook. Consider a 1988 episode devoted to making his mother's recipes. He begins the episode with a parade of jokes. "When I was a little handsome kid growing up in China, my mother did all the cooking," he says. "She never let me into the kitchen. But with that wok, I was a rebel. So I jumped right in anyway. See? That's me!" A black and white photo of a small child sitting in a wok flashes across the screen. "I have such a good time with my wok that I still have the same wok. That was about sixty-five years ago." (Yan, of course, was much younger than sixty-five when he said this.) But that gag gives way to a splendid culinary performance: He chops shiitake mushrooms and garlic as if he is making music, his eyes rarely making contact with the cutting board.[33]

The crowd marvels at such displays of culinary aptitude. Yet, throughout the 1980s and 1990s, there seemed to be a growing gulf between what the masses responded to in Yan's work and how the American press assessed his stardom. Combing through decades-old newspaper archives would confirm my worst fears about the way that people in power spoke and wrote about Yan, which was often, to put it in plain terms, racist. Even the compliments had a touch of racism. "The only way to describe transplanted Hong Kong Kid Yan is a modern version of Jerry Lewis' frenetic Oriental houseboy, with better teeth," wrote Eve Zibart in an otherwise appreciative assessment in the *Washington Post* in 1989.[34] That same year, the writer of a *Chicago Tribune* piece, Maria Goodavage, would characterize Yan as "the non-Asian's stereotype of an off-the-wall Chinese chef, broken English and all."[35]

As the years went by, more members of the press seemed to find glee in taking aim at Yan's accent and appearance, as if he was standing in a room where he did not belong. In 1993, Bryan Miller of the *New York Times*—a paper that has long been responsible for setting cultural trends in food—referred to him as "a hyperkinetic, cleaver-wielding man whose teeth flash like headlights when he talks." Adding to this unkind physical description, Miller continued that "Mr. Yan's cooking comes second to his clowning." I wince when I read these passages today, their racism so overt and bruising. That they appear in what is ostensibly the most influential paper in the country is especially troubling. Critics from other corners, too, would become louder in later years. A 2008 article in the *San Francisco Chronicle*, for example, covered the accusation that he was faking his accent, as if he was donning a racial costume.[36]

Understanding all the criticism that Yan has invited from many parties—those who express racist disdain for him, others who denounce him for being a traitor to his people—has deepened my sympathies for him. On the surface, Yan's life is an inspirational tale of a man pulling himself up by his bootstraps to establish himself in the United States. Conversely, detractors might just reduce Yan's entire career to one extended stunt, claiming he was just making a series of assimilationist compromises in order to make it in America. But Yan was not born with privileges that would make it easier to thrive in this scenario. Neither was I. Yan has spoken in past interviews about the fact that he did not deliberately seek out mass affection; it came to him unexpectedly. He had no choice but to accept it. "I never projected myself as a star," Yan told one newspaper in 1988.[37]

Some might scoff at this claim, considering the fact that Yan is very much a star. But I buy the sincerity of his intent. Yan cooked because he needed to live. He did not have any other choice. "In my whole life, I was never afraid of failure," Yan reminds me. "I don't know what failure is."

Notes

1. "Make Some Noise for THEE Martin Yan," KQED, https://www.facebook.com/KQED/videos/171326984183814/.

2. "8 Treasure Rice Pudding," *Yan Can Cook*, KQED, https://www.youtube.com/watch?v=aYbj3u4HeSk; "How to Make Beijing Pizza," *Yan Can Cook*, KQED, https://www.youtube.com/watch?v=V0faeTZgzQo; "Make Dim Sum at Home," *Yan Can Cook*, KQED, https://www.youtube.com/watch?v=T20umka2D_U.

3. "About," *Yan Can Cook*, https://yancancook.com/home/about/.

4. Ruth Gebreyesus, "Martin Yan Was a YouTube Celebrity Chef Before There Was YouTube," *KQED*, February 3, 2020, https://www.kqed.org/bayareabites/136185/martin-yan-was-a-youtube-celebrity-chef-before-there-was-youtube.

5. Katie Jackson, "Amid Coronavirus Pandemic, Chinese Restaurants in the US Are Emptier Than Ever," *Today*, March 10, 2020, https://www.today.com/food/amid-coronavirus-panic-chinese-restaurants-us-are-emptier-ever-t175326.

6. Chinese Dessert Recipes, *Yan Can Cook*, KQED, https://www.youtube.com/watch?v=01ro-Hhfukc.

7. Martin Yan Makes Crab Soup, *Yan Can Cook*, KQED, https://www.youtube.com/watch?v=uwI-PoawRhU.

8. Jenny Banh, "Culinary Ambassador Chef Martin Yan Speaks," in *American Chinese Restaurants: Society, Culture and Consumption* (Routledge: New York, 2020), 219.

9. Randy K. Schwartz, "The Tough Years Before 'Yan Can Cook,'" *Repast* 32, no. 3 (Summer 2016): 3; Diane Stoneback, "Have Wok, Will Travel: Chinese Chef Martin Yan to Explore Other Asian Cuisines," *The Morning Call*, March 26, 1997, https://www.mcall.com/news/mc-xpm-1997-03-26-3127000-story.html.

10. Schwartz, "The Tough Years," 3.

11. Banh, "Culinary Ambassador," 220.

12. Kevin Pang, "Martin Yan Is Chinese Cooking's Greatest Evangelist," *The Takeout*, July 23, 2018, https://thetakeout.com/martin-yan-is-chinese-cookings-greatest-evangelist-1827818967.

13. Schwartz, "The Tough Years," 3.

14. Amanda Gold, "Martin Yan's Can-Do Attitude," SFGate, February 20, 2008, https://www.sfgate.com/food/article/MARTIN-YAN-S-CAN-DO-ATTITUDE-3293824.php; Amy Wu, "Frugal Gourmet / Why Martin Yan Is Proud of the Holes in His Socks," SFGate, October 19, 2004, https://www.sfgate.com/business/article/Frugal-Gourmet-Why-Martin-Yan-is-proud-of-the-2680841.php.

15. Schwartz, "The Tough Years," 4.

16. Natalie Haughton, "Celebrity Chef Martin Yan Takes You on a Chinese Tour," *Los Angeles Daily News*, February 7, 2008, https://www.dailynews.com/2008/02/07/celebrity-chef-martin-yan-takes-you-on-a-chinese-tour/; Maria Goodavage, "Can Yan Cook!" *Chicago Tribune*, April 13, 1989, https://www.chicagotribune.com/news/ct-xpm-1989-04-13-8904030930-story.html.

17. Schwartz, "The Tough Years," 4.

18. Gold, "Martin Yan's Can-Do Attitude," https://www.sfgate.com/food/article/MARTIN-YAN-S-CAN-DO-ATTITUDE-3293824.php.

19. Shirley Fong-Torres, "Yan Can Cook Well," *AsianWeek*, June 2006, 17.

20. Schwartz, "The Tough Years," 3.

21. Hadley Meares, "The Remarkable Madame Wu," KCET, February 24, 2015, https://www.kcet.org/food-discovery/food/the-remarkable-madame-wu.

22. Sylvia Wu, *Madame Wu's Art of Chinese Cooking* (Toronto: Bantam, 1976), 34.

23. Schwartz, "The Tough Years," 5.

24. David Kamp, *The United States of Arugula: How We Became a Gourmet Nation* (New York: Broadway, 2006), 110.

25. Paul O'Neil, "Comedian in the Kitchen," *LIFE*, December 5, 1969, 56.

26. Kamp, *The United States of Arugula*, 110.

27. "Distinguished Achievement Award 2013: Martin Yan '73, M.S. '77, https://alumni.ucdavis.edu/news/distinguished-achievement-award-2013-martin-yan-73-ms-77

28. "Distinguished Achievement Award."

29. "Distinguished Achievement Award."

30. Kathleen Collins, *Watching What We Eat: The Evolution of Television Cooking Shows* (London: Continuum, 2009), 93.

31. Dana Polan, "Joyce Chen Cooks and the Upscaling of Chinese Food in America in the 1960s," WGBH, http://openvault.wgbh.org/exhibits/art_of_asian_cooking/article.

32. Ralph Blumenthal, "Chinese Restaurants Flower Following Diplomatic Thaw," *New York Times*, July 27, 1972.

33. "Recipes from Martin Yan's Mom," *Yan Can Cook*, KQED, https://www.youtube.com/watch?v=F6mCs07Uy-g.

34. Eve Zibart, "PBS' Feeding Frenzy: A Raging Appetite for Cooking Shows," *Washington Post*, April 30, 1989., https://www.washingtonpost.com/archive/lifestyle/tv/1989/04/30/pbs-feeding-frenzy/b61d2b74-fdba-417c-b618-0a48fa4f7b48/.

35. Maria Goodavage, "Can Yan Cook!"

36. Amanda Gold, "Martin Yan's Can-Do Attitude."

37. Lynne Helm, "Cooking Turn Ons: Innovative Chefs Are Channeling Their Energies into Television. Here's a Look at Them," *Southern Florida Sun Sentinal*, July 13, 1988, https://www.sun-sentinel.com/news/fl-xpm-1988-07-13-8802100788-story.html.

Martin Yan's Hot Walnut Soup

"Can you imagine doing something totally new with walnuts? Walnuts are available everywhere so why not use them? Here's a dessert to start with!"—Martin Yan

Method

Roast walnuts in 325°F oven 10–15 minutes or until fragrant and lightly browned. Grind walnuts to powder in blender.

Combine walnut powder, rice flour, sugar, and water in a large sauce pan and slowly bring to a boil. Reduce heat to low and simmer, stirring continuously for 15–17 minutes.

Stir in milk and bring to a second boil. Serve hot.

Yan's Remarks: If you cannot find rice flour, soak 4 tablespoons long grain rice for 3–5 hours. Drain and blend for 2–3 minutes in a blender.

If rice flour or long grain rice are not available, use cornstarch as a substitute.

Place rock sugar in a paper bag and hit with the flat side of a cleaver to crush.

¾ cup (200 ml) walnuts, skinless preferred

¼ cup (60 ml) rice flour (long grain)

6 ½ tablespoons (97 ml) rock sugar or brown sugar, crushed

4 cups (1 L) water

¼ cup (60 ml) evaporated milk

6

Pound Cake and Puri

FERNAY MCPHERSON: I was born and raised in San Francisco, but my family came here during the Great Migration from the South. My great-grandfather was a porter on a train and traveled around to different cities as he worked, but when he came to San Francisco he really fell in love with the city and decided to move his family here from Texas. He came out first with my great-grandmother to look for a home, and later brought my grandmother, my aunts, and my uncles to San Francisco. My dad was also born and raised here, actually in the same neighborhood that we live in now. My parents are still in my childhood home, and I live on the same block that I was raised on. My mother migrated from Texas as well; my dad's family came from Amarillo and my mother and her family came from Port Arthur. Their reasoning for coming to San Francisco, too, was work. My grandfather worked for the post office and landed a job in San Francisco, and that is how my mother and her siblings and my grandmother came—again, my grandparents coming first to find a home, and then later bringing the children.

My mother and her siblings traveled on a train, and this is where the pound cake and fried chicken come in. They traveled on a train for, I think, three days to get here, and the food that was packed for them was fried chicken and pound cake. Back in the day there were flyers that were mailed out to southern states letting folks know that there was work in San Francisco at the port, and that is how a lot of

Geetika Agrawal and Fernay McPherson spoke with Philip Gleissner and Harry Kashdan over Zoom in December 2021. During the two-hour conversation, Agrawal and McPherson reflected on their own familial histories of migration and discussed how they have made homes for themselves in the San Francisco food scene. The transcription has been edited for length and clarity.

people ended up here during that Great Migration, for better opportunity. When my mom's family was traveling, and even when she was back home in Port Arthur, Texas, she would be so fearful because my grandmother was not one that obeyed segregation. My grandmother would go into the bathroom for the whites only. My mom was young, she didn't understand what my grandmother was doing, and it scared her. It was a relief to migrate here from Texas, because there weren't those same Jim Crow laws here, although they did face a little racism here too. Still, it was a little relief, because my mom didn't have to be scared of what my grandmother was doing—which, of course, she was *supposed* to be doing, because it wasn't right to have to go to a whole other part of somewhere to use the restroom or to get a drink of water or just to even eat. But for my mom, that was a little bit of a relief.

Minnie Bell's, the name of my restaurant, is a combination of my great aunt, Minnie, and my grandmother, Lillie Bell. My grandmother passed away twenty years ago. My aunt is still here, and she's eighty-eight years old. I go to her for as much as I can, but she was very young when they migrated here. During that time, San Francisco had a huge population of African Americans. The neighborhood, the Fillmore, was once considered the Harlem of the West. My grandfather just fell in love when he came to the city and came into the Fillmore. I always tell people my neighborhood was my grandmother and my great aunt's Fillmore, it was my dad's Fillmore, and it was my Fillmore, and those are three very different times, you know? We have all experienced our neighborhood at different times, and we have a different vision of what that neighborhood was. My grandfather really gravitated toward what he saw in the neighborhood culturally. I didn't get to witness that strong, rich, African American culture here in the neighborhood like they did. By the time I was coming up, it was dwindling down a lot, and it was in the midst of the crack epidemic, so it was very much deteriorating.

GEETIKA AGRAWAL: My family are migrants too, we just feel earlier in our journey and I wonder, listening to Fernay, where we will land.

I'm the first one in my family to fall for San Francisco, and while it was different from the city Fernay's great-grandfather fell for, it was a love for the city that brought me. I came here and had, for the first time in my adult life, the energetic feeling of belonging, of this being a place I wanted to make my home.

My dad moved from India to Madison, Wisconsin, to get his PhD in computer science. He was married already to my mother, but as many Indian men did at the time, he came first, checked it out, and got everything settled—as much as one "settles" in a one-bedroom graduate school apartment. My mom came to America on November 4, 1980—I know because she texts me every November 4th to remind me. She had never been on a plane before she came, alone, to start a new life in America with a man she was just getting to know. She spoke English, luckily, but my mom probably would have never left India. She would have liked to have your life, Fernay, she would like to be living down the street from her parents. She was not an adventurer.

The first foreign land she set foot on was in Paris, at the Charles de Gaulle Airport. Her brother-in-law, my dad's younger brother, had driven her to the airport and befriended somebody who was going to fly all the way to Wisconsin so that she could do the layover. My grandmother—her mother-in-law—packed her puris and pickles for the journey. Puris are a classic dish of the state I am from, Uttar Pradesh, and they hold well so they are as popular at home as they are on a journey, or a picnic.

I have this really great picture of my mom during the first snowfall. She is wearing a sari and a coat and she has it shoved into her snow boots. She figured out everything with other women who, just like her, were joining their husbands and navigating a new country. There was one auntie who figured out how to drive, so they would all pile into the car and drive to the grocery store and wander around the aisles, trying to understand what things were and what things could be turned into foods that were familiar to them and what things were just new and delightful. My mom's favorite American thing is Wonder Bread; she just doesn't let herself eat it as often as she used to (or you know, she "settles" for the fresh-baked Tartine bread around the corner). Back then, frozen pound cake and Wonder Bread felt more exotic than the puris, rotis, sambars, and *idlis* of home. My mom used to make my dad lunch every day and meet him between classes, and she would make Wonder Bread and mayo sandwiches. My dad says, "We didn't know anything about nutrition." They thought, "You come to America and

Geetika Agrawal

everything's obviously got to be great for you." I ate all the sugary breakfast cereals as a kid—they didn't know!

We lived in New Jersey briefly, and then I mostly grew up in California. My parents still live in the South Bay, which never really resonated with me, so I always knew I wanted to go away. San Francisco did not really leave an impression on me until my early twenties—probably because most of our visits were confined to the tourist highlights—crooked streets, sourdough bread bowls, and seals at Pier 39. I cannot give you an exact reason why, but what I know for certain is that I just felt *right* in the city. I have lived in the city now for fifteen years, with a break in the middle, and am today in a spot four blocks from my first house—I walk by it all the time. When I first moved here, for me it was about claiming a place that was mine. What I think a lot about with regard to migration is living in this third space: when I go to India there is a part of me that feels really at home, but it also feels very clear that I don't quite fit. I don't think I have ever felt like I fit in with American culture, either. Claiming San Francisco was an act of claiming something that was mine. At its best, even with the changes, it still feels like that kind of place in spirit, where everyone belongs. Maybe it's a port city spirit. I don't think this city is truly as progressive or welcoming as its reputation, but I do think that San Franciscans, especially the ones that really identify deeply as San Franciscans, have an openness of "You do you, and I'll do me." I feel like there is a real respect for not being afraid to be yourself in this city. That really means something, especially when you don't fit in anywhere else.

FM: I think it is definitely that. I think that is why so many people love it here. It is a true space where you see culture, and you see it in so many different aspects that San Francisco is full of. Geets, I remember you telling a story about your mom when you went to school. You have to share that story.

GA: My mom cooked us a full Indian dinner every night growing up, but she sent me to school with her best attempt at an "American" lunch. For most of elementary school I had a snappy *Return of the Jedi* hard plastic lunchbox, in which I would have a bologna sandwich one day and a PBJ another day. Except my PBJ was Skippy and mint jelly. That's right, mint jelly.

In my imagination my parents must have wandered down the grocery aisle, encountering more brands and flavors of jams than ever before, and my dad, being the adventurer, chose the most exotic-sounding flavor. "Let's pick mint jelly. Who makes jelly out of mint?" My whole family ate it—it was a pantry staple in our vegetarian household. I had no way of knowing what mint jelly is actually used for until I was in college. One day in the dining hall they had lamb, and they had the mint jelly next to it. I was like, "What the . . . Oh that's what mint jelly is for!"

FM: My mom has two sisters that still live in Port Arthur. Right before the pandemic was the last time we were there to visit, and we haven't been able to go back since. I am praying that next year we can go to visit them. When I went in 2019, that was the first time I had gone back in well over twenty years. It was really good to just go see. It has changed a lot, because I just remember dirt roads and red ants when I was a little girl. But it is really good to be able to go back and see the changes. My great-grandmother's house is still there, so I was able to go out and take a picture of that. It was pretty dope to see. As a kid, we would have these smoked beef links. So that is one of the things that I always have to do when I go: get good beef links.

Most of the family is in Houston now, so when we went to visit we were in Houston. But my aunt said, "Well, no, we'll drive to Port Arthur." My mom said, "Oh, but it's so far." I said, "But we going. Okay? You not driving, for one, so you could just sit back and enjoy the ride." I wanted to just drive and explore the city. That is one thing that I love to do when I go anywhere, really. My grandfather was able to come with us that day, and just hearing him talk: "Oh yeah, right over here, this used to be this and this used to be that." Just being able to learn, and hear from his voice what it was like, was just so intriguing to me. He remembered the streets. He would say, "Hey, make a left right here, make a right right there." To be able to be with him and hear the stories and be directed by him through the city that I am so connected to, but also not connected to—that was intriguing.

GA: My family is from the state of Uttar Pradesh. My parents got married in Allahabad, which was renamed to Prayagraj in 2018. My mom was born in Lucknow and then moved to Allahabad. My dad was born in Khurja and then the family moved around until they built a house in Ghaziabad, when it was still underdeveloped in the late 1960s. It is one of the satellite cities of Delhi, like Gurgaon and Noida. I love going to Ghaziabad because it has still maintained a lot of the ways of life that westernization is changing. Gurgaon, on the other hand, is where a lot of the tech companies are headed, but it is missing so much of what I love about going to India—the street vendors, the dirt roads, the old open-air markets. It has more modern chains and Indian versions of Western brands.

I have an aunt that has lived in Gurgaon for twenty-five years. I remember how her building was one of the few towers. Back then it was fields and a few call centers that would be open at four o'clock in the morning when we were coming in from the airport. Now, I can take the metro from Delhi. When I was a kid, it was an hour and a half drive from the airport. Then in the mid-2010s it would take four hours to make the same drive because of how much traffic and car usage had exploded and the infrastructure had not caught up yet. I went right before the pandemic in February 2020 and it is back to taking an hour and a half. It was always such an event—we used to come in at two o'clock in the morning, and everybody would get up and there would be a whole meal. It's such a homecoming. This time my cousin ended up coming to meet me but, if she hadn't been able to get away from work, my aunt suggested, "Just take that—thing—the Uber." I thought, "Whoa, okay. Things are different here now. And more similar to what I know from America."

Growing up, my mom's side of the family still lived in Allahabad, and we would take an overnight train to see my grandparents after visiting family in and around Delhi. The aunt seeing us off would pack us pickles and puri for the journey–and we'd sip on chai sold to us through the window at stops along the way. As soon as you get off the train, you'll encounter *aloo ki sabzi* and puri; it's one of Uttar Pradesh's regional classics.

My grandparents wouldn't let me eat at the station, lest my "American belly" give out, but there was one place I could get my hands on some *aloo ki sabzi*. The Ganga River ran by my grandparents' house, and there is a famous temple there, Lete Hanumanji, where the idol of

Hanuman is horizontal instead of vertical and bright orange. We would leave our shoes with someone we paid to make sure they didn't get lost and then would walk barefoot down muddy paths in the beating July heat to visit the temple and feed the pilgrims and others living off alms that lined the temple gate. Feeding those asking for alms was part of the visit and there were a handful of *aloo sabzi walas* who would sell you plates in orders of thirty to give as offerings. As a kid, the whole experience was uncomfortable for me, but I never complained because after everyone was fed we would each get our own plate. The payoff of the crispy puri dipped in cumin-flecked tomato broth with pillowy potatoes was always worth it.

FM: I always think about loving to eat as a child, loving to see that food on the table. My mother has this picture of me, I was probably maybe two or almost two, but I have on this little apron and a bowl of soap suds that my mom had given me. I was making my cake with soap suds. As I whipped them to the point of nothing, she would just keep replenishing them. I think that my love for cooking started all the way back then, without me really knowing. I think it has always been there for me, and I just went through life to get a little older to realize that cooking is where my journey is.

Growing up, I was fascinated with seeing my aunt and my grandmother cook so much food during the holidays. On Christmas morning we would open gifts at home. My Aunt Minnie lived just one block away, so we would open gifts at home and then walk to her house. When we got there, she had a table full of food ready at like nine o'clock in the morning. It would be everything: cakes, pies, the cornbread dressing, the turkey, mac-and-cheese. At nine o'clock in the morning! I just loved it, and I knew she would have the red and green layer checkerboard cake I always looked forward to seeing—and eating, of course. But that fascinated me. How did she do this? Did she just get up that morning and cook all this food? It was magic.

My Aunt Minnie is my father's auntie, but she was like his mom; she helped raise him. My grandmother Lillie Bell is my mother's mother. We would go to my aunt's Christmas morning, and then that night we would go to my grandmother's house. When I got there, it was the same, a table full of food. I was this little chunky girl with big poofy ponytails, and it was just my favorite time because I could really eat whatever I wanted. My parents weren't paying attention because they were all up dancing.

I learned how to cook dishes with my grandmother, mom, and aunt at an early age. As a teenager I was helping cook huge family meals, but I never thought of it as a career until I was older. I remember my mother getting recipes from my aunt and my grandmother. My aunt would come over to teach her how to do the cornbread dressing, or we would go to my grandmother's house to do gumbo. My mother hates to cook, but she cooked when we were kids. It was four of us and we had two cousins who lived with us, so she definitely cooked, but it was not one of her favorite things. I remember my Aunt Minnie was teaching us how to do the peach cobbler, my grandmother was teaching us how to do the caramel cake. My mother pulled from both of them, which was pretty dope for me because I just did the same thing. I can still call my auntie for different recipes.

One thing my grandmother did with us for years was in Paterson, California, where there were farms. Every summer we had to go pick our vegetables. This was all the way until I was in high school—I guess a little after high school is when my grandmother started getting a little sick. We had to go early in the morning, and we would get a packed pork chop sandwich or a sausage sandwich to take with us. We picked green beans, okra, snap peas, green tomatoes. After we picked all the vegetables, we would go back to the house, and my aunt would fry the green tomatoes for us to snack on, while the rest of us had to wash everything, bag it, and freeze it. That was our only opportunity to go to the farm and pick fresh vegetables. It was so hot, and when I became a teenager, I just thought, "Ugh, I do not want to go to these fields," but I didn't have a choice. I appreciate it so much now, you know, that it was something that we did, and that we did as a family—all of us, cousins and my aunties and my uncles. In that neighborhood now it is just homes, it is redeveloped into communities. Now I wish I could take my kids to a farm and make them pick all day like I had to. They would have a different appreciation for life, for sure.

I didn't go to culinary school until I was thirty years old. I worked for AT&T—I was there through the phases of Pacific Bell to SBC, and then it turned into AT&T. It was so many different changes within the company, and I went through a lot of different surpluses and redundancy layoffs. After my last one I was already a mother of two, and I decided, "You know what? I'm just going to go to culinary school. I'm going to do something that I like to do. I like to cook. I am tired of this corporate world, I am tired of going through these corporate changes and issues and name changes and big moves." This was in 2008, and from there, my journey started. I still had to work, of course. I was in Sacramento at that time, and that is where I attended culinary school. I moved back to San Francisco right before I graduated and worked and did things in the community. I did my externship at a restaurant in Oakland, and I also just taught cooking classes in the neighborhood and catered small events. After I left the Oakland restaurant, I couldn't really find much opportunity in the culinary field here in San Francisco. It was hard for women, and being a Black woman made it that much harder, so that is what forced me to create my own lane in cooking. I thought it was just going to be a journey of cooking for people and catering events, but now I am sitting on this screen telling you all my story. I did not see the vision. I honestly didn't see it. I just thought that I was going to be doing something that I enjoy doing, which is cooking. But so much has happened in that journey. Finding the La Cocina culinary entrepreneur program and being able to formalize more and just meet some amazing people that would help me to see things through a different lens than just, "Oh, you're cooking for somebody." I didn't know people wanted to know my story. I never, never thought that.

GA: I remember almost every meal that any entrepreneur cooks for me. The way other people catalog something else, I can catalog meals. I grew up with food being really important.

In my family it is how we best know to show our love. When we would arrive in India at two o'clock in the morning, not only was everyone up but the kitchen was humming. Snacks on the table, hot cups of chai, sweets stuffed in your mouth–that was the way to say, *you've arrived, welcome home, we've missed you.* "Geetika, another *ladoo*, I made them special, are you trying to get skinny?" was what my grandmother said instead of "I love you."

My grandparents are gone, and my older relatives are getting older, but my uncle still calls me starting a month before I arrive and demands, "What are we going to eat when you get here?" When we eat together just after you are done eating (or really, before you are done) he always asks "Okay, what are we going to eat next? Okay, and then what else do you want to eat? And then what else?"

There is this phrase that any aunt will always say to you when you ask, "Oh, should I put it out?" The answer is always *Hoga tho khalengi*— "If the food's there, everyone will eat it." It's true. Nobody is ever sad when you put out food, and I have come to see the wisdom of it.

My mom always cooked a full Indian meal every night, which is something I took for granted. Bread, dal, one to two different vegetable dry curries, homemade yogurt, fresh rice—every night. Thursdays she fasted, so that day would be the non-Indian night. I remember my brother and I would be such butts about it when we were kids, saying, "Mom, everything tastes like Indian food!" She would make pizza and it would have garam masala potatoes on it. Her chow mein would just have Indian spice. There would always be cumin in everything, no matter what cuisine it was. In high school I took over Thursdays. I thought, "I need to show you how to cook American food. I'm the expert on this." I remember very clearly the first dish I made was from Allrecipes, and it was a feta and sundried tomato spaghetti. I felt like I was a gourmet. So did my parents—just because it was different.

My mom's older sister died of COVID-19 in May. For the first time ever my mom and I could participate in the grieving process. In the past we could never really afford to fly, so I missed every funeral and every wedding ever. This time, we joined a Zoom call at five o'clock in the morning with all these relatives. This aunt was *the* cook in the family, the one whose food made people say, "Oh my god." Every single person at the end inevitably reminisced: "I remember her tomato chutney. I remember her *poha*. I remember her by this." She was remembered by each person by their favorite of her dishes. I am actually working on collecting a cookbook that is not going to be her recipes but each person's memory of their favorites. That is how we define who we know: what they cook, and what they love to eat. If you asked my family to profile each other that's what people would tell you.

FM: That is so dope. That's so fascinating to hear. I love that.

GA: My nuclear family doesn't always get along, but we will get along at the dinner table. Whatever it is, everybody will sit down and eat.

So, it sticks with me. I love to cook, and I love to cook with people. I think in the pandemic everyone else started cooking and I stopped. I made a lot of pies. I do not know if I also got a little burned out on cooking and running around before the pandemic just trying to be a working mom and do the nine to five and find a way to make myself lunch and also leave food for my kid and just . . . I got tired, I think. My husband stepped up on the daily, and now, in a surprise to both of us, my daughter calls him the family cooker. When I met my husband, he lived on peanut butter and jelly sandwiches and canned tuna. We had a peanut butter and jelly sandwich bar at our wedding for lunch. I still love to cook, but these days I'll take over a project. One Saturday morning I decided to make this Indian Andhra dish, where you make a curry and you soak the omelet in the curry. It is three stages, and I was an hour late, but my family knows how I am, and they will just feed themselves snacks because (usually) it's worth the wait.

I actually cooked my first official American Thanksgiving this year. As a kid, Thanksgiving was always a source of frustration, especially when we were in New Jersey, where I was the only Brown, nonwhite kid. Everybody else would be talking about all these dishes that seemed so delicious and exotic to me. I would get to some auntie's house. They would have ten beautiful curries and all I could think was, "Where are the sweet potatoes?" This year we made nine different casseroles and I realized, "Holy shit, this is so much work." It took us two days doing nothing else. We didn't even make the turkey. It is insane. I do not understand how people do it.

FM: I changed the format of Thanksgiving after culinary school. Before, we would literally get up and do this stuff early in the morning, me and my mom. It was an all-day thing. After I started learning some prep techniques, I decided, "We're going to do this a little different." My mom was gasping, "I could sit down before everyone gets over!"

Now, for our holidays I will have the mac-and-cheese, candied yams, fried turkey, and cornbread, and Minnie Bell's has that fried chicken and it also has that pound cake on the menu that my mother had with her on her trip to San Francisco. I do not cook the same way on a daily basis. It is rare that I fry anything at home. At home, I cook very light, very, very light. I might throw a salad together, or some broth with some shrimp and some vegetables. It is usually just roasted chicken, roasted vegetables. Last night, we had ramen soup. I do eat out a lot; there are so many options here in San Francisco. I just love different food. When Geetika was talking about holidays with her family and the different curries, I thought, "Oh my goodness, that sounds so good." But the food that she wanted was something that I had every day, all the time.

GA: Michael and I found a way to eat out during the height of shelter-in-place. We figured out which sub sandwich places were open for takeout, and I had a lot. I did a minor study in Dutch crunch in San Francisco. I would say, "Oh, okay, let's go to these five corner stores and we'll walk there." That was our pandemic activity.

FM: When we first went into shelter in place back in March last year—2020, was that 2020?—when we first went into shelter in place, we thought, "Okay, we're closing down for three weeks." We had the option to stay open for take-out, but no one was coming in. Everyone was scared then. So we closed for three weeks, and during that time I was able to just see how much time I didn't give myself between running the business and being mom. I gave myself nothing. And I just looked around my house and saw how much needed to be done in the house, because I was forced to sit with myself. I was able to see how little I gave myself and I really shifted that. I definitely have realized what I can do at Minnie Bell's and what I cannot do. I can't run every aspect of the business and then go at my counter every day and take orders. I was taking shifts myself! We have a schedule, and my name was on the schedule: Fernay is on the counter, Fernay is on the fryer. I definitely changed that, and now make sure that I have employees for every shift. I am able to actually look and see what I should be refining. The pandemic helped me to just slow myself down a little bit and listen to my body, listen to things that I need. I can keep going and going and going, but if I just tire myself out nothing is going to come of it.

GA: I'm with Fernay. I realized that I am last for myself all the time. I feel that there is a lot of performance about equity and support and self-care, but not enough collective action to shift as a society into healing and co-support.

Eating is among the first things to fall between the cracks. I am tired of not having time to make myself a reasonable lunch and sit down. I work in food, I talk about the power of food all the time, I talk about these beautiful meals, but can I have an hour and a half, every day, to make myself a fresh lunch and sit down and eat it? Can you take an hour to sit and have a lunch meal with me without feeling like you need to be in fifty other places and that this is a waste of time? With me, it started at a dinner table and it will end at a dinner table. That conversation is where ideas and connection come from, and at the end of the day that is all I am doing, in my job and in my life. I struggle with whether we're going to make space for that.

It's harder, I know, for food business owners. And for me, they are also the cornerstone of a healthy, vibrant place. They nurture our souls and define the cultural identity of a place. They also hold down and feed a web of other local vendors—farmers, dry goods suppliers, plumbers, contractors, sign painters, photographers, banks, and more. A successful food business is a network of human relationships that, to me, make a place feel like a living, breathing space. This is one of the things that is hardest for me to watch change. I really struggle to find peace in it.

Fernay McPherson at her restaurant Minnie Bell's

FM: Businesswise, it is still up and down, up and down. The last few months have been good, but now we are back to numbers all the way down, and we have to turn down work because we don't have the capacity to do it. And then it turns out, "This day was slow, so I really could have done that catering." It's just so hard to be able to know at this point with the pandemic. I have turned down so many catering jobs just because the food needed to be individually packaged and I didn't have the capacity to do it. I'm not back at 100 percent capacity. I used to be open seven days a week, from eleven to eight. Now I am open five days, from eleven to seven or eleven to five. That has been a major adjustment. Traffic is still not where it was prior to the pandemic. I was just looking at my numbers today and for the year. I still have December to go, but I am probably down 30 percent of what I did in 2019. Rent is back to normal, so I am not getting that support anymore. We didn't see catering at all, really, in 2020. It was a lot of food relief programs. We were doing individual meals for the community. We weren't open at full capacity when we were doing those, so it was easier for me to provide some hours for staff and do these meals because it would be 200 meals here, 200 meals there.

This year I have seen a shift in holiday parties, in fact, so we're able to do some holiday party catering. But now everyone has to have food individually packaged, so then that puts me in a position where I have to figure out, "Okay, how do I open up for service and then try to do these individually packaged meals for 150 people?" I find myself having to turn down some of that work, which sucks because it's turning money away, but it is hard to be able to do those individually packaged meals at this point and stay open for customers to come in and buy. That's a big revenue stream that I have to turn down.

It has just been so hard to be able to know how to make decisions, because things just change rapidly. Now we have this new variant out and the number of walk-ins has gone back down. The day that I might turn down some catering, we may be down $1,000 because we didn't get enough people to walk in and buy food. Those things right there are the things that I am struggling with right now. Trying to make the right decisions, but not knowing how.

GA: Do you have staffing shortages, too? Are you feeling that?

FM: Yeah, I'm definitely short on staff. That is what's causing me to be closed those two days. I can get maybe three people, but three people are not going to be able to do the whole day from eleven to seven. I don't want to open for half-days because I feel like customers get confused if the hours change. I would hope that we do not have another variant. I wish this virus would just disappear. Just kick rocks. Leave.

GA: Goodbye!

FM: Go! I'm tired of masks. I'm tired of not being able to see people's faces. I hope that we are back to normal in 2022. Back to normal, no virus, and that people are able to just get back on track. In January 2020 I got my liquor license, and 2020 was supposed to be Minnie Bell's biggest year. It ended up being the lowest. I still haven't had an opportunity to really realize the liquor license vision. It would bring in another good revenue stream, but I haven't been able to do that at all. I do these really fun Kool-Aid cocktails, it just really fits the theme. Now all of our cocktails are bottled. I really wanted to have a guest bartender come in on Friday nights and make some nice drinks. I haven't been able to do those things and be able to serve not a crazy expensive bougie cocktail, but just a really delicious cocktail in a nice glass that looks good, for people to have an experience. Most people, when you go out to a bar and to drink you're not trying to get a bottled cocktail, you want to sit and drink with the people you're with.

GA: Fernay, would you say you're at 50 percent of 2019? 60 percent, roughly, of sales? Where would you say?

FM: I'll need to compare 2019 to this year, but I'll take a guess and say that I'm at about 70 percent.

GA: I have this theory that we're all at 75 percent in everything. We're at 75 percent energy, 75 percent of everything.

FM: Yeah, I would say about 70 percent because I'm still, like I said, closed two days a week. The thing about it is that I'm trying to still make sure I'm giving hours to the crew that I have now. I am so scared to cut their hours because it's so hard to get people now. I am only at 70 percent, but I'm still paying out their hours.

GA: It was really interesting for me to hear Fernay's thoughts. Our La Cocina entrepreneurs have to bootstrap up, they don't have cash that they can just speculate on. So quite a few of our entrepreneurs found a way to use catering in offices and big events to get some steady cashflow that allows you to start hiring steady staff and building systems.

The pandemic has shaken up that office revenue, and it feels like these days, more tech workers might look for job flexibility and remote work over free food offered by their employers, which will change the opportunity we have been able to leverage for the past decade. We at La Cocina and the entrepreneurs are looking for new ways to get to customers as that shakes up.

The other thing I think about a lot is that with the pandemic people have returned to comfort foods, familiar foods. And with the rise of delivery and people not wanting to go into grocery stores and even restaurants, the opportunities to just try something new have decreased. That is another interesting trend. I really believe in La Cocina's ability to drive flavor and drive taste, but I think we are going to need to innovate around that. How do we create opportunity? How do we create new food experiences? Because people still want them!

Another thing that I have noticed is the labor and service shortage is really showing up in the high-end dining experience. You go out and you pay a lot more money than you used to, and you are not getting the same service experience. You will see two servers working the floor when there were normally five. It's the same in the kitchen. Before the pandemic there was this explosion of higher-end dining in San Francisco, and I am curious as to what is going to happen to that trend.

Food quality does still feel consistent in owner-operated food businesses. There are so many threats to small businesses that we all know, but I continue to see them as the most resilient and valuable to a local economy. If it is family owned, there is a level of resiliency built in around staffing. So many restaurants in SF have changed menus and reworked operations but found a way to keep a human connection. The pandemic has given me a new understanding of what it means to be a long-standing business.

The last thing that is important in the food business is rents. What Fernay said is a real thing to pay attention to. Landlords have returned rents at the beginning of 2021 back to normal, and even in 2020, the rents did not always reflect the reality of the market, or the impact that was happening. As somebody who worked across thirty-six leases, I know the reality of what was actually given. It was not as much as people say. It wasn't enough even then. Fernay, if you're at 70 percent of 2019, that is pretty dang good, but rents are at 100 percent, so something is not going to pencil. And supply chain issues are real. For example, we're running into a cost increase because epoxy, which was a cheap sealant to keep your floor food safe, has gone up ten times because of plastic shortages in the supply chain.

FM: About the supply chain, we're seeing that with food. For three weeks we may not be able to get product that we need. We're improvising. It's gone for three weeks, and then it comes back and something else is gone. I am dealing with that a lot. I'm running around to five or six stores looking for just some Crystal hot sauce. Tomorrow is my day to pick up my order, so we'll see. What am I going to be missing tomorrow that is going to be gone for the next two weeks and that I'll have to look for in three or four different stores?

GA: The word you used, Fernay, "improvising." In my nine years at La Cocina I have seen this improvisation at work in every aspect of business. Part of me thinks it comes from having to adapt your food, your concept, your life to a foreign place, in a way that becomes second nature to how you think. The first couple months of shelter-in-place my mother relied on grocery delivery and didn't visit her Indian stores, and she said it reminded her of her early days in America, of searching through unfamiliar ingredients to re-create a taste of home in an unfamiliar land.

As we have been talking, I have been thinking about Fernay's observation that everybody in her family is obsessed with food and defined by a dish. When she said that I had a moment of realization—that's not just how everyone thinks? It makes me appreciate how telling my own story is as an opportunity to understand something new about myself.

My favorite part of working with the entrepreneurs was teasing out those stories—why this food? Why this business? Why now? It helped me understand them and their vision and what was going to be important to them. At best, I am hoping to support the entrepreneur in going where they want to go, a thoughtful wayfinder. For me, knowing their story and why it matters to them, beyond the business opportunity, is always such a critical piece.

Before I forget, I wanted to add one note, Fernay. Do you remember we did that media dinner at La Cocina and you brought your great auntie Minnie? I remember that meal so well. Fernay had fried all the chicken, and I convinced her that she needed to make pound cake for this media dinner. I loved hearing you, Fernay, tell the story of Minnie Bell's to the media while we all ate fried chicken and sat at the table with your auntie.

FM: What I think was even more cool is that for my space in Emeryville I did a soft opening on my auntie's birthday. That was really, really dope. We were able to bring the family out. I needed to test the equipment and stuff, so I just cooked for the family. We had cake and we celebrated her birthday, and then we did our soft launch to the public that Monday. That was special in itself, to be able to have her there. I spent a lot of time with my aunt. My aunt was like my caretaker because she was so close to us. She was already retired, so she helped my parents tremendously when I was growing up. She would always say, "I'm not gonna live to see your kids," and I would say, "Yes you are." Now I have two granddaughters. She's eighty-eight years old, and she's going to be eighty-nine; not only has she seen my kids, but she has seen my grandkids. She saw me on Thanksgiving and she said, "Oh my gosh, this food! You just get better. I feel like I was a little girl in the projects and them old women was in there cooking that food, that's how your food is tasting now." And I'm just like, *I've made it. I've made it.*

GA: You have made it.

FM: If it's tasting like the ancestors' food, then I've made it. That's when I know I'm doing right.

Sour Cream Pound Cake

Method

Preheat oven to 325°F. Butter and flour a large Bundt pan or coat with baking spray. Combine the flour, salt, and baking soda in a large bowl, whisk together and set aside.

Cream the butter and sugar until light and fluffy. Add the vanilla, then the eggs one at a time while mixing on medium speed, scraping the bowl down twice or so. Add the flour mixture and sour cream in alternating batches, mixing on low until just combined.

Use your spatula to finish the batter off, scraping the bowl down and mixing any errant sour cream or flour in. Transfer the batter to your prepared Bundt pan and bake at 325°F for about 1 ½ hours or until a skewer comes out clean from the center.

Cool in the pan for 10 minutes before inverting.

Sift confectioner's sugar on top.

3 cups all-purpose flour

1 teaspoon kosher salt

1 teaspoon baking soda

1 cup butter, room temperature

3 cups granulated sugar

6 large eggs, room temperature

1 tablespoon vanilla extract

1 cup sour cream

½ cup confectioner's sugar (for topping)

Puri

Yield: 20 Puris

Method

In a large bowl, combine the flour, salt, and spices. Pour in the melted ghee and add enough water to form a stiff dough, about ½ cup. Incorporate ingredients using a wooden spoon and turn the dough out onto your countertop. Knead well until it comes together to form a smooth dough, about 4 minutes. Cover and rest the dough for 30 minutes.

Heat the oil over medium-high heat to 325°F.

Divide the dough into 20 equal pieces. Roll each ball of dough into a thin, 5-inch-wide circle.

When the oil is hot, fry each puri, gently pressing it down with a frying spoon to puff it up. Once puffed, flip the puri and cook the other side. When the puri is a light golden brown, about 1–2 minutes, remove from oil and drain on a cooling rack.

Eat them as hot as you can handle. They will keep as a traveling snack for a day or two.

2 cups atta (whole wheat flour)

1 teaspoon kosher salt

½ teaspoon ajwain

4 tablespoons ghee, melted, or canola oil

Oil for frying

Teta Thursdays: Conversations on Food, Culture, and Identity during a Global Pandemic

7

The pandemic turned me into a sourdough geek. I had always been intrigued by the craft of baking with sourdough but never had the time to explore its doughy intricacies. The pandemic changed all this. Fascinated by the sourdough craze I read about online, I decided to give it a try, even adopting the practice of naming your starter baby—mine was Umm Kulthum, the iconic Egyptian contralto from the early 1900s. But as I got more into the fad, and despite the fluffy interior and crusty edges of the loaves Umm Kulthum grew up to be, I felt disconnected. As a queer Arab American food writer, I have come to see the value of food in the context of community. Whether I am curating pop-up dinners inspired by my research or connecting on social media with food writers from around the world, social connection and storytelling are central to my work. Communal food practices integrate source and consumer, nourishing bodies and society. How then to build connection amid so much disconnection? How to maintain the health of the body in quarantine, but also of the self in relation with others?

At first, the extra time felt like a novelty. Amid mandatory lockdowns, the world was thrust into an eerie, slow-paced (for some) isolation with a surplus of time that no one anticipated. The way people used this time reveals much about us, our relationship to the present, and our idea of an imagined, often idealized, past. Many treated the initial days of COVID-19 like an unexpected vacation in the comfort of home. In a matter of weeks, a microscopic, airborne virus had disrupted the heartbeat of global capitalism: supply chains were crippled, markets (temporarily) crashed, and human activity around the globe came to a screeching halt, revealing just how vulnerable we are to the whims of global markets. People, in turn, sought comfort amid the uncertainty, albeit in isolation.

Back to Umm Kulthum. Bakers and nonbakers, at least those fortunate enough to work from home, flocked to their kitchens. Flour flew off the shelves and gave birth to countless sourdough babies. Mine was born on April 20, 2020. I shared photos with an online community of friends, many of whom I have never met face to face. The pandemic forced the world to reckon with our digitally connected reality. I spent many early-pandemic afternoons reading about the science of sourdough (and watching Instagram Reels of other people's cats). Prior to the advent of commercial yeast in the mid-1800s, all leavened bread was possible because of sourdough. Our ancestors transmitted this knowledge through practice, over millennia. In the past, someone had to teach you their craft. Today, we have the internet. You could learn how to bake with sourdough by yourself. I read hundreds of online recipes. I scoured videos on YouTube to gauge the ideal consistency and the correct types of bubbles that indicate success. Umm Kulthum lived up to the online descriptions I read about. But I was the only one there to give her a taste.

One of the markers of modernity is our independence, not from other nations, but from each other. For much of human history, the prospect of living in isolation would have meant near-certain death. Cooperation has been an essential element of the human experience. Although we continue to rely on others to this day, perhaps even on a global scale, much of this cooperation has been commodified and abstracted. There is something truly modern about cultivating your own sourdough starter in order to bake bread for yourself. In its contemporary incarnation, sourdough conjures an idealized, forsaken past. Although the ingredients and preparation have remained largely the same, the context could not be more different. Baking sourdough for myself during the pandemic felt wasteful. Each time I "fed" Umm, I had to discard all but a spoonful in order to make room for the new flour and water (otherwise she would grow uncontrollably). At twice daily feedings, that is more bread than any one person should consume by themselves. This is a modern problem. In the context of a community or a local bakery, there is no discard. The scale inherent to communal styles of baking allows for efficiencies that are not possible when baking in isolation.

Although there are thousands of creative recipes to use leftover discard, they address a symptom. Recipes for "discard crackers" or "discard pancakes" do not take into consideration the effort to prepare the pastry and the energy needed to fire up the oven, all in the name of "saving" the discard. I found that these recipes ultimately mask some of the tensions in baking bread for myself. Throughout the pandemic, I found myself discarding lots of starter in order to keep up with Umm Kulthum's voracious appetite. Most home bakers end up storing their bubbly starters in the refrigerator in order to extend the time between feedings. The cold temperature slows the fermentation process, and in turn "liberates" us from the burdens of reciprocity and exchange of communal baking.

Although we still depend on others, our dependence has been abstracted and commodified. This abstraction is justified in the name of scale and efficiency, although noticeably different than the scale and efficiency of communal baking. It is more efficient and, thus, more economical to buy flour from a grocery store than it is to develop a relationship with a local farmer who grows, harvests, and mills their own grain. Modern capitalism enables us to exchange money with a corporation that will cheaply and reliably provide flour at the lowest prices the market can yield, assuming no collusion or monopoly. My point is not to demonize or glorify this transformation, rather to ask how this transformation has fundamentally shifted our relationships to each other and the environment.

Little Umm isn't to be blamed for her isolation. She is a product of our time.

Umm Kulthum, Antonio Tahhan's sourdough starter

Although modernity has altered how we learn about sourdough, the underlying principle has remained the same: mix flour with water, and naturally occurring yeast and bacteria from the environment will colonize the shaggy, porridge-like dough.[1] Depending on environmental factors, such as temperature, a flourishing colony of voracious microorganisms typically forms within a few days. So, you see, maybe Umm Kulthum wasn't as isolated as she seemed. Her own chemistry is a testament to her interdependence with others, even as she is caught up in systems of capital and global supply.

There was something alluring about cultivating my own starter, especially during a global pandemic when commercial yeast became almost impossible to find. On the one hand, this practice felt like a humble nod to tradition. On the other, baking with sourdough felt like a revolutionary act. Fermentation revivalist Sandor Katz argues that fermentation is a co-constitutive transformation where practitioners and agents of fermentation depend on and nourish one another. In the case of sourdough, the yeast and bacteria in the starter break down the wheat, making it easier for humans to digest. This process is often referred to as "predigestion." It results in bubbles of carbon dioxide that get trapped in webs of gluten, ultimately giving bread the light and airy texture that is so desirable.

Sourdough is not the only example of food that is mutually beneficial for humans and bacteria. All fermented products rely on thriving colonies of microorganisms that transform the foods they inhabit into a myriad of new and complex flavors and textures. Olives, for example, would be inedible if not for the transformative process of fermentation. Straight from the tree, olives are incredibly bitter and difficult to digest. The signature deep, umami flavor of soy sauce is also a tasty by-product of fermentation. The benefits of fermentation are not limited to predigestion and novel flavors but also to preservation. Prior to refrigeration, fermentation enabled humans to extend the shelf-life of foods that would have otherwise rotted and gone to waste. Fermenting milk into yogurt or cheese extended the shelf life of dairy from a few hours (prior to refrigeration) to weeks, months, and even years in the case of some hard cheeses.

As a food writer interested in traditional food practices from the Arab world, I wanted to explore these shifts in our foodways with my peers. I wanted to understand and contextualize why certain practices disappear and what it means if or when others make a comeback. More importantly, I wanted to have this conversation at a time of deep reflection in the food community as many restaurants closed their doors and people around the world found themselves isolated in their kitchens. An underlying motivation, however, was also to create a sense of community where the pandemic had left a void. On March 23, 2020, I launched *Teta Thursdays: Conversations on Food, Culture, and Identity.*

The series was structured around live conversations with some of my favorite food writers, chefs, and researchers in the field of Arab foodways. The word *Teta* is the Arabic term for grandmother. I chose this title based on my own experience as part of the Syrian diaspora. My grandmothers were the conduits for the culinary traditions that I grew up with. Food was one of the central ways that I experienced and understood my Syrian identity. I remember that many of the dishes my grandmothers cooked required hours of preparation and many hands. Cooking was as much practical as it was social. For many, our grandparents are the keepers of the culinary knowledge and traditions that we often take for granted. I wanted this series to shine a light on the implications of these traditions for our relationships with each other and the environment.

The series would not have been possible without the thoughtful contributions of my friends and cohosts of the series.[2] I am grateful for the nourishing conversations we had at a time when so many around the world were isolated from friends and family. All this thinking about Umm Kulthum and her microbial connections (plus the real-life diva's signature hour-long songs that kept me company in the kitchen) led me to reflect more deeply on food origins and preservation practices, and how we can give birth to new and meaningful connections as we emerge from isolation. How can we draw on the precapitalist contexts in which these traditions emerged and use the knowledge we developed in isolation to create a new post-COVID-19 reality, where the labor of baking by yourself is integrated into community?

Mouneh as Resistance

One of the recurring themes in many of the *Teta Thursdays* conversations was the practice of *mouneh*. In the Arab kitchen, *mouneh* refers to the practice of preserving seasonal foods so they can be available in times of scarcity and unpredictability. Barbara Massaad, author of the Lebanese cookbook *Mouneh*, traces the etymology of this traditional practice to the Arabic word *mana*, meaning to store. At our own time of unprecedented unpredictability and scarcity, I asked each participant to take us into their pantry. I wanted to learn about their most treasured *mouneh* traditions.

Quarantine was not new for Palestinian food writer Mai Kakish, who grew up in Jerusalem during the First Intifada and the Gulf War. During our *Teta Thursdays* conversation, Mai recalled what life was like under curfew whenever there were periods of unrest. For her, "the pantry is the base of the kitchen . . . it's the place where you start thinking of your meals and then the fresh ingredients come into play." Mai refers to her pantry using the traditional Arabic term, *namliyeh*, which is derived from the Arabic word for ant, or *namel*, reminding us of the fact that traditional pantries in Palestine were protected with a fine mesh screen to keep ants and other bugs away from the valuable *mouneh* that was stored inside.

There is something inherently anticapitalist about the practice of *mouneh*. In a capitalist society where goods and services are commodified, the expectation is that you do not need to preserve ingredients because corporations can give you what you need, when you need it (as long as you have the capital). In many industrialized countries, the contemporary grocery store is often owned by a large corporation that gives the illusion that seasons are irrelevant. If you want blueberries in the dead of winter, you can purchase a container of blueberries, typically picked in the southern hemisphere, packed in plastic, and shipped halfway around the world. Most fruits and vegetables that are transported long distances are picked when they are not ripe so that they can withstand the long journey without bruising or rotting. These fruits tend to be less flavorful than their seasonal counterparts that are picked ripe and harvested locally.

Economy of scale is one of many factors that shape the ingredients we cook with. For Mirna Bamieh, the politics of the Israeli occupation is another. Mirna is an artist and cook. She is the founder of Palestine Hosting Society, "a live art project that explores traditional food culture in Palestine, especially those that are on the verge of disappearing." During our *Teta Thursdays* conversation, Mirna explained how foraging restrictions on popular Palestinian plants, such as *aqub* and *luf*, have affected Palestinian cuisine and the traditions. Extensive checkpoints and apartheid separation walls that have broken up the Palestinian homeland have limited the places where Palestinians can forage. Israeli authorities have also instituted policies outlawing the practice. These policies are implemented under the pretext of environmental concern, which is misguided in the context of small-scale consumption that is typical of individual households. The reality is that these policies are part of a broader, systematic effort to sever the historic connection between Palestinians from the land of their ancestors. Forgetting how to forage is one step in forgetting what it means to be Palestinian.

For Mirna, the dishes she researches represent a lineage that connects Palestinians to smells, tastes, and practices that some barely remember or perhaps never experienced. Mirna curated a performance dinner around the practice of foraging for wild plants. An important component of this dinner was the research, not only in identifying the plants but also in learning and reclaiming the indigenous cooking practices that have connected Palestinians with their land for generations. One plant in particular, *luf*, can be toxic if it is not handled properly. Mirna points out that the scientific name for this plant, *Arum palaestinum* (arum of Palestine), is a testament to this plant's ties to community, identity, land, and history. If you place a tiny piece of this raw plant in your mouth, it will make your tongue tingle. Indigenous Palestinians have a special way of preparing *luf* that rids it of its toxic properties. It involves rubbing the leaves with salt several times and squeezing out the resulting liquid. Mirna laments how the occupation has limited this practice through its restrictive policies against foraging.

Mai Kakish's family instilled in her the importance of living off the land. Her grandfather planted apricot and olive trees around their house in Jerusalem so that future generations can eat from their fruit.

Her grandmother taught her the valuable lesson that "a house with lentils and olive oil will never go hungry." From a very young age, Mai learned the value of preserving what is in abundance for times of scarcity. In Palestine, these practices are not simply about living a traditional life. Preservation takes on a different sense of urgency amid the looming threat of curfews, incursions, and calorie-counting import restrictions. In Gaza, for example, the Israeli government went so far as to calculate the number of daily calories Palestinians trapped in the enclave need as part of an effort to keep the Gazan economy "on the brink of collapse"—although the Israeli Defense Ministry denies that the government ever made use of these calculations.[3] Mai's practice of *mouneh* was dual purpose. As much as *mouneh* helped secure her family's access to food, Mai was also connecting with her grandmother and upholding generations of Palestinian culinary tradition. The seemingly small act of maintaining a pantry is a noteworthy act of resistance to both the capitalist grocery store and the Israeli occupation. It nourishes both the body and the self in relation to others.

Although Mai grew up in Palestine, her family encouraged her to go to university in the United States. Mai recalled that at first she was isolated and miserable studying in a new place, away from the familiar foods and warmth of her grandmother. One thing that brought her comfort during this period was the occasional care package of *mouneh* that her family would send her from Palestine. During our Instagram Live conversation, Mai showed me bags of homemade *za'atar* blends and grape leaves from her grandmother's vineyard packed in air-tight plastic soda bottles. The bottle she showed during the interview was packed in 2017. Mai told me that she wants to keep this bottle intact as a memento from her grandmother. Mai's grandmother passed away a year after our conversation. Her vineyard continues to grow in Palestine. Mai has started foraging for grape leaves in Chicago and wants to try preserving the leaves in air-tight containers.

A distinguishing element of *mouneh* is the inherent transformation of food. The point is not to have access to the same foods every day of the year, but to preserve seasonal ingredients at their peak by way of transformation. A sun-dried tomato is not the same as a fresh tomato. Milk is not the same as yogurt or cheese. Turnips are not the same as pickled turnips (*m'khalal lifit*). The techniques for preserving foods are varied and rich: from air drying and curing to steeping in vinegar and cooking in sugar. The result of this transformation is a more varied and complex cuisine.

I cannot help but think of Mai's grandmother in the context of preservation and transformation. The point of her grandmother's *mouneh* is not to re-create for the sake of maintaining an idealized imagination of the past, but rather to put into practice the meaning of these traditions in our own lives and consumption habits today. This is not to detract from tradition for tradition's sake, but to acknowledge the practical context in which these traditions emerged. Unlike me, a privileged sourdough enthusiast, Mai's grandmother did not necessarily have the luxury to engage in romanticized aspects of preservation and fermentation for the sake of novelty.

Part of the value of such practical and seasonal culinary traditions is their defiance of neoliberal forms of consumption. The apricot and olive trees that Mai's grandfather planted produce fruit at a particular time of year. The expectation is to transform these fruits at their peak into nourishing *mouneh* that can be shared and enjoyed throughout the year, particularly during times of scarcity and uncertainty. These issues of seasonality, transformation, *mouneh*, family, communal connections, and resistance are inseparable.

Gender and Labor

To prepare for my *Teta Thursdays* conversation with Mirna Bamieh, I baked *khubz smeedeh*, a special ring-shaped bread from Tulkarm, a Palestinian city in the West Bank. Historically, this bread was prepared at funerals and weddings. I first tasted *khubz smeedeh* at Mirna's "Menu of Dis/appearance," a special performance dinner at Bard College in November 2019. Mirna opened the dinner by asking guests to break the ring-shaped bread and make a wish. As we pulled the ring apart with our hands, we were greeted with the scent of cinnamon from the fragrant toasted wheat stuffing. This was one of the last public events I attended before the start of the pandemic. The theme of disappearance and the flavors from the performance dinner shaped much of my *Teta Thursdays* conversation with Mirna, who participated from her home in Palestine.

Khubz smeedeh is a labor-intensive bread that is stuffed in a peculiar way, from the inside out. The dough is perfumed with anise, fennel, nigella seeds, turmeric, and earthy olive oil. The dough itself is savory and does not contain any sugar. The sweetness comes from the fragrant filling, which is made from coarse cracked wheat seasoned with a generous amount of cinnamon. After the filling cools and the dough has rested, comes the complicated part: stuffing. When I attempted to prepare the *khubz smeedeh* before my conversation with Mirna, I watched the tutorial she shared on her Instagram from when she learned to prepare the dish in Tulkarm. The video shows her friend Mu'men and his mother shaping a big batch of bread rings together.

Similar to my experience with sourdough, I found myself learning to prepare this dish alone. I revisited Mirna's video several times as I tried to perfect the filled ring shape. You start with a mound of dough that you pierce in the center to create a volcano shape. Then you have to stretch the dough along the perimeter in order to make room for the sweet filling. The trick is to make sure the dough around the opening remains thick. Once you add a generous amount of the filling, you have to delicately pull the inner edge of the dough around the filling to form a seal. Then you have to take the outer seal and pull it into the center, which helps ensure that the filling will not ooze out from the bread as it bakes. Feeling a little lost? It is a complicated routine.

As I spent hours shaping a single tray of Mirna's recipe, I reflected on the social significance of this labor and its implications in a capitalist economy. In a capitalist society, where a person's worth is tethered to the amount of capital they can amass, it becomes difficult for a home baker to justify spending hours shaping a single tray of *khubz smeedeh*. There is a prevailing contemporary discourse around food that seeks to simplify dishes for the sake of efficiency. To demonize this trend, however, is to miss the point. The point is not whether it is "good" or "bad" to find shortcuts in cooking, but to interrogate what it means when the entire act of cooking is driven by speed and efficiency. Who in a society has the privilege to cook dishes that require more time?

Perhaps more importantly, who is expected to do the labor of cooking complicated meals that involve hours of painstaking preparation and often uncomfortable environments?

Questions about food, tradition, and community have led me to reflect on the past, and in particular on the history of gender in cooking. Prior to modern industrial capitalism, most families practiced subsistence-based agriculture. This typically meant that all members of the family had to contribute to the production of food for survival. According to feminist Marxist theory, capitalism altered the hierarchy of labor. Whereas all labor in sustenance-based agriculture was critical for the survival of the family unit, capitalism ascribed a wage to labor outside the home, rendering it more valuable than domestic labor. When capital is the sole measure of value, unpaid domestic labor becomes worthless, both in terms of dollar amounts and social standing. This critique of capitalist gender dynamics and the idea that a "woman's place is in the kitchen" is important for reimagining social expectations of who belongs in the kitchen today.

Notwithstanding this critique, we should be careful not to romanticize the precapitalist past in which domestic labor was not rendered worthless. From tilling the soil to grinding grains and plucking the feathers off chickens, the past is replete with examples of grueling work in precarious conditions. Not producing enough food for the family often meant hunger and misery. In a provocative piece titled, "A Plea for Culinary Modernism," Rachel Laudan argues that we should celebrate modern advances in food production for what they have provided: more shelf-stable foods, modern kitchen gadgets, and less hours in the kitchen for women. She describes the opening of a McDonalds in Rome as one step in a long history of fast-food establishments that date back to "the days of the Caesars." Laudan uses the term "culinary Luddites" to describe cooks who view food history through rose-tinted glasses and bemoan industrialized foods. She points out that the "[culinary] Luddites' fable of disaster, of a fall from grace, smacks more of wishful thinking than of digging through archives."[4]

Recognizing the harsh context of this labor, however, should not blind us to the insidious aspects of contemporary domestic labor. While some kitchen tasks have been rendered trivial through industrialization, the context of this labor has changed. This led me to wonder, how can we contextualize labor beyond the physical toll it takes on our bodies? Maybe some of the less coercive (admittedly labor-intensive) food traditions of the past that brought communities together in socially productive ways are worthy of our reconsideration. My intent is not to qualify whether the food traditions of the past and the domestic labor that produced them were "good" or "bad," but rather to interrogate how we can think about cooking, and the labor around cooking, today. For this, I have my mother to thank.

Affective Labor

I was born to a Syrian family in Venezuela and grew up in Miami. When my family moved to the United States in the early 1990s, we did not know anyone. In a sense, this was a form of cultural isolation, one that shaped my mother's relationship to food and cooking. My mom felt compelled to continue the culinary traditions of a Syrian homeland she never lived in. I remember coming home from school to elaborate meals I did not fully appreciate until I started cooking them for myself. My mom used to roll entire pots of grape leaves alone in the kitchen while my brothers and I were at school and my dad was at work. She used to spend hours meticulously coring squash in order for us to experience the flavor of *kousa mahshi*, or stuffed squash. I later learned that my mom's recipe for *kousa mahshi* is a traditional Aleppan preparation that she learned from her mother, which calls for lots of minced garlic, a generous amount of dried mint, and a few glugs of pomegranate molasses in the broth. She simmers the squash stuffed with spiced lamb and rice in a fragrant broth until the skins became tender and the rice is perfectly cooked.

In Aleppo and Caracas, these dishes are often prepared with the help of many hands. It is a social activity. I often refer to this style of cooking as a team sport. Somehow, chopping a small mountain of parsley for tabbouleh seems more enjoyable when surrounded by friends and boisterous laughter than when you are alone in the kitchen. When we visited extended relatives in Venezuela every summer, I experienced the social style of cooking that has shaped my perspective on how food ought to be prepared. This is the affective quality of food labor that has the potential to socially bind us. But my mom in the United States experienced what Laudan describes as the drudgery of handmade meal preparation. Unfortunately for her, alone in her kitchen and far from Venezuelan Syrian relatives, there was no modern gadget that could have alleviated some of the labor of individually wrapping grape leaves as Laudan would have it. What might have been better, though, is if my mom's newly adopted home in the United States would have had the social infrastructure for communal cooking that she could have tapped into more readily. Rolling dozens of tiny grape leaves over a conversation with a dear friend can have a different affective quality than the same act in isolation.

As we are still in the midst of a global pandemic, many of us remain in isolation in our own kitchens. Some of the hardships of cooking in quarantine today mimic the hardships of past domestic labor. And yet, I want to encourage us to think of the affective qualities of this labor that enrich its social value. Perhaps technology can be a temporary aid for us in this endeavor. Holding the phone camera up to a pile of chopped parsley for Mom to see, sharing photos of our sourdough starters to an online community of friends, or hosting virtual conversations on foods—these are not altogether unpleasant activities. In the longer term though, as the need for social isolation from the pandemic subsides, I hope that we emerge with a renewed sense of communal food preparation. Having seen the darkness of the isolated kitchen, the brightness of each other's company should be all the more clear.

The gendered aspect of cooking is also not lost on me. When I was living in Aleppo in 2010, the most curious aspect of my research was that I was a cisgendered man interested in what is largely a woman-dominated space. Why would I want to know about these recipes and traditions? A few of my interlocutors jokingly suggested that I should find a wife who could cook these dishes for me. Little did they know that I was more in the market for a husband. My own experience as a queer person forced me to contend with the heavily gendered aspects of the kitchen. And yet, my sexuality has also given me access in some ways to this space. Although the women cooks I learned from in the kitchens of Aleppo did not know that I was gay, I knew that my experience as a gay man gave me the courage to enter that space and engage with them. My entire life has been a lesson in not conforming to societal expectations of what I should or should not do. In the process, I imagined for myself a less gendered, less heteronormative culinary tradition. Queerness demands a reimagining of social norms that are based more on equity and agency. It is not sufficient to say that a woman's place is *not* in the kitchen. All genders should have a place at the proverbial table. Just like *mouneh* can be read as a form of resistance, queerness in the kitchen is also subversive. Queer politics makes space for marginalized identities to exist in unexpected places. For me, that place was the home kitchen as a cis-man.

Reflecting on my mom's experience in relation to mine, agency stands out as an important element in the joy of cooking. Although my mom was not forced to re-create an imagined authentic Syrian cuisine that cost her hours of labor a day, she felt compelled to continue these traditions. My mom was not one to cut corners. Even her kibbeh fritters maintained their signature pointy ends and the impossibly thin casings that speak to the skill of their maker. My mom has always been an excellent cook, even though she felt the labor of cooking more acutely in the absence of the social fabric she left behind in Caracas. It is not that my mom lacked agency—it is that her social culinary options were limited.

The question of agency and the gendered pressures of culinary tradition also came up in my interview with Reem Kassis. Reem grew up in Jerusalem and moved to the United States for university. She never imagined she would end up having a career in the food world because her studies were an escape from some of the gendered expectations of a home cook in Palestine. She received a master's degree in business administration from the Wharton School in 2010 and continued her studies at the London School of Economics. It was not until Reem had her first daughter that she realized the value of food as a vehicle for national identity, which for her was the turning point. She wrote her first book, *The Palestinian Table*, with her Palestinian American daughter in mind. When I asked her what the process of writing the book was like, she described it as "a labor of love"—an intense, yet socially productive, experiment. Regardless of whether a publisher was going to print it, she knew she wanted to preserve these recipes and family stories for her daughters who never lived in the homeland that she left behind.

"It was less about the food we were eating . . . it was more everything that was around it," she said. "In different seasons, we would go pick olives at my father's village . . . in the summer, we would pick okra and *molokhia*." She reminisced about the summers in her mother's village where they used to pluck *molokhia* leaves together and chop them by hand, a process that required many helpers and hours of preparation. Unlike my mom, Reem was drawn to the kitchen under different circumstances. While she came to the United States to study and distance herself from the kitchen, it was her first experience eating dining hall food that made her miss home cooking. So what did Reem do? She decided she wanted to learn how to make *maqloobeh*.

In the hierarchy of Arab cookery, *maqloobeh* is an Olympic-level dish. It requires masterful layering of rice, chicken, eggplants, cauliflower, and other vegetables into a large pot. You have to cook the different components separately so that they finish cooking at the same time. Once everything is cooked, you carefully flip the pot onto a large tray. At this point some people will do a ceremonial drumroll on the pot, both for dramatic effect and to dislodge any pieces of eggplant or crispy rice that may have stuck to the bottom of the pot. If you do everything correctly, the dish is supposed to come out like an inverted savory cake, which is how the iconic dish got its name, which means "upside down" in Arabic. In hindsight, Reem admits that she should have picked an easier dish to start off with. After several long-distance phone calls to Palestine, Reem's mom offered to fly to the United States and cook the *maqloobeh* for Reem. Reem laughs, adding that this was a time when international calls were still prohibitively expensive. In the end, Reem had so much *maqloobeh*, she fed her entire dormitory and she still had plenty left over.

Authenticity in the Diaspora

Cooking in the diaspora is riddled with concerns over authenticity. Phoning home is one way to ensure that recipes turn out as we remember them. For the inaugural *Teta Thursdays* episode, I invited my dear friend Abeer Najjar, a Palestinian American food writer who grew up in Chicago. Abeer has grappled with her own questions of tradition and authenticity. One of the signature recipes that Abeer writes about on her blog is a dreamy *tres leches* cake infused with cardamom and rose water. She encourages readers to use a boxed cake mix if they do not have time to make the classic yellow cake base from scratch. Abeer's no-fuss approach to cooking mirrors her warm, affirming personality. She explains that this recipe was inspired by the Latinx community that she grew up alongside on the South Side of Chicago. Abeer is attuned to the ways in which recipes travel and transform as they change hands.

For Abeer, food tells a personal story. One of the recipes on Abeer's social media that caught my attention is an unusual *molokhia* "salad." *Molokhia* is a dark leafy green that is part of the okra family. It is typically prepared as a stew or a soup across the Levant and North Africa. More importantly, it is served hot. I had never heard of raw preparation before that is served cold. Each time Abeer posted photos of this salad on social media, she was met with intrigue. Abeer learned this recipe from her mother, who in turn, had learned it from her grandmother. Although her mom's side of the family is from Yaffa, her mom grew up in a refugee camp outside Ramallah as a result of the *Nakba*. The term literally means "catastrophe" in Arabic and refers to the forced displacement of hundreds of thousands of Palestinians in 1948, when Israel became a state. At the refugee camp, it was common to dry the fresh *molokhia* leaves during the peak summer months when they were most abundant. To make the *molokhia* salad, which Abeer's family calls *buraniyye*, you first grind the dried leaves into a fine powder and mix the powder with diced tomatoes, minced garlic, lots of chili peppers, freshly squeezed lemon juice, and a generous amount of olive oil. The result is a salsa-like consistency that you mop up with freshly baked bread.

Although the precise origins of Abeer's *buraniyye* remain unknown, I later learned that there is a very similar preparation of *molokhia* in Upper Egypt. Both versions are prepared with dried, ground *molokhia* leaves, both are served cold, and both call for a similar set of ingredients. The version from Upper Egypt is called *shalowlo*. Some recipes for *shalowlo* omit the tomatoes while others call for a slightly different combination of herbs and spices, but the composition of both dishes is undeniably the same. Whether or not there is a direct link between *shalowlo* and Abeer's *buraniyye* is unclear, but what remains certain is that there is no single version of *shalowlo* or *buraniyye*. In other words, while we may not know whether *shalowlo* became *buraniyye,* or vice versa, we do know that versions of this dish exist in Upper Egypt, a refugee camp near Ramallah, the South Side of Chicago, and most recently, in Baltimore, where Abeer and I cooked her version of *buraniyye* in October 2019. To ask whether one dish "became" the other is to do an injustice to the omnidirectional, knowable, and unknowable influences that leave their mark on the flavors, textures, and rituals of that dish. For Abeer, it is the stories that connect these dishes to the people in her life that give them more meaning.

There are myriad reasons for why or how a dish can evolve, which prompts us to expand our parameters of authenticity. *Muhammara*, for example, is a classic red pepper and walnut dip from the northern Syrian city of Aleppo. A drizzle of pomegranate molasses gives this fiery dip its signature sweet and tangy profile. The secret to Chef Mohamed Orfali's *muhammara* is an intensely caramelized onion. He sautés it in olive oil until it develops a sweet, smoky flavor, and adds a small spoon of Arabic coffee for a deep, almost chocolatey flavor profile. He learned these techniques from his Aleppan grandmother, Teta Fatoum. Chef Orfali is an Aleppan celebrity chef and restaurant owner based in Dubai. He also has his own cooking show, *Al-Matbakh Al-Mu'aser*, or *The Contemporary Kitchen*. When Orfali attended culinary school in Aleppo, the curriculum was Western, based on French techniques from the 1960s and 1970s. The more he cooked foreign dishes, the more he realized the importance of memory in cooking. Although the French dishes he was learning to prepare at school tasted fine, he felt they were devoid of social meaning, divorced as they were from his world.

During our *Teta Thursdays* conversation, Chef Orfali explained how the food from his childhood shaped his identity as a chef. These memories of his childhood in Aleppo inspired him to dig deeper into the traditional food practices of the region. He read about distillation methods in medieval cookbooks. He learned about classic preservation techniques, including the use of a soy sauce–like condiment made from fermented barley that was prevalent in thirteenth-century Syria. One of Orfali's pet peeves is when people do not consider Syrian cuisine to be innovative. He has built his career around dispelling this myth, much to the chagrin of Aleppan grandmothers who write to him saying that he is ruining tradition. In response, Orfali points to the distillation of rose petals to make rose water and the use of *kilis* or calcium hydroxide to make a classic candied eggplant jam, to suggest that the region has a history of embracing innovative techniques and that we should look both backward and forward when thinking about our foodways. Orfali draws much of his inspiration from the rich terroir of the villages surrounding Aleppo, including the town of Urfa, where his family is from. We concluded our conversation by reminiscing about some of our favorite Aleppan dishes like *kabab b'karaz* (cherry kababs), *lahme b'ajeen* (Armenian meat pies), and *heytaliyye*, a floral milk pudding that made its way to Aleppo from China along the Silk Road. All these dishes were innovations, to some extent, yet gained their place on the "classic" Aleppan table over time. From the regional varieties of *buraniyye molokhia* salsa in Palestine and Egypt and cardamom rose *tres leches* on the South Side of Chicago to *muhammara* spiked with a spoon of Arabic coffee, tradition evolves over time and space informed by the people who inhabit those planes.

In a recent conversation about sourdough and communal practices, a friend asked me, "What's the solution?" What a question! As we adapt to our new pandemic reality, a lot of us are left wondering how we can apply lessons from this collective experience to creating a different framework for understanding our relationship to food—one that is not dominated by corporations with special interests or exploitative forms of consumption/production that wreak havoc on the planet. How do we resist being folded into neoliberal forms of consumption? This is a tall order. As modernity seeks to liberate us from one another through the commodification of goods and services, I propose a more entangled, mutually beneficial existence, one that mimics the co-constitutive relationship between us and our wild ferments. As I reflect on the stories from the *Teta Thursdays* conversations, it becomes clear that tradition is less about the specific foods we seek to re-create in a contemporary context than our relationships to each other and the past. A practical way of thinking about this is through the lens of affective labor. It is not enough to re-create foods in a vacuum, devoid of the meanings they hold. The same dishes prepared in different contexts can draw out wildly different emotions and social flavors. Enjoying a perfectly baked loaf of homemade sourdough alone in my kitchen, while pleasant, is not the same as baking with others or supporting a local baker who does this for a living. As capitalism seeks to commodify our existence so that we become reliable consumers, we ought to push back by examining the structures of power that are embedded in every aspect of our lives. There is no single right way to resist. The intent is not to re-create a bygone era or become hunter-gatherers, nor to romanticize either. Instead, we should be conscious about the sustainability of how we grow and source our food in a more collectivist sense to avoid the trap of elitist Luddism. We should reexamine the ways we prepare food to work with our seasons and preservation practices, or *mouneh*. This approach is about the health of our bodies and our souls in this challenging pandemic era.

Notes

1. It is important to use flour that has not been bleached or processed in a way that can hinder the growth of the bacteria and yeast that make up sourdough.
2. I want to thank (in order of appearance): Abeer Najjar, Kathryn Pauline from Cardamom and Tea; Mai Kakish from Almond and Fig; Nadia Hubbi and Deanna Kabakibi from Sweet Pillar Food; Mirna Bamieh from Palestine Hosting Society; Sami Tamimi, Anny Gaul from Cooking with Gaul; Reem Kassis, and Mohammad Orfali.

3. Maayan Lubell, "Israel Gaza Blockade Study Calculated Palestinians' Calories," Reuters, October 17, 2012, https://www.reuters.com/article /us-palestinians-israel-gaza/israel-gaza-blockade-study-calculated -palestinians-calories-idUSBRE89G0NM20121017.

4. Rachel Laudan, "A Plea for Culinary Modernism," *Jacobin*, May 22, 2015, https://jacobin.com/2015/05/slow-food-artisanal-natural-preservatives/.

Kousa Mahshi
(Aleppan-Style Stuffed Squash)
Serves 4–6

Method

Rinse rice under cold water, drain, and set aside. Do not worry about getting every drop of water out.

Mix rice, meat, tomato paste, olive oil, seven spice blend, and salt until well combined. Be gentle while mixing the stuffing so as not to break the rinsed rice.

With a vegetable corer, carefully hollow out the squash making sure not to puncture any of the sides or the ends (save the squash "meat"). You want to get as close as possible to the edge of the squash without puncturing the skin. This takes practice. Do not be discouraged.

Stuff the squash with the rice and meat mixture, stopping about half an inch from the top. Make sure the stuffing is not compact. You want the broth to be able to get into the squash in order for the stuffing to cook through.

If your pot has a thin bottom, cover the bottom with a layer of sliced carrots to protect the squash from sticking or burning.

Carefully position all the stuffed squash inside the pot.

In a mixing bowl, combine the beef broth with the lemon juice, dried mint, pomegranate molasses, minced garlic, and salt to taste. Check for seasoning. Adjust any of the seasonings to your taste.

If you have any leftover filling, place it in aluminum foil and crimp the edges to form a small pouch. Poke holes small enough to let

8–10 Mexican gray squash (*calabacitas*)

1 lb ground lamb

½ lb medium grain rice

2 tablespoons olive oil

5 cloves of garlic, minced

2 tablespoons tomato paste

2 teaspoons seven spice blend

4 cups beef broth

½ cup lemon juice, freshly squeezed

3 teaspoons dried mint

2 tablespoons pomegranate molasses

Salt, to taste

1–2 carrots, thickly sliced (optional)

broth in, while not allowing the rice to fall out. Set the pouch over the squash.

Pour seasoned broth over the squash and pouch. Place a heavy, heat-proof plate on top to weigh the squash down and keep them from floating. Add water to make sure the squash are fully submerged. The amount of water will depend on the size pot you use.

Bring the pot to a boil and then reduce heat to maintain a light simmer for 45–60 minutes.

Notes: You can typically find seven spice blends in most Middle Eastern grocery stores. They are sometimes labeled as "Lebanese" or "Syrian." You can also make your own blend at home. Every house has their own ratios. Mine is mostly allspice (~75%), some cinnamon (~10%), and a little bit of cardamom, black peppercorns, nutmeg, cloves, and ginger. Alternatively, you can use ground allspice if that is all you have. If you do not have access to ground lamb, you can use ground beef. If you find lamb to be too gamey, I recommend mixing it with ground beef (50/50) to cut some of the gaminess.

8

The Map to Myself

I don't know if I have found what I was looking for. I don't know if anyone ever does. I have learned a lot about myself through my journey though. From my emigration to my immigration, I have looked for my reflection in a largely white society. I knew I was different, but I have turned into a chameleon. I have learned to camouflage to blend into my constantly changing environments. I realized pretty early on that my idea of how people viewed me and their actual perceptions of me were not the same, but I learned to use this to my advantage. I came to understand what people needed me to be; a friend of color, an ethnic entrepreneur, a minority business owner, an immigrant—almost like an adult version of show and tell. I have absorbed every ounce of that, and it has become my superpower. I have learned to read people and use it to my advantage. I became a better chef, a stronger woman, a parent that could draw from multiple cultures, a successful business-woman. I learned to navigate my parallel paths. I came to the United States to be someone else, and now, try as I may, the world I would like to go back to does not exist.

Being an immigrant, by choice or otherwise, teaches you to mold into a different character than the role that was given to you. It forces you to look beyond the obvious and find a new reality, a new you. To leather your surface and brace your emotions. At least that is what was necessary for me to adapt; to wear this new skin. I had to be single-minded in my drive. I had to overcome the hurdles that came with being a desi girl and break the ties of tradition at home, and I also had to face the challenges that came with being a desi girl in the United States. The accent, the slang, the dress code, the music. All I wanted was to blend in. But when you have chosen to bend the rules across continents, it is not so easy to disappear. You sort of stick out in every situation.

All of that adapting and adjusting over the years was preparing me for this very moment in time. The year of COVID-19. This is the year that broke the best, but for me, this year was an awakening. Since I molted from Sangeeta to Sang, I have been coasting along. I didn't leave my home behind to come here and coast. I came here to chase dreams. COVID-19 reminded me of that. What a strange blessing to be smacked over the head with. What an unexpected wake-up call. It was time, once again, to rediscover myself. To reinvent myself.

As with all roads, mine has been full of misadventures, unexpected turns, and failed plans. Isn't that the one constant in life though? It seldom reflects your dreams. As a seventeen-year-old, I fought and cried and raged until my family finally caved to my demand to go to art school in the United States. So this crazy, rebellious teenager from Bombay came to conquer the quiet streets of Ohio. After a short detour at my aunt's house in Dayton, and a few other escapades over the next year, I walked into the hallowed halls of the Columbus College of Art & Design. I knew, for sure, that my name was going to light up the bill-boards, given the opportunity. From poetry to painting, my art was going to shake the world. My pain, my words, my experiences, were the end-all. I was going to awaken souls. Nobody understood the world like I did. This was fact. This was also, as the kids would say, a true LOL moment. I had no idea what any of that meant. I was raised in an elite world. I knew no real pain. I had never sacrificed anything. I had no life-changing experiences. I came here naive, hungry, and wide-eyed.

I took art school by storm. I was a rare bird. There was only one other student from India during those years. I liked how the other students fawned over my words, my stories of home, my exclusiveness.

My new friends were so curious about my life and why I came to the United States. The biggest shock to them, and to me, was the confusion over my mastery of the English language. I did not expect to teach history when I got here, but I enjoyed having an upper hand in this situation. I also had a little fun at their expense. I taught some facts: India was colonized until very recently, and even though Gandhiji drove away the tyrants on an empty stomach, we held on to the queen's language. But, for my personal amusement, I also told them that our mail was delivered via camels.

I understand that I had led a privileged life and had traveled a lot, but I expected a lot more from college-age students in a first world country. I was a little shocked at the level of ignorance about other countries and their cultures. It was a substantial part of our education in India. So I took advantage of it. After all, I had come here to reinvent myself. The images of India that they had come to recognize via *The National Geographic* were completely shattered when they saw my pictures of home. Come on, I had to get some pleasure out of this interaction! I really enjoyed being in art school. The freedom to be whoever I wanted, dress however I wanted, think for myself, create, feel, lose myself so I could ultimately find myself, these were all novel notions to me, and I was in love with all of it. Until the day that I realized that I didn't want to be an artist.

I had always known that I was creative, but I didn't know what that meant. I don't know if it was a label my parents forced on me along with all the art and music classes, or if I took it more seriously because I needed that outlet in my childhood, but I don't think anyone thought it would be permanent. For as much as my family supported women being educated and chasing their dreams, at the end of the day, that dream was supposed to come to rest at the feet of the perfect marriage. Only then did the woman truly have time to be creative. She could paint her pretty watercolors while raising her adoring children and making sure her husband was well taken care of. But in my small world, poets, writers, and artists were creatives. To me it was a title. Little did I realize that it was a philosophy. A way of being. An idea that could be transformed or transform all things around me. Had I misinterpreted my dreams? Had I come all this way to find out that I was wrong?

I missed home. I really missed the food more than anything. Food is such a huge part of what ties us to our memories. Certain tastes and smells transport us so effortlessly. I had lived a privileged life and had never learned to cook. That was my grandmother's crown to wear. She decided the daily menu, she yelled at the staff till perfection was achieved, she knew exactly which auntie or which cousin favored certain foods, she knew when we had exams or sports meets and would make sure it was reflected in what we ate that day. She told us stories of ancient times and fables as she slowly coaxed small bites into our mouths. I had never thought about where the food came from; it was just always present. Now, here I was, a million miles from home. I was surrounded by all these colors, but my life lacked flavor. To look back on my childhood, I wonder how much these memories played into my choices as a chef. The importance of being able to travel to distant lands or conjure up places through taste. The value of building those relationships around food or at the table. I have heard friends over the years share stories of making pies or canning fruit at their grandparents', but it just doesn't seem to compare with my memories from home. Be it weddings or mango season or Diwali, the Festival of Lights, our house would fill up with aunties. Related aunties, neighborhood aunties, aunties young and old would gather around my grandmother. Knives and tongues sharpened for the day. How I wish I could go back to those days of cooking and storytelling. A constant banter of matchmaking and gossip. The house was filled with pungent, spicy, sweet, and sour aromas of pickles and mangoes, jaggery and chilis. Days that I shrugged off in my preteen years. Voices I shut out because I did not want to hear about how I was ruining my chances of a good match. That is what I was homesick for, but those moments were gone. They would never be re-created.

So I went in search of myself again. I moved to London. I reinvented myself once again. I worked, made new friends, applied to art school but never followed through. Something didn't fit. I met so many new people, travelers from across the world. Everyone had an amazing story. I met a lawyer from South Africa, out to see the world; I met some models from France, in search of work in London; I made some really good friends from Serbia who came hidden on the backs of trucks, got deported, and snuck back in on another truck. I met Filipinas and learned how to cook adobo. I drank vodka with the Serbians, I ate cheese with my French friends, I ate goulash and fish and chips; I went to Wembley and ate all the Indian food I had missed over the last few years; but again, something was amiss. I blended in too easily. I felt like I had moved across the world, but yet I was completely surrounded by familiarity. Almost like I had come back home. There were so many Indians and as many Britons that had some connection to India. How was I to grow if I stayed the same?

As homesick as I was, I knew that if I fell back into the comfort of familiarity I would never push myself to be the person I was chasing. I was still on this path with no end in sight. I still did not know what I was chasing. I knew, for sure, that once I had picked a trade, I would be the best at it. But what was it? Maybe I was meant for the United States. That promise of a certain freedom. The allure of being whoever you wanted to be. The rebelliousness and mischief of being American, that is what I was about. No matter how liberal a family one might grow up with in India, there are limits. My family traveled and placed importance on education. We were allowed to wear shorts and eat meat. We were allowed to go to clubs and dance the night away. But everything was within a box. We were Indian first. We showed respect to our elders by bowing down and touching their feet. We dressed modestly when we were around family. We crossed our legs and spoke in hushed tones. We studied hard and stayed disciplined. We were allowed to dream, but we knew our dreams were only dreams. We did not choose our own futures. Our families made the bigger decisions. They would choose our colleges and careers, and when the time came, our husbands.

America was, to me, the land of opportunity, the promise of freedom. A place where eighteen-year-old kids were considered adults and were no longer answerable to their parents. American kids were allowed to dream, and then chase those very dreams. There is a fearlessness about kids here. Failure is an option. The world looks at Americans with disdain, but to me, the idea that you could be whoever you chose to be outweighed everything else. I could come to the United States, hold on to my Indian beliefs, and still be able to carve my own future. I wanted to have my own experiences. I wanted to live a life that did not end with finding a good husband. I wanted to laugh and meet people outside what was expected from me. I did not want to be stuck in my social environment. I wanted to know who I was if all the chains were broken. So I came back to Columbus, Ohio.

My family still lived in Mumbai (Bombay to those of us that lived there). They were becoming very annoyed with me. This was not typical behavior for a good Indian girl. For any Indian girl, really. I should have been well on my way to medical school or pursuing a law or business degree. Here I was, floundering across continents, unsure of everything, but stubborn to the core. I refused to go back home. I just did not belong there. The slights of racism I witnessed in the United States were equal to the slights of sexism I had witnessed at home. I choose to use the word "witnessed," and not "experienced," because I have always been able to look at slights against me from outside myself, like those things didn't happen to me. In a sense it is my defense mechanism. I do not want other people's actions defining me or taking anything away from me. In India, women are constantly subjected to shame. As a woman, you have no worth besides what is bestowed upon you by a man. In the United States, the same skewed logic applies toward people of color. You have no worth besides what is bestowed upon you by white society. I was a misfit there, as much as I was here. The difference was, in India, in those years, I would have just disappeared into a life chosen for me. I would not have had the strength to fight my family if they were facing me. Here, I was not obligated to entertain anyone else's whims. I had to find another place in the world; at least until I knew who I was.

I started working at a little pizza shop close to me that had just opened its doors. That was my first kitchen job. I loved it instantly! I fell in love with the chaos and culture of the kitchen. I fell in love with the equality between the punk rock server, the delivery driver trying to pay for college, the dope head that was just content with his life, and everyone else in between. I fell in love with the idea of this simple dish that united all walks of life. And then, I fell in love with my boss. I dated, worked, went to shows, got tattooed, drank, smoked, and did all the things a twenty-one-year-old American kid does. I was having the time of my life. Still restless and looking for a challenge, I became more engrossed in the workings of Hounddog's Pizza. I really came to love the hands-on work. I slowly started getting interested in the business end of the restaurant. A year later, to the chagrin of my traditionalist Indian family and my partner's born-again Christian family, we got married. I looked beyond race and religion. I was a step closer to finding my place. Because of my "shocking" ability to speak English so well, and my ability to converse with most people, his family slowly started accepting me. Thirty years later, my own family is still learning to accept me. Together we grew this little family business into a campus institution at Ohio State. When the space next to us opened up, we added a twenty-four-hour dining room. We worked all the time. As we built the business, we kept growing the menu. This was the first time since I left home that I felt a sense of comfort. We had two boys in the midst of all of that, and I slipped into yet another role. Another space opened up next to the restaurant, so we opened Ravari Room, a music venue named after our kids, Ravi and Ari.

Now that I had kids and I was so far away from home, I craved familiarity. The only way I knew how to raise children was how I had been raised. I wanted home-cooked meals. I missed the smell of spices frying, hot chapatis and ghee. I missed mango season, and the endless jars of pickles. I missed the sounds of the mortar and pestle and the shrill whistle of the pressure cooker. So, I started to teach myself how to cook. At that time, there was one little Indian store in Columbus, and it wasn't very well stocked. I improvised. I taught myself how to blend spices and create familiar flavors with whatever was at hand. I wasn't really cooking Indian food, but I was learning how to mold American dishes into more cross-cultural meals. My memories were playing tricks on me. I knew how the dishes I craved should taste, I thought, but it had been so long that I wasn't sure anymore. I never did develop a palate for most American foods and could not bring myself to feed my kids premade, processed foods, so I started spending more time in the kitchen. I had found my creative space.

I learned some things about myself in those years. I need constant change. I was restless because I like to be challenged. I need rules, so

I can bend them. I need problems, so I can find solutions. I need things to break, so I can fix them. So, eight years later, when my marriage broke, I slipped very easily into my next avatar. Single mom and entrepreneur.

I opened Bodega, a little neighborhood bar in the Short North Arts District of Columbus. By then my appetite for cooking had grown by leaps. I tried my hand at culinary school, but, once again, school was just not for me. So, I taught myself. I tried every kind of food I could. I learned about wines. I developed a taste for the stinkiest of cheeses. I was ravenous. I opened Bodega with a partner who had vision and an uncanny entrepreneurial spirit. We created a unique draft list and a small, but creative menu. We were way ahead of our times in Columbus. Within a year, we had fifty microbrews on draft, hundreds of hand-picked beers and wines, and a crafty little menu consisting of small plates, soups, and paninis. Business boomed, and I slipped into the comfort of my role. Everything was exactly how it was supposed to be. Bodega received more awards than I could have imagined. No matter where I was in Columbus, people recognized me. My kids were in awe of the fact that everyone knew them. We always joked that they could never get lost in Columbus because they were always two people away from me. It never occurred to me that I might be recognizable because of my ethnicity. Because I was one out of maybe two or three Indians in Columbus that were in the restaurant industry, other than those that owned Indian restaurants.

It never crossed my mind that I stood out for any other reason than my hard work and talents. With every interview, with every new conversation, with every new friend, the questions were consistent: Where did you learn to speak English? Why did you come here? Isn't it hard being a woman of color in this arena? At some point, I started questioning myself. I began to wonder *why* I was being asked those questions. I had fought so hard, for so long not to be recognized for my ethnicity that I couldn't even remember why. When I first moved to the United States, I noticed that people here had a very particular idea about Indians. We all spoke English with accents, we smelled like curry, we were super nerdy, and then came *The Simpsons*, with the iconic Apu, and America finally had its validation. I had left behind the walls that stifled me in India, and I was not about to give this country the privilege of reducing me to an Indian stereotype.

My name wasn't on billboards like I had predicted years ago, but it was in every local magazine. It felt like a stepping-stone. There was more out there. There were more accolades. More mountains to climb. More walls to tear down. As my network grew, so did my appetite for knowledge. For the first time, I started noticing my environment. Not just the space around me but more so the people that filled it. The relationships people had with food. I started talking to our vendors, and customers. Now that my kids were older, it was harder to take our annual pilgrimage to India. School, sports, and work, all seemed to get in the way of our month-long excursions. As I traveled back home less frequently, I noticed the things that I had taken for granted before. Everything in India came from "farmer's markets"; everything I was consuming in the United States might have started its journey on a farm, but the produce had been so altered along the way that I was certain it should no longer be called vegetables. People around me spoke of farmer's markets like they were only for the privileged, or something you visited while touring California. No one really questioned where their food came from. It was just the way it was.

So I started a new venture. The Table. A locally sourced, globally inspired restaurant. With that came new challenges, and new wins. I had learned so much, I had grown so much, I felt like I was at the top of my game. I vowed to make The Table a teaching kitchen. I wanted to share my knowledge and skills with my staff. From an education standpoint, I knew that school was not an option or choice for everyone. I had learned, over the years, that to hone a skill, real-world practice was the most efficient tool. The best thing I could do for anyone entering the culinary world was to immerse them in all the knowledge I could share and give them the space to create. From an entrepreneurial angle, I wanted to teach them how to dream big, and also to know that dreams can turn into a reality. I wanted to teach them how to write a business plan, how to manage food and labor costs, and, most importantly, how to lead and nurture their own teams. The Table would be my legacy. I wanted to share my immigrant journey through food. I would take my guests on trips all across the world. I worked hard to teach my staff about global flavors, and watched the guests lap it up. I teamed up with farmers across Ohio and shared their products and stories with our staff and guests. I was disciplined about food waste and took a holistic approach to sustainability. I had, firsthand, experienced the challenges of being a woman in my field, so I made it my mission to staff the line with female cooks and bakers. I taught them how to ignore the boys' club and be proud of themselves.

Slowly, but surely, I was getting recognition as more than an entrepreneur. I was being noticed as a chef. I was being invited by other chefs to cook alongside them. I got opportunities to work with a lot of amazing people and showcase my talents at a number of events. I was invited to take part in James Beard dinners, and got a page in *Truth, Love & Clean Cutlery*, a guide to exemplary, organic, sustainable, and ethical restaurants edited by Alice Waters, the grande dame of the farm-to-table movement in the United States. I was recognized as a leader in hospitality by the Asian American Commerce Group. The restaurant was getting a lot of press. With every interview or write-up there was always an underlying query about how I, an immigrant woman, had succeeded. Because, obviously, I should be running an Indian restaurant. I was upsetting the world of the white male chef.

I was now much more in tune with the raised eyebrow. I recognized the pale scent of racism and sexism much more easily. Nobody was ever directly confrontational about my achievements, but there was a low-level hum that I became accustomed to. It wasn't just the media; it was other chefs too. I also noticed that it wasn't just about what I could bring to the table (the pun is unavoidable!) but that I offered diversity. I made them look good; not only did they have a female chef to work alongside but a woman of color to boot. It had the best effect on me. It made me stronger and more determined to be true to myself. I started shaking off Sang, a name chosen for me in high school when we tried to form our own identities; I was Sangeeta once again. I made it a point to introduce myself by my full name. I dug my heels in, and for the first time in a long time, I felt comfortable in my skin. I was finally there. I had reached my pinnacle. Everything would be smooth sailing from here on out.

On March 14, 2020, Governor DeWine issued the order to shut down all restaurants in Ohio. COVID-19 had broken the world. It is one thing to say, "The rug was pulled out from under me"; it is a whole other feeling to be standing on said rug as it gets pulled out from under you. It doesn't just take your legs out, or even knock the wind out of you; you feel every part of yourself sinking, from your breath to your heart to your stomach and then your legs. At some point I made contact with my brain and registered the shock. The staff slowly started trickling in at the restaurant. When you are faced with a once-in-a-lifetime moment, you are not really sure what to do with it. How do you process something you just cannot grasp? We all stood around wide-eyed, as though at a funeral. I knew we had to get the restaurant organized. There was food to take care of and a kitchen to be cleaned. There were open bottles of wine to be dealt with. We made a decision and did the most important thing first. We drank all the wine. Then we opened a few more bottles for posterity and drank those. I bid everyone a safe trip home, we called our respective rides, and went home to pass out. I remember waking up at three o'clock in the morning, but not in that soothing gentle way one opens their eyes after a restful night. More like someone that has stopped breathing and finally gets air pumped into their lungs. I awoke in an absolute panic.

I knew there was so much to be taken care of. The first thing I did in those early hours was to start a fund drive for the team. I knew only too well how tough this was going to be for service staff. Service industry staff is like an army of ghost warriors. We are there to share in all your celebratory moments, and we are there for all your heartbreaks. Whether it is the servers anticipating every need, the mood, helping to create the perfect proposal, staying in the shadows during an important work dinner, or maybe even inserting a joke at the right moment to help you break the ice at a first date; or the bartender that has ears for days, can make multiple drinks while listening to one customer and reminding another that one heartbreak does not end the world; or the true invisibles working long hours in hot kitchens and airless basements to make sure that every morsel dances on your tongue. Together we take you away to distant lands or a much-needed two-hour vacation or the perfect wedding, all without being noticed.

The next day I cried. I cried until the tears had dried up, and then I cried with my entire body. Almost like dry heaving. I didn't recognize the sounds coming out of me, some dark sadness from the depths. Like a scene out of *Aliens*, where your body contorts and writhes until something unrecognizable tears through. It was time to change again.

Restaurants had been shut down for about two weeks when another local chef and I started chatting about the service industry. We had both had to lay off multiple staff members and had a similar sense of foreboding. We knew how truly difficult this shutdown was going to be. We could not sit around and wring our hands when it was time to roll up our sleeves. We are leaders in our community, in our industry. That doesn't change when ships are sinking. We knew it was time to step up and make a difference. So, we started making calls. We called everyone in our network, and some outside it. We realized very quickly that people were looking for ways to help, but they just didn't know how. Within two weeks, with a small army of amazing, creative, generous, kind, and incredibly hard-working people that barely knew each other, we launched "Service! Relief Effort for Hospitality Workers." Our goal was to help as many people in the service industry as we could.

By April 4, three weeks after the state shutdown, we started doing the one thing we knew how. We started cooking. We were donated space in a commercial kitchen, and thanks to some seed money from a few local companies, we were able to move forward. We hired some of our immigrant staff that we knew would not be able to get unemployment, even though they paid taxes, and we got to work. For the next eight weeks, we put out two hundred meals a day for out-of-work industry workers and their families. These were well executed, chef-driven meals just like they would have enjoyed at the restaurants they used to work at. It was a fast turnaround for a grassroots nonprofit! Within a few days of us launching, funds and volunteers were pouring in. Most of it was through word of mouth and social media, but individuals started donating whatever they could. We were a small team of acquaintances that became fast friends in our effort to do the right thing. The kitchen staff worked their behinds off because not only were they incredibly grateful to have a job, but they knew that these meals were going to feed their friends, colleagues, and coworkers, and it flamed an unspoken will to work even harder. As friends came together to design websites or fundraise, or old staff members volunteered to pass out meals at the pick-up locations, our intentions deepened. There were so many lessons to learn. I had always given time to charitable organizations, but I had never been part of building one from the ground up. The one thing that will stay with me is how easily people open their hearts. To watch the community in Columbus come together and give time, talents, money, and support is one of the most gratifying experiences I have had.

We chose a few locations around town where people could come pick up their meals. It was the first few weeks of the quarantine, so the streets were dead. Initially people were a little hesitant to stop by. Being in the service industry, we are not used to going hungry. There might be a lot of other debts looming, but hunger was hardly an issue. Most restaurants provide some version of a staff meal. Standing in a food line was a little scary or maybe even humbling for some people. But in a tight-knit community like ours, word spreads fast. As the lines grew, so did our interactions with the community. We heard stories of unemployment failures, fear of other bills looming, families stuck at home with no incomes and an inability to provide the basics. We talked endlessly to people that were just lonely. To come from such a customer-driven background and to suddenly be isolated can be brutal. That brief interaction while picking up dinner also provided a place for people to share their experiences and know that they were not alone in this. It gave all of us a sense of purpose. We gathered resources such as unemployment help, free food, local and national grants, job openings, anything that could help lessen the burden, and added it to our website and emails. We knew we were on the right track, and we had to keep pushing forward.

The Service Relief Pickup Station during lockdown

The Map to Myself

As people started getting their feet under them, and restaurants were partially reopening, a fresh new wave of pain and anger threatened to drown us. The country had taken to the streets to fight for equality. With the protests in the foreground and COVID-19 surging in the background, businesses were at a standstill. People were not comfortable going out to pick up meals, and workers were finally getting some relief from unemployment benefits. So we took a break from serving meals to reevaluate the needs of the industry. Let me remind you that while all this was going on, my own restaurant had struggled and finally shut its doors. I was lucky enough to have settled up with our vendors and staff, but the bank and the IRS had a noose around my neck. Reopening under the new rules was just not an option for us, and carryout was too unpredictable day to day to sustain us. As that struggle carried on, I continued to fight to help others in the industry.

After a brief survey, we came to learn that people needed fiscal help. Now that deferment programs were coming to an end, and everyone from utilities to landlords were knocking on doors, a lack of funds was the number one issue. Service! had created enough buzz locally to be included in some larger fundraising efforts. NBC4 made us the recipients of a telethon, The Big Give brought us in under their umbrella, private donors were reaching out, magazines, marathon runners, coffee shops, you name it—for round two of Service! We handed out $250 grants to twenty-five applicants every week for the next eight weeks. We wanted to touch as many people as we could. Hospitality workers went through our website and answered a few questions and turned in some basic paperwork to prove that they were working in the service industry or had recently been laid off. If everything was turned in, they got the money. We did not want to make it any more difficult or shameful for them to get the help they so desperately needed.

The majority of the applicants were immigrants. They worked mostly at the convention center or at hotel banquet halls. A lot of them struggled with English and could not navigate the unemployment maelstrom that was still a cause of frustration. A lot of them were unsure of how to get any other help, or where to even look for it. Most did not have any other experience to put on their résumés, besides banquets, to qualify for another job during such an unstable time. A majority of businesses were on a hiring freeze or being very selective. Immigrants had it much worse in this scenario. They could not fall back on the skills they had and were lacking resources to find new employment. Now we were into the fall of 2020. As much as restaurants were trying to regain "the new normal" (probably the most hated phrase of 2020, along with "pivot"), and staff were trying to get employed again, the limits put into place by the state made it very difficult for day-to-day operations. Staff weren't able to get enough hours, and restaurants were constantly shutting down because of contamination. To add to the uncertainty and stress, there seemed to be a huge divide over the mask mandate, which made an already fragile moment even more strenuous. Every day we would hear of more restaurants shutting their doors for good. But it was not just about restaurants. What we failed to see was the bigger picture. Our stakeholders. Restaurant shutdowns had a terrible effect on farmers, breweries, beverage vendors, linen companies, local craftspeople, and so many more businesses that rely on restaurants purchasing their product. As much as I wanted to help everyone, we had to stay focused. We were committed to helping service industry workers. So we went back to work. We worked on raising more money, we sent out updated resource lists, we sent out links to job openings as they came about, and we gave out turkeys and sides for Thanksgiving. There is always more work to be done.

As we keep growing Service! we hope to use our collective knowledge of the hospitality industry to lay groundwork for some real change. If there is anything I have learned after twenty-five years in this industry it is that we have perpetuated a broken and antiquated system. There need to be more resources, mentors, and stalwarts to help the next generation of industry workers. We need to educate one another and be prepared so we do not find ourselves in this position again. I never thought that I would do anything besides work in the restaurant industry, but working behind the scenes to support the industry has been so much more gratifying. And so here I am, slipping into yet another role.

It seems like the longer I stay away from home, the more I come back to my roots. My grandparents had set up charities and resource centers to help women and children, to teach them skills, help them learn trades, educate children, assist with medical bills, and so on. I had always looked up to them for being so intent in their giving. For their times, in a regressive society like India, my grandparents fought for women's rights. My grandfather, a doctor, treated the underprivileged and took care of the women that were forced to work in the red-light district. He brought his family to the bright lights of Mumbai in 1940. He made sure his siblings had the best education while he was still in residency himself. He built a beautiful home. He made sure his wife, siblings, and kids would never want for anything. As he amassed his wealth, he made sure he reminded his family of their obligations as a community. He was a powerhouse. The sound of his footsteps on the front stairs brought the whole house to a standstill except for us, his grandchildren—those footfalls were what we waited for. He never walked into that house without gifts for us. Every single day.

My grandmother was the proud daughter of a lawyer. She brought the lessons she had learned in her youth to her husband's house. She ran that house like it was her crowning jewel. She was always dressed in the finest saris, perfectly pleated and tucked; hair combed back into a neat little bun; a red bindi placed directly in the middle of her forehead, and the faintest smell of roses. She was most definitely the woman behind the man. Ultimately, every decision was made by her. There was a constant stream of visitors to our house. Everyone that came by was looking for help in some form, whether it was financial, a reference, help resolving a family disagreement, advice on a wedding match, or sometimes just wisdom. Nobody walked away empty-handed. More importantly, nobody walked away hungry. All matters big and small were taken care of around the table. No matter what the answer was, my grandmother made sure the guests were well fed before they left. My grandparents gave their time and money with open hearts. That selflessness, I believe, was latently instilled in us. My father feeds hundreds of cancer patients and their families every week, patients that come from all over India to the only free cancer center without a penny in their pockets. A lot of them sleep on the streets outside the hospital, elderly and babies alike. With no roof over their heads, and no money to buy any food, these hapless families wait around for weeks or months while their loved ones are in the hospital. My father decided to carry on his parents' legacy by donating money for hot meals and making sure to hand out as many meals in person as he can. He listens to their struggles, wipes away some tears, and maybe sneaks an extra pack of cookies to some little kid. I feel like the years of service in my family have come home to roost within me. I am the carrier of this legacy, and I could not be prouder.

In the downtime between Service! projects, I started cooking again. I did not pursue the quarantine sourdough challenge, or perfect any baking skills. Instead, I took to cooking Indian food, the one cuisine I had pushed away for so long. For years I cooked Indian like I cooked Thai or French or anything else. Peripherally, with no real attachment. But now it was different. Maybe it was because I was homesick. Maybe it was because I had more time now. Maybe it was because I needed comfort and wished my great grandmother or my grandma were coaxing little bites of *khichdi* (rice and lentils cooked together) and *dahi* (yogurt) into my mouth. I am not sure what sparked this need, but I was all in. Every auntie's eye roll came to mind as I worked on the perfect round chapati. According to the mother of all auntie superstitions, a woman could not find the right husband unless she could roll a perfectly circular chapati. In my case, I already had the perfect man, now I just needed to use my round chapati–making guiles to keep him happy forever. I labored over marinades and curries and blended all my spices from scratch. I got recipes via WhatsApp from family members and housekeepers in India and tried to re-create dishes from my past. As I shared the dishes with friends and family here, I told stories of home, and I realized how much I had buried. As I conjured up these forgotten recipes, along with them came memories. I came to understand how intertwined food and my memories of home were. So I cooked more.

The more I remembered, the murkier the waters got. It has been so hard to explain to my family, both in India and in Columbus, what I am going through right now. I am desperately trying to reclaim my heritage, bring my memories to life. But the harder I try, the further I get from it. The India of my past, Bombay from over thirty years ago, does not exist. India is a booming economy full of tech wizards and future software gurus; Bombay is now Mumbai. The little corner shops we ran to after school to buy crazy neon-colored candies and cute little scented stickers have now been replaced with Hermès and Rolex stores. The street food vendors that we all lined up for, salivating and hoping they didn't sell out before it was our turn, have been replaced by brick-and-mortar chef-driven restaurants using molecular gastronomy. My grandmother's reign over the kitchen and the importance of perfect spice blends have been usurped by store-bought, prepackaged masalas.

My mother, a child of the feminist movement, fought her way out of the kitchen. She has no interest in sitting around the table and coaxing bites of food into her grandkids' mouths. She has no time to dwell on the past. My grandmother took the stories with her. My family in India marched on without me. Their lives kept evolving, but I was not a part of those anecdotes. My kids are grown. They were raised with me cooking elaborate meals and regaling them with stories of my childhood, but they have nothing to connect them to. On our rare trips home, they do not recognize the places from my stories. I guess I don't either.

I have freed myself from guilt and expectations. I can still be anyone I want to be. The world still has room for my dreams. As my name rolls off my tongue effortlessly, I wait patiently as people try to pronounce it. I am Sangeeta Lakhani, and once again I stare at my next chapter, naive, hungry, and wide-eyed.

Murgh Makhani (Butter Chicken)

Serves 4

This dish brings back so many memories of my childhood. I can recall in an instant sitting at Shalimar Restaurant with my family. Sunday nights were our nights together. My grandad always wanted to go to the same place, even though the food was better at other restaurants. We were raised in a vegetarian household, but on Sundays at Shalimar, we were allowed to eat anything we desired. For me, it was always murgh makhani *and* roomali roti, *tender pieces of marinated and grilled chicken cooked in a creamy tomato sauce and a handkerchief-thin, soft flat bread to soak it all up. There was a dance floor with a live band; and as my parents took over the dance floor to boogie to the disco beats of ABBA and the Bee Gees, all I could do was dream of eating the same meal next week. This is a two-part recipe, first the tandoori chicken and then the gravy. You could just stop at the tandoori chicken and enjoy that as it is, but it is worth the extra step to make the butter chicken!*

Method

Add the ginger, garlic, and green chili in a wet grinder and blend to a smooth paste. Mix the yogurt with the gram flour in a bowl to get rid of any lumps to form a thick paste consistency. Add the ginger, garlic, chili paste, paprika, chili powder, garam masala, and coriander powder. Also mix in the ground cinnamon, saffron, and salt. Stir well and add the chicken pieces. Mix well, making sure to coat the chicken pieces in the thick marinade. Leave to marinate for a few hours or even over-night if you prefer.

Soak wooden skewers in water. Preheat the grill on medium. Shake off the excess marinade and thread the chicken pieces onto the skewers

For the tandoori chicken

1 lb (450 g) skinless, boneless chicken thighs cut into bite-size pieces

2 tablespoons thick yogurt/Greek yogurt

2 teaspoons chickpea flour/gram flour

4 cloves garlic

1-inch piece ginger peeled

1 green chili

1 teaspoon mild paprika

½ teaspoon chili powder (or a little more if you would like it spicy)

½ teaspoon garam masala powder

1 teaspoon coriander powder

Pinch cinnamon powder

Pinch of saffron crushed

Salt to taste

Butter for basting

1 teaspoon *chaat* masala*

Juice of ½ lemon*

For murgh makhani (butter chicken)

1 ½ tablespoons unsalted butter

5 green cardamom pods, lightly crushed

1-inch cinnamon stick

4 cloves

1 small onion, finely chopped

1 heaped tablespoon grated ginger

2 green chilies, slit lengthwise

1 teaspoon Kashmiri chili powder (or mild paprika)

½ teaspoon garam masala powder

3 tablespoons tomato puree

5 ounces (150 ml) heavy cream

2 tablespoons honey

1 tablespoon *Kasoori methi* (fenugreek leaf powder)

Salt to taste

Chopped cilantro for garnish

and place them on a wire rack. Cook under the grill for 15–20 minutes. Turn the skewers every 5 minutes and baste with melted butter until the juices run clear and they are cooked through, slightly charred around the edges. You can also do this step in an oven instead of a grill.

*If you are stopping after this step, sprinkle the tikka (grilled chicken pieces) with the *chaat* masala, juice of ½ lemon, and cilantro. If you plan on continuing, omit the *chaat* masala and lemon juice.

Once the chicken is cooked, set aside and proceed to make the *makhani* sauce below. This can even be done a few hours or a day in advance.

Heat a heavy-bottom sauce pan and add the butter. Add green cardamom, cinnamon stick, and cloves. Fry for 20 seconds, add the onions and sauté for 5–7 minutes on medium heat until they take on a light brown color.

Add the grated ginger and slit green chilies. Fry for a further minute and add the chili powder, garam masala powder, and the tomato puree. Stir well and cook for a couple of minutes. Now gradually add the double cream, stirring continuously to mix all the spices with the cream. Simmer and cook for 2–3 minutes.

At this stage add a splash of water if the curry is too thick. Stir in the honey and the fenugreek powder. Season to taste. Now add the cooked chicken pieces and simmer the curry on a low heat for 8–10 minutes. Garnish with cilantro and serve with roti or paratha.

9

There Will Always Be a Sea

Being Filipino means there will always be a sea.

Whether it is the water between the beaches of California and the Homeland, or whether it is a space between a parent and child who disagree on what "homeland" means: being Filipino means there will always be a sea. A sea of sacrifice between me and my family who immigrated before; a sea between my "perfect English" and the sounds the elders make with their mouths when they want to keep a secret. Being Filipino means there will always be a sea. Like drowning in a mass of people, chanting in protest under the summer of 2020 sun, wondering if you can say you are not racist, remembering how badly you once wished you were white. Being Filipino means there will always be a sea. Maybe it is the tidal wave of news of the latest typhoon, or the flood of numbers like "nearly a third of the nurses who've died of coronavirus in the US are Filipino, even though Filipino nurses make up just 4% of the nursing population nationwide."[1] Being Filipino means there will always be a sea. Even when your bedroom becomes an island, when the sidewalk becomes a shoreline; when COVID-19 lockdown makes you a castaway to the island of your own life.

Still, being Filipino means there will always be a sea.

Like the sea of brown bodies speckling the patio under the hot sun of summer 2021: laughing, mouths full of garlic and chicken

Kitchen of the Restaurant
Kasama in Chicago

adobo, pushing all the two-top tables just to sit together. Like the tide of orders spanning expo and the wave of sizzling *longanisa* and *tocino* grilling over charcoal. Like the roll of Chicago rain, pouring over the streets as you eat Filipino barbecue with your coworkers in a crammed car, and talk about how you don't pray anymore, but it seems like a prayer answered: how you all came to work at Kasama, a restaurant named "togetherness" in your mother tongue, to reconnect with people like yourself: people who have felt like an island, apart from each other.

Being Filipino means there will always be a sea. But someday, that sea might be the eyes of a coworker, who understands what it is like to come back, humbly, to a culture you left behind. Sharing a quiet moment together, when you notice each hand preparing a serving of your favorite childhood dish is a hand like yours, with brown skin, and a history of sea tattooed on them too.

Note

1. Catherine E. Shoichet, "Covid-19 Is Taking a Devastating Toll on Filipino American Nurses," CNN, December 11, 2020, https://www.cnn.com/2020 /11/24/health/filipino-nurse-deaths/.

Kasama Chicken Adobo

Method

Start by dissolving 1 heaping teaspoon of salt in 4 cups cold water. At Kasama we use a 2 percent brine to add salinity and moisture to the chicken. If your recipe is smaller or larger you can adjust the brine by using whatever amount of water you see fit and then adding 2 percent salt by weight.

Add your chicken to the brine and let sit for 24 hours in the refrigerator.

After your chicken has been brining for at least 24 hours you can remove it from the brine.

In a medium pot, add your oil and begin to brown your minced garlic. Once the garlic begins to brown, add your chicken to the pot. Add the soy sauce, vinegar, 7 Up, bay leaves, and black pepper to the pot. Put a lid on the pot and cook in a 350°F oven for 45 minutes.

After 45 minutes, remove your pot from the oven and let your chicken rest in the pot without the lid for an additional 35 minutes.

Remove the chicken from the liquid and let it rest on a tray. Add 1 cup of dark brown sugar to the remaining liquid and on medium/low heat allow the sugar to dissolve and the sauce to reduce slightly. Once your sauce has thickened you can remove the pot from the heat.

You can then grill your chicken and use the reserved chicken adobo sauce to baste with a grill brush. The sugar in the sauce will help your chicken to caramelize on the grill. If you are cooking inside, you can use your broiler to finish the chicken adobo. Enjoy with steamed rice or some roasted veggies!

2 lb chicken thighs

1 heaping tablespoon salt (20 g)

4 cups water (1,000 g)

1 cup soy sauce

1 cup white vinegar

1 cup 7 Up

6 cloves minced garlic

2 tablespoon canola oil

4 bay leaves

½ teaspoon ground black pepper

1 cup dark brown sugar

Food and Caring during the Times of COVID-19 on the U.S.–Mexico Border

10

The Past Guiding the Present

In March 2020, the community of El Paso, Texas, received stay-at-home orders and recommendations to isolate and quarantine because of the coronavirus pandemic. As soon as we got this notice, I remember posting a food tip on social media based on a lesson I grew up with: buy a burlap sack of rice and one of beans and complement them with the food you have in your refrigerator, freezer, or pantry. My parents were migrant farmworkers. At that time, there was no unemployment insurance available to farmworkers, so they did not get paid if they did not work. We had to be creative and resourceful in stocking up on food to build a modest pantry. I remembered that my parents bought rice and beans for us to eat to offset food insecurity during the times that they were seasonally out of work and in between harvesting periods. There were times we had to wait two or three weeks before the fields were ready enough to harvest whatever fruit or vegetable was in season.

When I was growing up, my family of seven usually bought food on the weekends to last throughout the week. As a teen, I would walk to the local supermarket with our $50 budget and figure out what to buy for the week. I do not know how I even planned meals with that amount, but I do recall that rice, beans, and tortillas were the most common staples I shopped for. I also bought chicken, beef, and fish to

Guillermina Gina Núñez-Mchiri

complement the rice and beans to make full meals. I remember that as a family of seven, we could all share one chicken. My dad usually had a drumstick, my mom would have a wing, and the five children ate the rest; the youngest one would always ask for the chicken breast. Now, we share one chicken among my family of three, and I usually serve it with a fresh salad, salsa, and tortillas. I remember that while growing up, a typical weekly menu included several chicken dishes, including chicken in the oven (sometimes with barbecue sauce), red chicken enchiladas, chicken mole, chicken soup with vegetables, and *pollo en estofado*—chicken with vegetables in a spicy tomato sauce. Grilled meat was most common on weekends when we had family and friends over for a celebration.

As I work from home and homeschool my son in the midst of pandemic quarantines, I have found myself thinking of these meals that I grew up on and drawing on the lessons I learned as a child of farmworkers. They have been guiding me as I navigate how to plan, shop for, and prepare nutritious, filling, and well-balanced meals during these present times of uncertainty.

Soups can be nutritious, comforting, and filling. My mom's *caldo de res* (beef soup/stew) brings me memories of warmth and comfort at home. We often laugh, saying Mexicans will eat *caldos* (soups) even if it is over 100 degrees outside. Mom made the most delicious *caldo de res*, and somehow this dish makes me remember her the most. My dad would warn us that it had too much cholesterol, while my mom and I would laugh as we enjoyed our bowlfuls. It had big chunks of beef and enough bone to make a savory broth. I learned a couple of strategies for making a good *caldo* from my mom. The first is to boil the beef about three quarters of the way, until it is soft enough to add the vegetables. Then you get Mexican spices (a pinch of cumin seeds, oregano seeds (not leaves), black peppercorns, and one clove) and you blend these with two cloves of garlic and a pinch of salt in a *molcajete*—a volcanic rock mortar and a pestle used to make salsas and blend spices for a variety of meals. This blend of spices gives the *sazón* (special seasoned flavor) for the broth and becomes the base of many of our dishes. My mom would add a quarter cup of water to the mix and then pour the crushed spices into the pan to sauté with chopped onion and tomatoes. Then she added the carrots, corn, potatoes, celery, *chayote*, one green chile, and green beans to the soup; once these were cooked three quarters of the way through, she would finish with the squash, cabbage cut into big chunks, and a handful of cilantro. She added sea salt and a tablespoon of Knorr beef bouillon to add more flavor to her *caldo*. She would serve it with corn tortillas, another handful of chopped cilantro leaves, a chopped serrano or jalapeño, and lemon. We usually had salsa in the fridge made from roasted tomatoes, chilies, onion, and garlic.

To accompany the *caldo de res*, my mom would also make her *sopa de arroz*, which was always perfect. It is a tomato-based rice dish rather than a soup, as one might expect based on the name; the notion of soup has much to do with the broth that the rice cooks in to give it its distinctive color and flavor. Although I make the *sopa de arroz*, it is not quite as good as my mother's. She had her own technique and *sazón* to her dishes. The key to making a *sopa de arroz* is to first brown the rice in oil, then add water and once it boils, lower the heat to the lowest setting possible, cover, and allow to steam for 15–20 minutes until it is done. Do not stir the rice after it boils, and whatever you do, do not lift the lid, so that the rice can steam through and not stick together. The *sopa de arroz* is typically served with the *caldo de res* and people can spoon it into the stew or eat it by itself as a side dish. The *caldo de res* is also served with corn tortillas in case people want to make tacos from the chunks of beef used in the stew, with a little added salsa for extra flavor.

Tortillas are a staple in Mexican kitchens. Depending on what region of Mexico you are from or what dishes you are seeking to prepare, you can choose from either corn or flour tortillas, or you can opt to have both available to make various dishes beyond tacos and burritos. For example, corn tortillas can be used to make *tostadas*, which are fried crisp and used as a base for diverse toppings, including beans, cheese, chicken, beef, chopped tomatoes, sour cream, salsa, and cheese. Corn tortillas are also used for enchiladas; they are fried and dipped in a spicy sauce and then filled with cheese, chicken, or vegetables. Flour tortillas provide flexibility and space to be filled with an infinite number of fillings to create burritos, which are quite popular throughout the U.S.–Mexico border region. There are so many dishes prepared with corn and flour tortillas that I would have to dedicate an entire chapter to this topic. Suffice it to say, they are versatile and practical items to have on hand during a pandemic or to eat at any time of the day. Being from southern Mexico, my parents preferred corn tortillas over flour tortillas. Corn tortillas are now sold in markets or can be made from fresh corn *masa* or from a dehydrated cornmeal mix that simply requires water. Corn tortillas can be pressed using a metal or a wood press or made by hand; the key is to press the dough into the signature thin disk shape and then heat them up one at a time on a griddle or directly on a gas stovetop burner. The flour tortilla is a lot more popular in northern Mexico; these are usually made with white (or whole wheat) flour, baking powder, salt, and *manteca*—pork lard (or other forms of vegetable fat for people who do not consume pork products). My mother never made flour tortillas at home; my dad was always watching his cholesterol levels, so he was particularly adamant about not using *manteca* at home (corn tortillas are made without added oil or fat).

Another lesson I recalled from our farmworking days is that we usually ate what was in season. This seems to be a good rule of thumb now that I am an adult cooking and caring for my own family during the pandemic and even prior to it. Because my parents worked in the lettuce fields, we had salads daily as a starter dish before having the main course. We added a variety of vegetables like cucumbers, tomatoes, celery, bell pepper, and carrots to the iceberg or romaine lettuce. There was a lot of crunch and texture to keep us chewing for a while before we even had the main dish. Perhaps this gave us something to help fill our stomachs and satiate hunger before digging into the main meal. I am so grateful that my parents taught us to eat fresh vegetables. Given our relationship to agriculture as farmworkers, we also enjoyed fresh fruit and regularly had platters of fruit to eat from throughout the day, including oranges, bananas, apples, papayas, pineapple, and mangoes. Eating fresh salads and fruit was one nutritious habit I grew up with that I intentionally sought to hold on to at home during the pandemic as a way of keeping us as healthy as possible.

Sometimes, I will make *huevos rancheros*, eggs over easy served on top of a pan-fried corn tortilla and smothered in red salsa made with onions, tomatoes, garlic, and jalapeños. Why have plain eggs when you can have a rich and beautiful warm salsa to smother them in? When available, I add chopped mushrooms to my *huevos rancheros*. A while back, I learned that mushrooms help boost your immunity during the flu season. Although I already got my flu shot, the climate is now getting cooler, and at times I feel the change in weather and the fatigue of working from home getting to me. At nights, I go for walks around my neighborhood. It takes me around thirty to forty minutes to walk around my son's former elementary school. As I walked through a park one evening, I saw teenagers hanging out in the street—not wearing masks. I see large groups of teens playing volleyball and their families standing around them—not wearing their masks. I have a hard time making sense of these behaviors. Could it be some people just don't care about getting infected, or do they think that they are immune to the virus?

Getting Food from Supermarkets during the COVID-19 Pandemic

Preparing meals during the pandemic made us reconsider what items we needed to buy to feed our families and how to go about getting these ingredients at various markets. People were responding to fear and panic of the unknown. Early in the pandemic, in March 2020, we knew little about how the virus spread and how to prevent or minimize the risk of getting the virus if we interacted with others. Minimizing exposure with other people meant staying at home as much as possible unless we needed to go out to work or get groceries, or for emergencies. People ran to the stores to stockpile on food and toilet paper. I began to see empty shelves in the supermarkets and at our local dollar stores. The food items that were first to go were canned soups, tomato sauce, spaghetti sauce, pastas, and ramen packages. People stood in long lines trying to take what they could find and afford. Although I had heard of empty store shelves in other countries, I had not lived through this experience until the pandemic.

I asked my friends what they usually did to get their groceries in El Paso during the first months of the pandemic. One friend ordered her food online and then drove to a local Walmart to have groceries placed inside her trunk without any human contact. Another friend had her groceries delivered to her door. My husband and I usually took turns doing a supermarket run, while our teenage son stayed at home. We used our facemasks, disinfected shopping carts, and went in and out quickly. Throughout the shelter-in-place orders, spending time in the supermarket strolling through the aisles seemed like a luxury to me. At a local Walmart near our home, some aisles had arrows with signs indicating what direction you were supposed to walk, though I have seen people coming and going as they please. I went on reverse once while trying to get a bag of corn from the frozen food aisle, and wondered how effective this system was in keeping people socially distanced. We generally visited the supermarket at least once a week to get fresh fruits and vegetables, though some of my friends reported going just once a month to minimize the risk of exposing themselves to other people who might be carrying the virus.

There are several supermarkets we go to, depending on what we are cooking. We get spices and halal lamb and chicken from the Arab shops. My husband likes going to a higher-end supermarket to get his olive oil and organic produce. I prefer going to Mexican markets to get my Mexican produce like chiles, cactus pads, guavas, papaya, and hibiscus leaves to make a cold drink. I like making a simple squash and corn dish, known as *calabacitas*, that goes well alone or as a side dish.

We go to markets en route to our home to pick up cereal, milk, or other household items. While visiting Food King, a supermarket with a large Mexican clientele, I struck up a conversation with the cashier about the empty shelves at other stores. She asked me, "Do you know why the shelves are not completely empty in the Mexican neighborhoods? Because people buy only what they can afford. They can't afford to hoard food like the rich people do." I walked out of the Food King thinking about the privilege of being able to buy whatever you need or want. In the past, we could go to any other store and buy what we needed. However, when the panic-buying began after shelter-in-place was ordered, even if we had money in our pockets, and plenty in the bank for our purchases, there was nothing on the shelves to buy.

I began to pay attention to how others shopped for food and what they were doing to make ends meet. A woman in El Paso uploaded images of her garden on Facebook. She complemented her meals with fresh items she grew herself: squash, chilies, and tomatoes. I admire people who can grow their own food. This seems like a skill worth learning. As a researcher, I would love to interview her about her garden in person, but, for now, I can report based on what she has posted on social media and the photos she has taken of her garden's harvest. Her posts inspire others to see what can be grown in our region, while maximizing space. She rents her home, so she makes use of a shared patio to grow food for herself and for others.

Social distancing regulations at the markets are usually followed, but not always. I felt a man standing behind me once, and I turned slowly toward him. He said, "It's okay, I am just waiting here. Sorry, I did not mean to startle you. I need to get to the eggs." I usually open the package to make sure the eggs are not broken. I checked and picked my dozen and scooted out of his way. Then, I noticed the man also opened and checked the package of eggs, just like I had done, before taking his selection. I walked away thinking of how we all have our ways of selecting our food and were now becoming aware of our shopping behaviors. With social distancing, we seemed to take a few more minutes to do things mindfully in order to give each other the space and time we all need to get through our days.

Sharing Pomegranates: September 27–29, 2020

On September 27, 2020, my colleague Terri H. sent me a message via Facebook asking if I wanted pomegranates. In Spanish, the fruit is called *granada*. Did I want *granadas*? Yes, I would love some. She asked me to go to her home to pick them up. Once I got there, Terri had a huge blue zip lock bag, the kind used to store away blankets, with about thirty or forty pomegranates. I had brought Terri a bowl of Mediterranean lentil soup I had made to reciprocate for her gift of pomegranates. Terri seemed grateful and excited to try my lentil soup. We were both wearing masks and chatted for a few minutes, six feet apart. After leaving I thought, "Who else would like some fruit?" I thought of my friends with families, so I dropped off some pomegranates at Ernestina's home (she has three kids), some at Natalia's home (she has two small kids), and then I went home. When I arrived, I saw that my husband was getting ready to meet up with his friend, Mokhtar, an Algerian in his mid-sixties who lives in Las Cruces, New Mexico—a town about forty minutes away from El Paso. My husband asked if I had any food made that I could send to his friend since he lived alone and did not have anyone else to share meals with. I asked my husband if he felt safe to meet with his friend, and he said his friend lived by himself, and as an Uber driver and a restaurant employee he was not working or interacting with anyone else since the businesses had temporarily closed. I understood why my husband had agreed to grab a cup of coffee with him: to help pass the time and break the silence of living alone. His friend has visited our home on several occasions in the past, though at this time my husband was reluctant to bring anyone home. I packed a plastic container with lentil soup and added a few pomegranates to the to-go bag to share with his friend. I reflected on how one bag of pomegranates had now gone to four homes.

On September 29, at night, Terri called to let me know that she had another bag of pomegranates. Her sister had just moved into town and her new home had a mature pomegranate tree that gave lots of fruit. I was glad to know that Terri had a sister to visit and hang out with her during this quarantine. I heard people in Canada are organizing pods of small groups of people committing to care for each other, who are willing to use caution and not interact with people outside their pods. Terri and her sister were now a pod and, thankfully, her sister brought her enough pomegranates to share with her friends. I got a bag of pomegranates, and now I too had something to distribute and share with my friends. Who would I share these fruits with? I looked around and thought: Hilda has four kids, Tania has three kids, Natalia has two kids, Maria has three kids, Maria's neighbor cares for her two grand-daughters, and her husband is a chef and dear friend of the family. It was already dark, so I left the pomegranates at people's front doors and on chairs or benches they each had outside. While dropping off pomegranates, I was listening to a debate that was taking place between presidential candidates on the radio. I did not want to stay home to watch it. Instead, I used this time to do my rounds and pick up and drop off pomegranates to my friends' homes.

I looked at the pomegranates on my counter and picked one to cut into four sections. My approach was to peel away the pomegranate pods to eat them slowly in small sections. On the plate I used to cut open the fruit, there was enough juice for me to tilt the plate and drink it. Every time I eat a *granada*, I remember the days my mom would buy one of these fruits for me to eat on my own while sitting in the back porch to avoid making a mess inside. I would run to switch out my clothes to wear a dark shirt or an apron to eat the pomegranate without tainting my clothes. I love pomegranates—*¡me encantan las granadas!* They are sweet, tart, and popping with flavor. Pomegranates are used on top of *chiles en nogada*, a complex dish that is usually prepared around the 16th of September to celebrate Mexican Independence Day. The dish has the three colors of the Mexican flag (red, white, and green) and is rich in symbolism and flavor. I cannot make *chiles en nogada* at home because my husband and son don't eat pork due to religious restrictions. So I enjoy them once a year by scouting for them at local Mexican restaurants during their season. As I have grown older, I have come to appreciate the colors, the textures, and the care that goes into making such a complex dish filled with a mixture of ground pork and beef, spices, dried fruit, fresh fruit, and raisins, and topped with a rich walnut cream sauce and colorful pomegranate seeds. I probably will not be making these *chiles en nogada* in my near future, so for now I will just cut a pomegranate into four sections and enjoy them one nibble at a time.

Remembering Our Ancestors and What They Ate: Late October 2020

It is seven months into the COVID-19 pandemic, and we are devastated by the thousands of people sick. The hospitals are filled to capacity, and people are posting pleas for prayers on social media, hoping their loved ones will make it through alive. A few of my students have been missing in action, and I am trying to figure out how to reach out to them. Today, October 27, 2020, it snowed in El Paso. This past Sunday, October 25, 2020, we received another stay-at-home order from our county and city officials closing the city of El Paso from ten o'clock at night until five o'clock in the morning. This seems like an effort to dissuade people from gathering in large groups and from going out to bars. Our communities on both sides of the border have been devastated by the impacts of COVID-19 on their physical and mental health.

It is getting close to Day of the Dead. Today, October 29, 2020, I made my father's oatmeal as a way of remembering one of the meals he had on most weekdays. I have been walking around the house thinking of what my dad liked to eat. He often made running commentaries about our food and the need to eat healthy. I remember his comment, "O comemos bien nosotros o come bien el doctor y su familia. Ustedes decidan"—"Either we eat well or we feed the doctors and their families well. You decide what it will be." Every morning, my mom prepared the oatmeal. She boiled a cinnamon stick in water and then added about a cup of oats. Once it had boiled for a while, she added condensed milk or whatever milk she had at home to make a creamy porridge. The oatmeal was an everyday breakfast item my dad would eat, except on weekends, when he would have eggs, bacon, and *frijoles* or a bowl of *pozole* or *menudo*. He was conscious of his high cholesterol, which is a problem that ran in his family. Oatmeal is supposed to be good for the heart.

I got up early to boil the cinnamon stick, then added the oats and a bit of condensed milk; it makes the oatmeal creamier, though it adds more calories and fat. I hope it all somehow balances out at the end. My mom's oatmeal was famous among our neighbors in southern Mexico. My dad would invite Cheo, who worked as a dump truck driver pulling sand from the river for construction projects. Sometimes my *tío* Pedro came over to have breakfast with my dad. As they ate, they discussed their thoughts on agriculture, the planting season, fertilizers, prices for the fruit per box of mangoes. Whoever came by, there was enough oatmeal to share, and they would comment on how different this meal was. They knew my mom made my dad's oatmeal unless she was mad at him, then it was my turn to make it. Mine was never as good as my mom's. Perhaps this was a sign my dad had learned to eat *como los norteamericanos*, like many people in North America: a breakfast meal that was warm, full of fiber, and sharable in a bowl. His choice to eat more fiber in the mornings, sometimes with a side of wheat toast and peanut butter, was an alternative to eating other breakfast items like eggs.

Today, I got up early to remember my mother making my dad's oatmeal. My husband and child do not like it. That's okay, more for me to eat throughout the day. My son has to make an *altar de muertos* for his Spanish class; perhaps I will add a bowl of oatmeal and one of *frijoles* next to Dad's picture printed on a coffee mug (a gift I received from my sister after his death). "We don't believe in that [altars], tell your teacher you are Muslim. You won't be making an altar," my husband says in the background. Remembering your ancestors does not need to be part of one religion, it is part of our culture, and they live among us in mind, in spirit, and in the meals that connect us *y ya*—and that is all. My altar has been sitting on top of a small round table in a corner of our house. Somehow my spouse is not yet aware that it is an altar to my ancestors.

The pandemic is at its all-time high rates of infection again. On Thursday, October 29, 2020, the El Paso County judge Ricardo Samaniego called for a two-week shutdown to end on November 11, 2020. The mayor of the city of El Paso, Dee Margo, did not agree with him. Several restaurants also protested and a long list of them continue to provide dine-in services. I drive around town and see people gathering in groups. On weekends, the parking lots of restaurants are packed with people: Village Inn for breakfast, Pelican's for dinner, and so many other locations throughout the city. The big chain restaurants are not as busy. I went to pick up rice, lentils, and turmeric at a local Arab spice shop. This pandemic has been a hard hit on small businesses and restaurants in El Paso. To support our favorite spots, we order take-out once a week. My son and husband like to get their weekly Subway sandwiches and, as a family, we like getting grilled chicken kabobs at Zino's Mediterranean restaurant or grilled chicken at Don Carbon, a Mexican restaurant specializing in mesquite barbeque-grilled chicken.

At home, we eat a combination Mexican-Mediterranean diet. We consume olive oil daily. In the mornings, we add it to our toast, and we cook our eggs in it. At night I use it to prepare dinner and add it to the dressing for our salads. My husband is from Tunisia, a North African country previously colonized by the French, so he grew up eating baguettes and wheat products. In the mornings, he has his coffee accompanied by toast dipped in olive oil, spreadable cheese, and fruit jam. He might also have some Greek yogurt with fruit. This is a typical breakfast for him every day unless I make scrambled eggs with olive oil, which is more likely to happen on weekends when I have more time to cook. I get tired of the same thing, so I usually look for almond butter or half an avocado to add to my toast. I also like having toast smothered in peanut butter with half a banana sliced on top. I eat one slice of bread on most days; I need to watch my carbohydrate intake because diabetes has already claimed several of my family members on my mom's side of the family, and she has been dealing with complications of diabetes for quite a while now.

What to Do about Lunch? Feeding a Mixed Ethnic Family: November 10, 2020

This week on Tuesday, November 10, 2020, we ran out of milk at home, and I did not have any to serve with our morning coffee or with my son's cereal. I had one carton of almond milk, which only I poured into my cup. No one else would try it. Little things like this get to me. Today, I ran off to my office at the university to log in for a meeting and avoid disruptions (my internet frequently cuts off at home during video conferences). The three of us at home are maxing out our internet capacity since we are all doing our coursework as students and as faculty during the same hours. On top of working full time, I co-parent a thirteen-year-old who consistently comes around and tells me he is hungry after just having eaten. For lunch I have my backup meals, mostly turkey sandwiches and tuna, which I add to shredded lettuce to make a quick salad. The routine and the mundane meals get old and unsatisfying, leaving us with limited meal options.

My husband recently started a PhD program and is taking his courses online in our home office on the second floor. He usually walks down the stairs to ask what's for lunch. I often have back-to-back meetings starting at noon or one o'clock and continuing through the afternoon. If I am in a meeting, I just shrug my shoulders, hoping he will figure something out. Even though I am working, the fact that I am physically at home means that my family still expects me to have food ready for them whenever they are ready to eat. There is usually food in the fridge and in the pantry, but they still come to me to address their food needs. When they notice I am working and cannot or will not listen to their requests, they go and get a sandwich. There is bread and tuna at home, and yet they prefer foot-long sandwiches from Subway. I challenge them to become more self-sufficient and care for themselves. I often say, "Have an apple or a banana until I finish my meeting, and then we will figure out what to make for lunch." I cannot help but think, why do we expect moms to take care of everyone's needs, particularly when so many of us work? The separation between work life and home life has become abysmally ambiguous during this pandemic. I have been reading and hearing so many stories of women stepping out of their careers to care for their families. There are simply too many requests to tend to and decisions to make. I hear from my colleagues that their smaller kids do not always understand why their moms cannot hold them while they are working. My teen son often comes around asking for a hug and for something to eat.

I tend to run out of ideas about what to make for lunch. I am usually pressed for time, particularly when a meeting or an interview is scheduled for 11:30 or when my child starts asking for food or I become keenly aware that it is past lunch time and no one at home has eaten. As a mother and spouse, I feel the pressure of the expectation to take care of my family's meals. Unless I am out of the home and not there to think about what to feed my family, I am the one mainly responsible for doing the meal planning and prepping. To be fair, my husband will go out and buy bread, yogurt, and other basic items he usually uses for breakfast. But when I am at home, he does not have to think of what meals to prepare throughout the week. My husband and son will pick up a sandwich or pop a frozen pizza into the oven at best, so they will not starve, though they will hardly cook on their own.

This pandemic has given me time to think critically about the roles and expectations that need to be redefined and reassigned to create more equity in the home. The time is long overdue to make the kitchen an accessible and inviting space for everyone in a family. It is imperative to learn to organize and create meals together. Petrified gender norms and expectations take a toll on life. My spouse and I were raised on two different continents, and these simple decisions about what to cook are not so easy in our home. He is from the Mediterranean and prefers meals with a spicy tomato sauce base. I like a variety of foods from Mexico, the United States, and other parts of the world. We both enjoy spicy food, fruits, and salads, so this gives us something to build on that we can all enjoy at home. Occasionally, our teenage son will ask for a Subway sandwich, chicken fingers, or a hamburger as a treat to alter the routine of everyday life during COVID-19. The truth is that I will consent to short trips at least once a week where he can get a meal he wants from a place he has been craving. I realize that ads online also get to our kids. Today he said, "It's footlong day, Mom!" Is that even a thing?

Working at home and trying to feed a family has taken a toll on my energy levels. Fatigue kicks in and it shows. I know there is food in the fridge and in the pantry, but it takes time to put meals together. I cringe when my child asks for ramen because it is full of sodium and carbohydrates. I have tried adding chicken to his ramen, and he will not eat it. I have made Mexican noodle soups, like *fideos*, but again, these tend to be high in sodium and carbohydrates. I try to get at least one salad in a day, but I need more than just salad. Sometimes I add a can of tuna or a boiled egg and beets—though my child will not touch the beets. I keep on thinking of creative ways to dress up a salad so that my entire family will eat it. I usually make a base Mediterranean salad with olive oil, lemon juice, salt, pepper, and dried mint dressing over lettuce, tomatoes, cucumbers, and slivers of red onion, or a Moroccan chopped salad with cucumbers, tomatoes, onions, bell peppers, and Kalamata olives in a lemon–olive oil dressing.

My son asks me often, "Have you found your own groove?" "My own groove?" I asked him the first time, to make sure I had heard him clearly. My own groove is a mess right now, *m'ijo*—my son. I know some people do meal planning, have lists of chores assigned to each person in the household, and distribute tasks equally among members of a family. I still don't know how they do this. I have heard friends and professionals say, "Push back, don't clean, don't cook, don't pick up after others." I have tried this approach, but at the end of the day, I have to make something to eat, and I need clean dishes to prepare and serve the food. Caring for others is hard work, and yet it is work that is often taken for granted and underappreciated. I do what I can when I can. A friend who specializes in massage and reiki therapy has suggested that I see these mundane household tasks as opportunities to practice mindfulness, gratitude, and meditation. I have talked to my family to express my needs, concerns, and expectations because the impacts of patriarchy are real, and they are exhausting. In time, my husband and son have gradually gotten better about picking up and washing their own dishes and looking out for themselves.

Food and Grief during the Pandemic: Early December 2020

It is now late in the academic semester, and both my husband and I are in the middle of final exams. The second week of December 2020, my husband's best friend lost his father. His friend is from Algeria, so going to his country to bury his father is not possible given the current travel restrictions. Because of the social distancing demanded by the pandemic, the ways we usually care for our friends during a death in the family has gotten complicated. How do we comfort others when we can't hug them? I went to the supermarket to pick up some flowers, chocolate cake, and a plant. To build their immunity, I added a bag of tangerines, also known as *mandarinas* in Spanish and in Arabic, to the cart as well. We have not visited with friends for some time, and it took me a while to find their home. I knocked on their door, using my knuckles and pressing the ringer with my folded finger to avoid touching the surface. When my husband's friend opened the door, my throat closed and my eyes swelled as I remembered the pain of losing my father years earlier. I mumbled, "I brought you this. We are sorry for your loss. Here is a plant and some other things for you. My husband is at school." I stood paralyzed in front of his door. I pointed to the items and asked him to take the things from my hands. I didn't know if people were coming over to express their condolences or to have coffee, so the cake and fruit might come in handy. He thanked me and asked if I wanted to come in for some coffee. I put my hand over my heart as I avoided entering the home and said, "Thank you, my husband will come by to see you later." They have a way of comforting each other as friends, as people of the same faith, and as immigrants who have both lost their fathers while being away in foreign lands.

In these moments of uncertainty and grief, we have so much to share with one another, and yet we still have to keep a physical distance to avoid spreading the virus. Until restrictions are lifted, a plant, chocolate cake, and tangerines will have to do to express our condolences, to offer comfort, and express our well-wishes during this time. I felt an overwhelming grief come over me. We stood on opposite sides of the door, both bearing our own sense of loss and grief. As I turned to leave, he asked how my mom was doing. I just remember saying, "She is still hospitalized due to COVID-19 complications, and I hope she will make it out alive."

Postscript: Food to Share with People Who Take Care of Your Family

After being hospitalized for five months with COVID-19-related complications, my mom is finally home at my sister's home in Southern California. I finished turning in grades and proofreading MA theses and dissertations, and then traveled home from El Paso to Calexico, California. On the 23rd of December, 2020, a nurse finally came to see my mother. She had been sent home without medications or items to care for her bed wounds. The hospitals and rehabilitation centers were overwhelmed and at capacity in Southern California. When the nurse saw my sister, he recognized her; she had been his high school teacher in 2003, and now, seventeen years later, one of her former students had come to provide home health care to our mom. He assessed her wounds and took her vitals, including her oxygen level, blood pressure, and sugar levels. I asked if he had eaten, and the young man just looked at me. I said, we will fix you a plate to take with you. A plate of lasagna, green salad, pasta salad, and potato salad with a plastic fork, a water bottle, and napkins. Later that evening, he called saying he lived in town and could come by and help if we needed additional support. He returned with bandages, echinacea, and a pill crusher for us to provide my mom her liquids and vitamins through her feeding tube. My sister gifted him some *buñuelos* (fritters made out of flour and topped with syrup or with sugar and cinnamon) and two baklavas I had gotten her for the holidays. He said they were short staffed and overwhelmed while working during this time. My sister said, "We will fix you another plate on Christmas Eve, I know you are still working through the holidays. Can you please come back to help us care for my mom?" My sister was interested in making sure we could hold on to his services as a home nurse. Having him come to our home to help us care for our mom, turn her, and address her wounds is a gift in itself.

We had our Christmas Eve meal at two o'clock in the afternoon. The turkey, ham, and salads are ready. This holiday season, we get to gather around our mother and with each other. We socially distance with spaces in between at the table, and we eat in rounds, keeping our face masks on when we are not eating or drinking water. We have a newborn in the family, and my mom is alive, we have each other, and we have food to eat at our table. The vaccines are coming, and we are alive to give thanks at the end of 2020. A new study indicates that people with low vitamin D were more susceptible to the virus so we went to get some vitamins yesterday at the local pharmacy store; everyone is getting vitamins for Christmas this year, and a roll of toilet paper to remember 2020. Staying at home has caused havoc on diets, routines, mental and emotional health, interfamily relationships, and so many of our social functions and interactions.

Dec 23, 2020. GGNM

Note

I would like to thank Andrea Sifuentes for her editing support, and Diana Riviera, my writing partner, for their encouragement to write about these experiences with food, memory, and culture on the border during the pandemic.

Red Chilaquiles

Method

Bring 4 cups of water to a boil. Wash and remove the seeds and the stems from 10 New Mexican red chile pods. If you can't find New Mexican chile, use *guajillo* dried chiles. Wash the chiles before adding them into a pot with the just boiled water. Turn off the heat and let the chiles hydrate. After the chiles and water cool off, drain, reserving one cup of the liquid.

In a separate pan, sauté two cloves of garlic in a tablespoon of hot corn oil. Remove after a minute and add the garlic to the blender with the chiles, reserved liquid, a pinch of dried Mexican oregano, and about 2 teaspoons of salt. Blend for three to five minutes until the sauce has no visible pieces of red chile. If you use a high-powered blender you do not need a colander for the chile sauce, but if specks of chile are visible, consider blending for a few more minutes or running the sauce through a colander to get a smooth sauce.

In the sauté pan, take a few slivers of red onion and brown them in 1 tablespoon of oil. Then remove the onion and pour in the chile sauce from the blender and let the sauce boil for five minutes until the sauce thickens a bit.

To make the chilaquiles, cut up 3–4 corn tortillas per person, using a sharp knife or a pizza cutter. Cut the tortillas in half and then into triangle-shaped chips. In a separate skillet, brown the tortilla chips in 3 tablespoons of corn oil on medium heat for about 2 minutes on each side until they are nice and crispy on both sides. Place the chips on a paper towel to drain extra oil.

10–12 New Mexico red chile pods (or *chile pasilla*)

4 cups of boiled water for soaking the chile pods

2 garlic cloves (peeled and chopped)

1 cup of the water you soaked the chiles in (warm, not hot)

1 cup of cold water

2 teaspoons of salt (or 1 tablespoon of chicken bouillon to taste)

One pinch of dried Mexican oregano

A few slivers of red onion

1 tablespoon oil

3–4 corn tortillas per person

Chopped onion

Queso fresco, cotija, or other Mexican cheese

Sour cream

Refried beans

Eggs

Once you are done frying your tortilla chips, add about 2/3 of the blended chile mix into the frying pan and add the fried tortilla chips to coat them on both sides. Let the chips simmer in the sauce for about one minute before serving them on a plate. You can heat up the left-over sauce to smother your chilaquiles if you want additional sauce.

Top the chilaquiles with chopped onion (red, white, or yellow), sprinkle queso fresco, cotija cheese, or any Mexican cheese blend, and sour cream. Serve chilaquiles with refried beans or with eggs (fried, over easy, or scrambled). Enjoy!

Intimate Tables: Food and Migration in a Time of Crisis

11

Our memories of the early months of the continuing COVID-19 pandemic are hazy and imprecise. They are memories of loneliness and loss, anxiety and isolation, and the struggle to maintain intimate connections with our friends and families and keep our communities together. Lockdowns, closed borders, and limitations on travel have been especially challenging for immigrants whose lives were built on mobility and the global networks of communication that broke down in 2020. As we are learning to accept that COVID-19 will likely remain a part of our world, and as we are facing the need to rethink our approaches to travel in light of a climate catastrophe, we are realizing that there cannot simply be a return to the way things were before.

Organizing this volume was a way for us to make sense of the experiences of the past two years by bringing together the diverse voices of immigrant chefs, food writers, and activists who so generously agreed to share their personal stories. Over years of conversations with the writers featured in this volume and with each other, *Resilient Kitchens* became closely intertwined with our own pandemic lives. The story of this book sits near the heart of our own pandemic experiences. As an afterword to this volume, we therefore offer our own narrative of food, isolation, community, and making meaning out of crisis.

We do not have clear memories of our conversations in the beginning of the pandemic. We know, for example, that we had our first virtual happy hour together on April 7, 2020, only because we found the Zoom link when looking back through our calendars. It was the day before Passover. Harry cannot fully recall how he celebrated the holiday that year. The annual cycle of observance is routine, but 2020 was nothing like years past, when his family set up a second dining table in the hall to host a riot of Russian cousins who immigrated to America after the fall of the Soviet Union. Jokes about celebrating Passover during an actual plague straddled the line between morbid and mordant. Harry and his family grasped for meaning in tradition but found it difficult to differentiate special occasions from the everyday when celebrations are deprived of their communal significance.

Only fairly recently did we fully realize how different our experiences of the pandemic have been. Philip's partner, who usually traveled for work much of the year, was finally at their house full time. What should have been an amazing period together felt on many days claustrophobic and disconnected from the rest of the world. To this day, Philip envies couples who describe how much they enjoyed the lockdown because they finally got to spend so much time together, and families like Harry's that were brought back together in a sense of security. In contrast, Philip feels like he ultimately failed at connecting with the only family he had in the United States.

In many ways, this volume is what has made us, Harry and Philip, a consistent part of each other's lives during a period of enforced distance. As might be expected given our work on this book, we have often talked about food during the last two years. Toward the end of 2021, these conversations increasingly became a window into parts of each of our lives that otherwise would have remained inaccessible to the other. We began the pandemic as colleagues at The Ohio State University, but have spent almost all of it apart. We passed months of lockdown in separate cities and finished this book while employed at different universities. As the pandemic accelerated, we each lived in our own world, until we tried building a new one in which we could remain connected.

Philip often seems to forget he is an immigrant, which is a luxury, in a way, although there's something melancholy about that too. He came to the United States ten years ago as a visiting student at Penn State, imagining an exciting year abroad before returning home to Germany, where he had dreams of pursuing an academic career in the German university system. Instead, he found himself attracted to the United States in ways he had not anticipated. As a teenager during the War on Terror, he shared Europe's ambivalence about American power on the world stage. But when he came to the United States in 2011, he marveled at how likeable he found it. Philip understood that American systems of power and access are far from equitable, but upon arriving in Pennsylvania he found Germany's strict, yet unspoken, system of class thrown into sharp and unpleasant relief. His path in Germany felt predetermined by the stifling confines of family history and local geography. He was the first in his family to attend university, and like many first-generation students—both in Germany and in the United States—he found academic hierarchies opaque and exclusionary. Having chosen what he only later discovered was the "wrong" university for his undergraduate studies, at the age of twenty-five his options already seemed limited.

In America, he felt that more doors were open. After a year at Penn State he began a doctoral program in Slavic Languages at Princeton; when he graduated he was hired as an assistant professor at The Ohio State University in Columbus, where he remains today. He married an American man during graduate school and began the Green Card application process soon after the wedding. Maybe it is not so much that he forgets he is an immigrant but that he is reluctant to claim that identity. Although Western Europe can be very different from the United States, cisgender white men enjoy similar privileges there as here, and in many ways his move from Germany to the United States was a lateral one between powerful economies and academic towers built in similar shades of ivory. Philip's English, too, is nearly unaccented. You probably wouldn't know he was not born here unless he told you, and that privilege of passing troubles his relationship to his own immigrant identity. Being an immigrant is both a core fact of his life and a label he often feels free to shrug off.

Philip's relationship with his own foreignness changed rapidly during the first year of the COVID-19 pandemic. With his Green Card not yet secured, his immigration status became subject to renewed scrutiny as his marriage dissolved. At the same time, his family in Germany, whom he was accustomed to visiting two or three times a year, suddenly felt inaccessibly distant. After the winter holidays at the end of 2019, eighteen months passed before he saw them again. During that extended period of familial separation, his grandmother died, his grandfather's dementia advanced to the point that he no longer knew who Philip was, and his relationship with his parents grew more distant as they struggled to understand the changes in Philip's life from so far away.

Harry spent the first five months of lockdown, from March to August, comfortably ensconced with his parents and sisters in the DC suburbs. He returned to Columbus to teach in the fall of 2020, but a series of family crises brought him repeatedly back to Virginia during that semester and the one that followed. Even during the worst of the pandemic, his movement never felt entirely restricted. He knew he *shouldn't* get on an airplane, but when it was absolutely necessary, he was always able to go home. To Philip, mobility never feels so casual. Even now that he holds a permanent Green Card, if he accidentally leaves his house without it, he worries about an encounter with law enforcement. He is often concerned about misplacing his papers, as replacing them would involve a lengthy, cumbersome, and costly bureaucratic process. It is in these moments of anxiety that Philip is reminded of his immigrant status, which he so often neglects to consider.

Our experiences of the pandemic—and even of the parts of it we have spent together—have often diverged. After Harry returned to Columbus in August 2020 he lived monastically, in a belated encounter with the shocking isolation many Americans had been struggling with since the first lockdowns in March. At the same time, Philip was trying to build new relationships. Harry experienced his return to Columbus as the imposition of a pandemic-era isolation he had thus far been fortunate to avoid; Philip experienced Harry's return as part of a bright moment in which he could begin to remake a queer social community that had fractured in March of that year. It was only as this book neared completion that we discovered the gulf between our states of mind that fall.

In December 2021, we decided to meet halfway between Columbus, Ohio, and Philadelphia, where Harry had moved for a new job. Sitting across the table from one another in a remote cabin in the beautifully named town of Friendsville, Maryland, we composed this chapter, a reflection on how each of our lives had unraveled over the last two years, and how we attempted to twine them together in new ways.

Ending graduate school also means leaving a close-knit community of peers and friends behind and starting a new social life from scratch. For many, it is a new chapter of adulthood centered on family. If you are queer junior or contingent faculty, it is less clear what your next steps are, or should be. We began our jobs at Ohio State six months apart—Harry as a postdoctoral scholar in the Department of French and Italian, Philip as an assistant professor in Slavic languages. After being introduced by a mutual friend, we connected over the sense of being strangers in Ohio, and shared a desire to explore alternative paths to building community. Our friendship unfolded at bars on Friday nights. By early 2020 we had a routine down: communal watching of RuPaul's Drag Race at Cavan's Irish Pub (an improbably named gay bar), followed by drag shows or karaoke and late-night pizza or a stop at Buckeye Donuts. Every week we would encounter the same cast of characters. The repetitive nature of these outings gave us a sense of being settled. The last time we went to Cavan's together in early March, we talked about what we then called "the novel coronavirus" but were unable to predict how it would affect our lives. We left for spring break not knowing this night would be our last at this bar together.

The worries that the early weeks and months of COVID-19 inspired were similar for most of us, yet we each experienced them in our own ways. Our university announced austerity measures that seemed to forebode a drastic restructuring. Junior and contingent faculty imagined that they would feel the implications of this most strongly. Harry, who was—and is—still searching for a permanent job, watched the academic labor market crumble. Job searches were canceled, and offers were rescinded around the country. Research accounts were frozen, and grant competitions were suspended. We were bracing ourselves for more hits to come. It would have taken rare optimism to imagine, then, the fiscal stability of our institutions a year later.

As spring break began, we were both waiting to hear from our university about grant funding decisions for projects that might, at first, seem distant from where our research has moved over the course of the pandemic. Philip hoped to collaborate with a group of scholars using digital and computational methods to study migration literature; Harry was planning to redesign his class on Mediterranean food culture to bring in chefs, restaurateurs, and food activists from around Columbus to speak and share food with his students over the course of a semester. At nearly the same moment that Ohio State announced spring break would be extended and classes would be moving online, the cycle of grant funding we had applied for was canceled. Instead, we learned that the university was offering a new grant program for projects that grappled with the COVID-19 pandemic, including a small budget for projects in the humanities.

We hesitated, at first, to even apply for this new round of grants. What did Philip's interest in migration literature and Harry's work on food culture have to do with a public health crisis? As we began to speak with each other about the interruptions we were already encountering in our work, however, our perspective changed. The earliest and most profound effects of the pandemic on the everyday lives of Americans who were not sick were felt in two ways: changes in the food system and interruption of the freedom to move. Restaurants were among the businesses hardest hit by lockdowns, and newspapers wrote breathlessly of the sudden American vogue for baking, which left grocery store shelves barren of flour and yeast, as well as toilet paper and hand sanitizer. Those of us who, like Philip, live far from our families found ourselves suddenly unable to visit.

Our research areas—migration and food—primed us to be alert to the importance of (im)migrant foodways during this time. The financial resources of a major American university offered us the opportunity to reflect on the present crisis. Despite moments of anxiety, we felt immediately that our own circumstances—Philip's stable employment and Harry's close family ties—insulated us from the magnitude of the disruptions that COVID-19 brought to other lives. We wanted to leverage the resources of the university to create a space for voices that are often absent from academic and public discourse. The volume you are reading represents the fulfillment of that drive.

Past pandemics, like the 1918 influenza, have in some ways been erased from cultural memory. It is human nature to shy away from grim death tolls and photos of makeshift epidemic wards. Through avoidance we find ways to forget these parts of reality altogether. Documenting recipes, we hope, is a way of creating a tangible (and consumable) record of how we made it through this time, both as a society and as individuals. Alongside our work on this volume, we started building a digital archive of pandemic-era food. We invited our own communities to contribute their stories, pictures, and recipes. We hope that this COVID Food Archive (covidfoodarchive.org), will grow in years to come, as we continue to reflect on how we have cooked and eaten during the COVID-19 pandemic—together with the ones closest to us, and alone in empty kitchens.

Several years ago, struggling with writer's block while in the midst of his dissertation on the history of Soviet literary journals, Philip decided to start a food blog. He wanted to explore his own origins by writing about recipes, and he hoped that the work would somehow generate inspiration he could bring back to his research. Truth be told, though, Philip was unaccustomed to thinking of eating as part of a rich cultural heritage—or at least not of his own. Celebratory feasting was not something his German Lutheran family embraced. On holidays and birthdays, his mother and grandmother were most satisfied when they ran out of food. Although they would never have formulated this belief explicitly, they found both leftovers and overeating offensive, as did many other northern Germans. A crowded table and costly ingredients made them actively uncomfortable. They did not celebrate austerity, either; they seemed simply to disregard food. Perhaps their interest in it was exhausted in the twentieth century, when domestic hierarchies assigned all food preparation to women. Philip's beloved grandmother, like many others of her generation, ended up in a West German household after her 1946 displacement from the former Prussian province of Lower Silesia, which fell to Poland after the war. Many of these displaced women never felt that they—or their cooking—were entirely welcome.

Regardless of what the reasons may be, Philip rarely feels that his origins align with the postcard romance of Old World traditions. His food blog was an attempt to assemble a new "old" identity for himself out of his local childhood culture and his readings on German and Central European food. He wrote in his blog about making picture-perfect dumplings and braised cabbage from scratch, sourdough bread, and poppy seed cakes. His family would not have taken pride in making a single one of these things themselves. Good-quality versions are readily available at stores in Germany and, to some extent, even in America. For Philip's family, elaborate home cooking would have been a frivolous waste of time. For Philip, though, cooking offered the chance to become someone else, by claiming—or constructing—his own German identity at a time when graduate school was chipping away at his confidence.

As he blogged, however, Philip could not help but feel that his claims about the deep importance of food were somewhat artificial. He ended the blog long before COVID-19 arose, although he continued making bread even after becoming an assistant professor. In his new environment, he wanted his baking to be about caring for and maintaining ties with others. His husband liked it when he made *tsoureki*, a sweet bread that played an important role in his partner's Greek Easter traditions. Philip felt competitive about it, trying to fashion a moist and flavorful version of a bake that oftentimes comes out stale and boring in order to earn the recognition of his new family. He approached Thanksgiving cooking the same way—several years in a row, he turned his patient sister-in-law's suburban kitchen upside down, trying to create a picture-perfect American feast. While Philip does not give much thought to his immigrant identity in his everyday life—with the exception of sporadic, anxiety-inducing administrative transactions—food is where it continues to play out. It offers an opportunity to be different and to connect with his own background, albeit in a very marketable way; and it became the playing field for assimilation. Philip made

Thanksgiving feasts that lived up to and even surpassed the expectations of his American family, trying to prove his worthiness to be considered a fellow citizen.

By Easter 2020, he had figured out how to make the most flavorful *tsoureki*, clandestinely referring to a German recipe for a different sweet, enriched bread. His husband liked it, as did their neighbor, to whom he gifted a personal ration every time he baked. They were impressed because he did something that they did not know how to do, something that appeared, to them, complicated and cumbersome. During the pandemic, many home bakers have discovered that while making sourdough bread does take some practice, once you have the process figured out all you really need is time and the willingness and liberty to schedule your day around proofing, folding, and baking. As he looks back on his own history of breadmaking, what Philip is most aware of is how tending sourdough, as well as his other baking and cooking, gradually became transactional, rather than rooted in real joy. Baking sourdough became a way in which he could still perform care for others, even when he felt like his emotions were failing him.

On a cold day in April 2020, Philip discovered another dimension of food. It was still frigid outside, and the sky over Ohio seemed threatening, empty, and endless. He was meeting Aaron, a close friend, by a river in Columbus. There was barely anyone around; most people had yet to discover the outdoors as their new social space, and even leaving the house during those early lockdowns felt somehow treasonous. As he was waiting, he caught snippets of a conversation between a few men in the distance. "Just a flu," one said. And then, "No atmosphere on the moon, the flag shouldn't fly."

"I have something for you," Aaron said as he arrived, reaching into the pocket of his vest. He dug through layers of fleece before he produced a small bag of cookies made by his own increasingly distant partner. He had mentioned them before: "They're my favorite cookies. Black walnut cookies. They are yummy." Standing an awkward body length apart, Philip and Aaron stretched their arms out to hand over the cookies. As paranoid as Philip was about transmitting a disease back then, he probably held his breath for the handover. For a brief moment, they were almost certainly closer than six feet apart.

Philip was worried about touching the same object as Aaron, and about bringing this food from a different household into the home Philip shared with his husband. His anxiety must have shown on his face, since Aaron quickly said: "You can throw them out, if it doesn't feel safe." It did not feel safe, at all, but the remark stung. To Philip, after all, throwing out food is beyond just wasteful—it is conceptually alien to his family's regime of carefully managed nutrition.

More than that, it felt like a double betrayal. Philip could bring the cookies home and put his husband at risk, or he could reject the gift that another person close to him had offered. It seems obvious, now, that the need to protect your household from risk of transmission should trump the social conventions of gift giving and receiving. In the moment, though, Philip felt caught between two unacceptable options: he couldn't bring a potential disease vector into the house he shared with his husband, but he also found it impossible to refuse the gesture of care contained in this gift of food. During the first weeks of an epidemic that we had barely any understanding of, food revealed a new layer of meaning: it was an expression of intimacy that had broken down even amid unprecedented public health efforts to contain and manage the spread of disease.

Until we forced ourselves to relive the early period of the pandemic during our conversations in December 2021, Philip had assumed that Harry's experience of being stuck at his parents' house would have involved levels of despair similar to his own in Ohio. But Harry found comfort and joy in spending a sustained period with his family. In suburban Virginia, they each worked in their own little corners of the house, went on long walks through the woods with their dogs, and exercised together in the basement. Especially in those first weeks, when we did not understand transmission very well, the possibility of contracting COVID-19 was the only anxiety-inducing part of Harry's experience.

In early March 2020, ominous warnings about COVID-19 were just beginning to circulate in Ohio. Harry, who was working in Ohio State's Department of French and Italian, was aware of the pandemic's crippling impact in Italy, and we were both concerned about friends and family in Washington State, New York City, Europe, and Asia. Given how much we still do not understand about the coronavirus, it is shocking to consider how much less we knew then. The day before leaving town for spring break, Harry went to a Mexican restaurant called Local Cantina, known for its chips-and-salsa bar. An Italian colleague in Columbus, perhaps more intimate already with COVID-19's horrors, refused to join the group. Harry ate indoors in the packed restaurant, unmasked, but asked his server to bring his table fresh chips and salsa from the kitchen so that he and his friends wouldn't have to risk touching communal tongs and spoons at the buffet-style salsa bar. With what we know now about airborne transmission, this clumsy attempt to make safe decisions looks, instead, like an early example of the hygiene theater we continue to stage, scattering hand sanitizer stations across public spaces and monitoring body temperatures daily rather than making meaningful changes to indoor airflow patterns in restaurants, offices, and schools. Frequent handwashing is always a good idea, but it does little to combat the airborne circulation of viral particles. Even with vaccines and boosters, being in a crowded restaurant remains a calculated risk, no matter how clean the utensils. We know now, but did not know then, about the critical importance of face masks.

A day later, Harry boarded a plane to Savannah, where he was meeting his family to empty out his grandmother's house. The woman next to him on the plane wore a mask; no one else did. Harry used an alcohol wipe to clean the armrests of his seat. By the end of the week, the university had announced that spring break would be extended and classes would be moved online for the remainder of the semester. Harry canceled his flight back to Columbus and got in the car with his parents and sisters to weather the coming storm as a family in Virginia.

Although we hesitate to generalize, Harry's family life, like that of many American Jews, has always revolved around food. He is blessed with two parents who are excellent cooks. Their division of labor is charmingly neat: his mother, Davida, specializes in traditional Jewish and Southern recipes from her childhood in Savannah; his father, Alan, has global tastes that were aroused during the two years he spent teaching English in Taiwan. Davida makes chocolate cookies and cakes; Alan is more interested in fruit-based pies and tarts. Davida is uncontested master of the Passover brisket; Alan is lord of the matzo ball.

As the child of accomplished cooks, Harry grew up in the kitchen, but he himself only cooked and baked occasionally. When, in the midst of a mental health crisis he took a semester off from college, his parents offered him a deal: they would pay for groceries if Harry cooked dinner for the family four nights a week. The responsibility of daily culinary invention is a familiar burden to most parents, but it was entirely surprising to Harry when, at the age of twenty, he took over the reins of his family kitchen. What followed was a four-month crash course in provisioning, during which he perfected a bolognese recipe, learned to trim animal proteins, and juggled the competing dietary preferences of his father, mother, and younger sister. When, as a graduate student years later, he began researching cookbooks, this experience formed a backbone of embodied knowledge that he used to approach food as an academic subject.

Harry's pandemic unfolded in three phases. The first five months were passed with family in the house he grew up in, surrounded by his parents and sisters and dogs, alternating nights of cooking. Almost every day, someone in the house would decide to bake something. Vast quantities of wine were consumed. It was a party that would not end, lent hectic texture by alternating relief at being together and anxiety about what was coming next. In the spring of 2020, he finished his teaching online. He and his father and sisters set up desks in different areas of the house; in the mornings they would "go to work," laughing at the absurd mimicry of their old structures.

By the end of summer Harry was desperate to get back to a semblance of his "real life" in Columbus, where, to his own disbelief, he was scheduled to teach in person, to a class of three masked students who had decided, for their own reasons, to try to make at least part of their semester feel normal. The following term he taught a course of sixty-odd students online, attempting to accommodate a wild variety of straitened circumstances while managing his own increasing isolation. Like many of us, he found minor salvation in culinary routines. On Sundays he would cook something elaborate; on Thursdays he would order take-out, indulging in a kind of laziness that he reframed through a virtuous lens as support for local businesses. In between, he gave in to what was, on good days, a quotidian ennui. On bad days, he lay immobile under the weight of major depression. Yogurt and cereal, that's a meal. Hummus and chips, that's a meal. Don't forget to eat fruit. Don't forget to eat something green. Don't forget to go outside. Don't forget to get out of bed. Many people struggled with the same grim inertia.

His contract at Ohio State concluded in June 2021. Harry returned to the Washington suburbs for two months in the summer before moving to Philadelphia for yet another limited-term fellowship, at the University of Pennsylvania. Over the fall of 2021 his patience with the pandemic, like that of many Americans, wore thin. In a university community where vaccinations were mandatory, the delta wave was largely an abstraction. He got his booster as soon as he was able, and aside from the mask he wore on buses and in meetings, his life began to stabilize.

Over the six years of their relationship, Philip's husband had grown accustomed to the peculiarities of his German in-laws' routines. His mimicry of Philip's mother's call "Kaffee!"—summoning the family members for the four o'clock cup of afternoon coffee with a pastry on the side—was hilariously accurate. In addition to the daily ritual, coffee and cake are also served this way at weddings, as they were when the two got married in Germany. They are also served at funerals. The plain crumb cake most common on both special occasions and regular coffee breaks is often referred to as *Beerdigungskuchen*, funeral cake.

In July 2020, Philip's grandmother passed away at the age eighty-nine. Travel to Germany, although technically possible, seemed unsafe, and so he spent the day of her memorial in distant Ohio. As common as it has become to attend family functions, such as birthdays, weddings, and graduations, on Zoom, dialing in to a funeral felt unusual, if not outright distasteful. Death seems to be the final frontier of virtual community. On the day of the service, Philip and his husband set their table in Columbus: a tablecloth they had brought from Philip's grandparents' house in Germany, the 1920s china from his great-grandparents, a photo of his grandmother, and an orchid. For a change, the parsimonious entertaining style he learned from his parents seemed apt. His husband had made a funeral cake. The two of them sat down at their table for what was possibly their last coffee, as later in the year they parted ways. Grief seemed to encroach on them from all sides. In an impossible situation, the performance of a meal gave them structure to hold on to, a way of connecting to the past and to each other.

Eating together, in a time of enforced distance, is salvatory. For us, it became clear that it was impossible to replicate this without physical proximity. Living on his own in the fall of 2020, Philip tried to break out of isolation by cooking elaborate Georgian recipes with his friends far away, by sharing photos of Christmas stollen, duck with dumplings and braised red cabbage—homemade, not store-bought—with friends and family. Harry established a routine with his grocery runs and weekly explorations of new recipes. On Sundays, we went on hikes together and had cheese and wine in the park. As the sun set earlier and earlier, we increasingly realized that, with all our tactics and work-arounds, eating alone at your house is still eating alone at your house. It was not until we aligned our quarantine protocols in a "pod" at the beginning of 2021 that we could finally start seeking rituals around food that gave us new ways of reconnecting our respective displacements.

Unable to justify another risky trip home before vaccines were widely available, in 2021 Harry celebrated Passover away from his family for the first time in his life. He made matzo balls with mixed success, he developed his own, Sephardic-inspired, charoset, and he devised a recipe for a lemon-ricotta-almond cake he hopes to make every year for the holiday. In Columbus, he did not have a proper seder plate, or an ornate dish for matzo, or the right kind of wine glasses for kiddush. What he did have, however, was the community he had created with Philip and, later, Aaron, who had joined Philip's life, their pod, and their meals. Harry invited them for a seder on the first night of the holiday. Harry led the seder in English as much as possible, speeding through passages he felt he had to recite in Hebrew in order not to lose the attention of what felt, at times, more like a curious audience than a table of dinner companions. But his mother had sent him a package of the same plastic frogs with which she whimsically decorates her own Passover table, and Philip and Aaron toyed with them

Harry Kashdan's Passover seder

whenever Harry left the table to tend to something in the kitchen, just like one of Harry's cousins always does at his family seders. Over the course of the seder, the relief of having this community away from home grew. Harry felt it in his body, as his shoulders relaxed and his smile widened.

Over the spring of 2021, when we shared a COVID-19 pod before Harry left Ohio State, we cooked and ate together often. On Philip's birthday, we constructed an enormous cheese board before digging into a family-sized savory *zelnik* pie that Harry ordered from a Columbus entrepreneur, Nontraditional Macedonian. We made Francis Lam's Singaporean braised duck from the *New York Times*, a tarte tatin recipe we found in Dorie Greenspan's *Around My French Table*, and Philip's own recipe for German *käsespätzle*, which he describes as a Swabian mac and cheese. Harry complained constantly about the lack of snacks in Philip's apartment; Philip responded by repeatedly (accidentally!) buying snack mixes Harry was allergic to. We ordered Korean take-out, drank copious amounts of prosecco, and whined to each other about the twenty-minute drive between our apartments, which kept us from spending even more time in each other's kitchens. There was desperation in our desire to be close to each other, but also the joy of friendship in a time of struggle.

We ate together, standing around Philip's kitchen island and sprawled on Harry's couch, at formally set dining tables and coffee tables with dishes spread haphazardly across them. As COVID-19 narrowed our social lives, sharing meals introduced new kinds of intimacy and vulnerability. The stakes of dining together were raised, and deepened. Many of us used food and cooking to build our own paths through the daily life of lockdown and quarantine; telling others about our evolving eating habits thereby became a way of letting people into our personal lives. We are grateful to the contributors to this volume for sharing their stories and letting us into their own encounters with the challenges of cooking and eating through a pandemic.

Hefezopf/Tsoureki (German-Greek Bread)

Yields one large loaf

This is where you can get creative in your pursuits of authenticity or individuality. German Hefezopf *is commonly made plain or with raisins. A real Greek* Tsoureki *should be flavored with orange zest or mastic resin, which has a unique pinelike flavor. My favorite additions are raisins soaked overnight in Ouzo or a combination of candied orange peel, walnuts, and chocolate—ideally a coarsely chopped chocolate bar for uneven and edgy chunks.*

Method

Dissolve the yeast in 1 cup of milk with a teaspoon of sugar added, let sit for 15 minutes.

Make a dough from the milk-yeast mixture, flour, sugar, butter, eggs, and salt. At this stage, also incorporate the orange aroma or others that you like. Knead for 10 minutes, either with a mixer or by hand. You are looking for a smooth and soft dough that is a little sticky. Keep adding another ¼ cup of milk, one tablespoon at a time, to reach the desired consistency. Let rise until doubled in size. This can take anywhere between 1 and 2 hours.

Put the dough on a clean surface and carefully fold in chocolate, fruit, or nuts of your choosing. Do not overwork the dough. Cover with an upside-down bowl and let rest for another 30 minutes. Preheat the oven to 350°F (180°C).

Braid the bread. It is very much in keeping with pandemic baking to research videos of braiding methods on the internet. Choose the one that

For the dough

1 ¼ cup (310 ml) warm milk

2 ¼ teaspoons active dry yeast

⅓ cup (80 g) sugar

3 cups (500 g) flour

6 tablespoons (80 g) butter

1 egg

½ teaspoon kosher salt

Flavoring and stuffing

1–2 teaspoons orange, vanilla, lemon, or anise extract

1–1 ½ cup raisins, dried cranberries, chopped dried fruit, chocolate pieces, nuts, or a mix thereof

Finishing touches

1 egg, beaten for egg wash

Slivered almonds or decorating sugar

appears most appealing and manageable to you. Transfer to a baking sheet lined with parchment. Brush the finished bread with the egg wash and decorate with almonds if you like. Let rest for another 30 minutes.

Bake for 30 minutes. Starting at 25 minutes, keep an eye on the bread. You want it to be golden brown and baked all the way through. Poke with a skewer to see if it is done. Once the skewer comes out clean, take your bread out of the oven and transfer to a wire rack to cool.

Almond, Lemon, and Ricotta Cake for Passover

A dense, sticky delight for the Passover table.

Method

Preheat oven to 350°F. Use a knob of butter to thoroughly grease a 9-inch springform pan, then dust lightly with almond flour, tapping out the excess. Line the bottom of the pan with a piece of parchment paper and butter and flour it as well.

Use your fingers to rub the lemon zest into the sugar in the bowl of an electric mixer. Add the butter to the sugar and lemon zest, and cream until light and fluffy. Then add the ricotta and continue creaming on medium-high speed for five minutes.

Add eggs one at a time, fully incorporating after each addition. Mix in the lemon juice, vanilla extract, and almond extract. In a separate bowl, sift or whisk together the almond flour, baking powder, and salt. Add dry ingredients into the wet and combine in the mixer on low.

Pour batter into the prepared springform pan, and bake for 65 to 75 minutes, until a cake tester or toothpick inserted in the center comes out clean. After 45 minutes, briefly open the oven and sprinkle the optional sliced almonds on top, then finish baking. Almond flour milled from unpeeled almonds is naturally brown, but you may choose to lay a sheet of foil loosely over the baking pan if you feel it is becoming too dark near the end of the bake.

Let the cake cool completely before removing it from the springform pan. Before serving, dust with powdered sugar.

For the cake

1 ½ cups granulated sugar

Zest of one lemon (about 1 tablespoon)

¾ cup butter, room temperature (12 tablespoons, 1 ½ sticks), plus a little extra for the pan.

1 cup whole milk ricotta

3 large eggs, room temperature

Juice of one lemon (about 3 tablespoons, a little under is fine)

1 teaspoon vanilla extract

Scant 1 teaspoon almond extract

1 ½ cups almond flour, plus a little extra for the pan.

½ teaspoon baking powder

½ teaspoon salt

For decorating (optional)

¼ cup of sliced or flaked almonds

Powdered sugar

Acknowledgments

We are grateful to the editorial team at Rutgers University Press, especially Jasper Chang, Kimberly Guinta, and Carah Naseem, for their support and their creative vision. Angelo Dolojan's thoughtful engagement with the essays led to the illustrations that give this volume its own visual language. Ryan Benyi patiently and expertly guided us through a last-minute food photography project. Gary Hayward at Ohio State was heroic in managing the administrative challenges that come with a volume of this kind.

This project was made possible by the Covid Special Grants initiative of the Global Arts + Humanities Discovery Theme at Ohio State and an award from the Hershey Humanities Against Racism Fund of the Wolf Humanities Center at the University of Pennsylvania. We especially thank Wendy Hesford and Puja Batra-Wells for their continued support of this project.

Notes on Contributors

GEETIKA AGRAWAL loves exploring the world through foods and the myriad of stories that come with them. She most recently spent nine years as the program director at La Cocina, a nonprofit that incubates food businesses run by talented women from communities of color—many of which are now internationally acclaimed Bay Area destinations. Geetika led La Cocina's COVID-19 response programs alongside seventy-plus entrepreneurs, all of whom survived the pandemic, so far. A migrant at heart, Geetika proudly claims the Mission District of San Francisco, California, as home.

ZEINA AZZAM is a Palestinian American poet, writer, editor, and community activist. She is the Poet Laureate of the City of Alexandria, Virginia (2022–2025). She volunteers for organizations that promote Palestinian rights and the civil rights of vulnerable communities in Alexandria, where she lives. Zeina also serves as a mentor for We Are Not Numbers, a writing program for youth in Gaza. Her chapbook, *Bayna Bayna*, In-Between, was published in 2021, and her poems appear in over forty literary journals, anthologies, and edited volumes. She holds an MA in Arabic literature from Georgetown University and an MA in sociology from George Mason University.

KEENAN DAVA is a taker of walks, lover of friends, gamer of boards, eater of foods, and drinker of drinks. Former server, current social media manager, future hermit, Keenan is often found awkwardly swaying to live Chicago music, lazily sipping bad coffee at Cafe Mustaché, scouring a thrift store, or writing silly little words. A close friend says that the meaning of life is to have as many good meals with as many people you love as possible, and then die. Keenan has been unable to find another answer.

ANGELO DOLOJAN is an artist based in Chicago, working as an illustrator and painter. Born in the Philippines, he arrived in the United States at age twelve. He studied art history in California, and, alongside pursuing a career in art, he ventured many roles within restaurants, which brought him to Chicago. His work is now a continued reflection of the many years spent in the restaurant industry, highlighting these special moments in food, people, and culture.

TIM FLORES grew up just outside Chicago with his parents, who immigrated from the Philippines in 1975. His first experience in professional kitchens was polishing dishes at Chicago's GT Fish & Oyster between college semesters in Iowa. Tim returned to Chicago and transitioned to GT's kitchen, where he met his future partner, Genie Kwon. In 2016 they helped open Oriole, a fine dining restaurant in the West Loop. In July 2020, Tim and Genie opened Kasama, a bakery and restaurant that serves modern Filipino food inspired by the dishes Tim grew up eating. Meaning "together" in Tagalog, Kasama is a reflection of both Genie and Tim's culinary backgrounds.

PHILIP GLEISSNER is an assistant professor of Slavic and East European languages and cultures at Ohio State. A native of a small town in Northern Germany, he first came to the United States in 2011 to pursue his graduate studies at Princeton University. He teaches and researches a variety of topics, including the Soviet literary press, transnational socialist cultural networks, and queer activism and community building in contemporary Eastern Europe.

STEPHANIE JOLLY is a manager of course development and online learning with an MA in food studies from New York University. A Pacific Northwest native, she has spent the better part of two decades as a digital nomad, teaching, writing, and editing from the United States and abroad. She has an avid interest in ethnobotany and the cultural politics of tourism.

HARRY ELI KASHDAN is a scholar of food and migration based in Washington, DC. After earning his PhD in comparative literature from

University of Michigan, he held fellowships at Harvard University, The Ohio State University, and the University of Pennsylvania. He has published widely on cookbooks as literary texts and on migration in the Mediterranean.

REEM KASSIS is a Palestinian writer and cultural critic. She is the author of the best-selling and award-winning cookbooks *The Palestinian Table* and *The Arabesque Table*. Her other writings have appeared in the *New York Times*, the *Wall Street Journal*, the *Washington Post*, the *Los Angeles Times*, and *The Atlantic*, in addition to various magazines and academic journals. She grew up in Jerusalem, then obtained her undergraduate and MBA degrees from the University of Pennsylvania and Wharton and her MSc in social psychology from the London School of Economics. She now lives in Pennsylvania with her husband and two daughters.

SANGEETA LAKHANI grew up in Mumbai, India, and moved to the United States at the age of seventeen. She studied at The Columbus College of Art and Design, followed by The Columbus State Culinary School. Sangeeta has been in the restaurant business for over twenty-five years and has won several awards for her restaurants in Columbus, Ohio. In 2014, she cofounded and created the menu for the farm-to-table restaurant The Table. In March 2020, Sangeeta leveraged her network to pivot her existing restaurant into Service!, a relief effort for hospitality workers. In her role as executive director, Sangeeta plans to keep growing Service! to provide resources and training opportunities for service industry workers.

FERNAY MCPHERSON, a native of San Francisco, began her culinary journey with Minnie Bell's catering and teaching youth cooking classes in the Fillmore district of San Francisco. Partnering with La Cocina, Urban Solutions, and Main Street Launch, Fernay has grown her business through roving pop-ups and by catering to big companies. In 2017, Fernay was chosen as one of the *San Francisco Chronicle*'s Rising Star Chefs. Minnie Bell's currently has a home inside The Public Market Emeryville.

BONNIE FRUMKIN MORALES is chef and co-owner of Kachka and Kachka Lavka. The first-generation American daughter of Belarusian immigrants, Bonnie grew up in Chicago in a large family that brought with them the distinctive food and drink culture of the region. She trained at the Culinary Institute of America, and in top kitchens in New York and Chicago. In 2014, she and her husband Israel opened Kachka in Portland, Oregon, a renowned restaurant inspired by the food of the former Soviet republics. The James Beard Award–nominated chef released her first cookbook, *Kachka: A Return to Russian Cooking*, in 2017.

TIEN NGUYEN has been writing at the intersection of food and culture for over a decade. Among other publications, she has written for the *Los Angeles Times* and *Lucky Peach*, and her work has been honored by the Association of Food Journalists. She is also the coauthor of several books, including *New York Times* bestseller *L.A. Son* with Roy Choi and, most recently, *The Red Boat Fish Sauce Cookbook*, which was named one of NPR's 2021 Books We Love. She teaches food journalism at the University of Southern California's Annenberg School for Communication and Journalism.

GUILLERMINA GINA NÚÑEZ-MCHIRI is Dean of San Diego State University Imperial Valley. She was formerly an associate professor of anthropology and director of women and gender studies at The University of Texas at El Paso. She is an applied cultural anthropologist with ethnographic and applied research experiences in the El Paso del Norte border region. Guillermina teaches courses on ethnographic and feminist research methods; urban anthropology; applied anthropology; death, dying, and bereavement; and the anthropology of food, gender, culture, and society. Her current work is on border narratives of food, care, and community building, a project funded by the National Association of Hispanic Journalists via the Ford Foundation.

KRISHNENDU RAY is a professor in the Department of Nutrition and Food Studies at New York University. He was the chair of the department from 2012 to 2021. He is the author of *The Migrant's Table* and *The Ethnic Restaurateur* and the coeditor of *Curried Cultures: Globalization, Food and South Asia.* He was formerly a faculty member and the acting associate dean of liberal arts at The Culinary Institute of America (1996–2005) and the president of The Association for the Study of Food and Society from 2014 to 2018. He is an Editorial Collective Member of the food studies journal *Gastronomica.*

MAYUKH SEN is the author of *Taste Makers: Seven Immigrant Women Who Revolutionized Food in America.* His second book, a biography of the Indian-born Old Hollywood actress Merle Oberon, is forthcoming. He is the recipient of a James Beard Award and an IACP Award for his food writing, and his work has been anthologized in two editions of *The Best American Food Writing.* He teaches at Columbia University's creative writing program and lives in Brooklyn.

ANTONIO TAHHAN is a Syrian Venezuelan American writer and researcher interested in the intersection of food, culture, and identity. In 2010, he received a Fulbright research grant to study the midday meal in Aleppo. Whether he is chasing the elusive tanginess of clay pot yogurt or mapping the global identity of *molokhia*, Antonio uses food as a creative lens for exploration and engagement. He recently completed his master's in Arab studies at Georgetown University.

Art Credits

Illustrations by Angelo Dolojan

Food photography on pages 24, 50, 76, 96, 118, 140, 166, 190, 198, 218, and 240 by Ryan
    Benyi Photography; food preparation and styling by
    Philip Gleissner and Harry Eli Kashdan

Chapter 1: Photograph on page 13 by Reem Kassis

Chapter 2: Photograph on page 31 by Stephanie Jolly and Krishnendu Ray

Chapter 3: Photograph on page 54 by Tien Nguyen

Chapter 4: Photograph on page 84 by Leah Nash

Chapter 5: Photograph on page 102 by Christopher Gregory-Rivera

Chapter 6: Photograph of Geetika Agrawal on page 123 by
    Eric Wolfinger; photograph of Fernay McPherson on page 133 by
    Jenny Love

Chapter 7: Photograph on page 147 by Antonio Tahhan

Chapter 8: Photograph on page 183 by Sangeeta Lakhani

Chapter 9: Photograph on page 196 by Kristen Mendiola

Chapter 10: Photograph on page 202 by University of Texas at El Paso

Chapter 11: Photograph on page 237 by Harry Eli Kashdan

Index

community, 15, 18, 128–129, 151, 186, 201, 210, 235; building of, 6, 17, 153, 223, 226–227, 236–237; food and cooking in, 145, 147, 149, 155–157, 162, 229; immigrant and ethnic, 8, 55–56, 61–63, 64, 71, 73, 82, 87, 160; organizing and organizations, 58, 66, 72; restaurants and, 68, 134, 182–183

cookbooks, 43–46, 54, 57, 101, 106, 150, 162, 234; writing and publishing of, 2, 8, 10–12, 84, 99, 130

cookies, 187, 231–233

cooking shows, 7, 55, 57, 100, 108, 113, 161; and Martin Yan, 99–100, 105–106, 108–113

corn, 39, 72, 203–204, 206

cornbread, 127–128, 131

corporations, 39, 126, 129, 147, 150, 162, 182, 185

crab, 102

cream, 45, 209

creativity, 110, 173, 182; in cooking, 147, 177–178, 201, 214

crème anglaise, 44

crème fraîche, 42, 47

cucumbers, 37–38, 40, 45–46, 57, 99, 204, 214

cumin, 127, 130, 202

curfew, 150, 152

curry, 33, 44, 131, 178

daal (dal), 41, 130

dairy, 45, 148

dan tat, 99

death, 1, 29, 48, 70, 104, 146, 229; of family members, 211, 215, 235

Delhi, 30, 126

desi, 172. *See also* Brown (racialized classification and identity)

dessert, 1, 7, 40, 101. *See also* cakes; cookies

DeWine, Mike, 181

Dia de Muertos, 210–211

diaspora, 149, 159

dill, 36, 41, 44, 47

dinner, 41, 133, 183, 211; as family ritual, 5, 16–17, 37, 124, 131; planning menus for, 32, 35, 42–46, 48; as (social) event, 16, 21, 91, 137, 151, 153–154, 180–181, 183, 236

disease, 2, 56, 59, 64–65, 68, 231–232. *See also* cancer

displacement, 71, 160, 230, 236

distillation, 162

donations, 92, 182, 187. *See also* charity

Doshi, Tishani, 29, 48

dough, 148, 154, 204

dressing, salad, 43, 212, 214

dressing, turkey, 127–128

duck, 55–63, 65, 72–73, 236–237

dumplings, 47, 93, 101, 230, 236

Dutch crunch, 132

Easter, 230–231

Eater, 54, 73